Have the Whole Boat

Also by Kim Kavin:

The Everything Family Travel Guide to Cruise Vacations
Tools of Native Americans: A Kid's Guide
The Everything Family Travel Guide to Timeshares

Coming in 2007:

The Everything Guide to Magazine Writing

Have the Whole Boat

✦

The Insider's Guide to Private Yacht Charter Vacations

Kim Kavin

iUniverse, Inc.
New York Lincoln Shanghai

Have the Whole Boat
The Insider's Guide to Private Yacht Charter Vacations

iUniverse books may be ordered through booksellers or by contacting:

iUniverse
2021 Pine Lake Road, Suite 100
Lincoln, NE 68512
www.iuniverse.com
1-800-Authors (1-800-288-4677)

ISBN-13: 978-0-595-40365-3 (pbk)
ISBN-13: 978-0-595-84740-2 (ebk)
ISBN-10: 0-595-40365-4 (pbk)
ISBN-10: 0-595-84740-4 (ebk)

Printed in the United States of America

For my husband, Sean Toohey,
who tends to our home and hounds while I go cruising

FIVE MOST COMMONLY ASKED QUESTIONS ABOUT PRIVATE YACHT CHARTER VACATIONS

Do I have to share a small boat with people I don't know?

Never. You cannot book a true private yacht by the cabin. Instead, you get to have the whole boat—and *you* get to decide who joins you onboard.

How can I possibly afford a private yacht charter vacation?

Actually, in many cases, a family of four will pay less for a charter than a cruise ship vacation. Even couples traveling with friends on high-end cruise ships can find comparable private yacht bargains.

Do I have to know how to drive a boat?

Absolutely not. You can learn, if you want to, but there are plenty of private yacht charter vacations that come with at least a licensed captain and sometimes a full-size crew to tend to your every wish.

Are those smaller boats as safe as the big cruise ships?

Private yachts are actually safer, for several reasons. They typically cruise far from the big tourist areas where pickpockets lay in wait. The only people onboard are you and your private crew—the yacht owner's personal staff. Private yachts rarely cruise where professional pirates do, and their crews are trained to international standards in case of the rare emergency onboard.

If charter is so great, why hasn't my travel agent suggested it?

Because she makes money selling cruise ship vacations. Charter is a smaller, unique segment of the vacation industry, and travel agents don't understand it the way professional charter brokers do. That's why your travel agent always suggests cruise ships. She simply doesn't know what you've been missing.

Contents

Acknowledgements

My deepest gratitude goes to the editors who allow me to write regularly about boats and charter. Richard Thiel at *Power & Motoryacht* and *Voyaging* took a chance on me a few years ago and has since become a terrific supporter, mentor, and friend. Betsy Frawley Haggerty welcomed me at *Offshore*, as have her successors, Darrell Nicholson and Tom Richardson. Laura Hughes at *Elite Traveler*, Elaine Srnka at *Celebrated Living*, Daphne Nikolopoulos and Kathy Becker at *Palm Beach Illustrated*, and Mark Nothaft at *Stratos* are always open to my ideas. Larry Bean and Michael Schulze are supporters of mine at *Robb Report*, as are Bill Klimas at *International Yachtsman*, Az Hatefi at *Transport & VIP Interiors,* and Ken Beaulieu and John Patrick Pullen at *Boston Whaler Magazine*. Bill Sisson at *Soundings*, Tim Sayles at *Chesapeake Bay*, Kate Simpson Lardy at *Dockwalk,* and Steve Connatser at *Traveler Overseas* always welcome my queries. Alev Karagulle has opened doors for me at *Nigel Burgess Magazine*, *Panache*, and American Express Publishing. Dave Funkhouser helped me bring yachting to the general public at *Northeast*. Kenny Wooton gave me my start at *Yachting*.

I also owe thanks to the charter professionals quoted throughout this book, and to many others within the industry. Retail brokers, wholesale brokers, marketing directors, operations directors, yacht owners, captains, chefs, stewardesses, deckhands—all have helped to teach me the business. So have magazine advertising salespeople like Terry Jacome and Lou Fagas. To the hardworking men and women who design and build these beautiful boats that we all cruise onboard, too, I say thanks.

Diane Byrne, a k a "The Shredditor," edited this manuscript for structure, content, and style. Few people in the world have the knowledge and skills for that task, and I am blessed to have her in my corner as both a colleague and a friend.

Shaw McCutcheon allowed the use of his beautiful photograph for the book's cover, Rupert Connor snapped a lovely author picture, and Dave Pollard created excellent illustrated maps for this book and its companion Web site, *www.CharterWave.com*. They are true artists, and I'm lucky to have my words alongside their work.

Thanks also to everyone who allowed me to reprint accommodations plans showing yacht interiors: David Hensel and Jonathan Cooper at Grand Banks

Yachts, David Ward, Stefan Wertans, and Jackie Phillipson at Sunseeker Charters, Don Gilman at Gilman Yachts, the team at *La Bonne Humeur*, Karen Kelly at Nicholson Yachts of Newport, Nancy Austin at The Hinckley Company, David Rohr at The Moorings, and Alev Karagulle at Nigel Burgess.

Fellow media professionals Kristin Baird Rattini, Dave Sheingold, Ellin Holohan, Diane Byrne, Liz Pasch, and Alissa DiGiacomo offered thoughtful, helpful suggestions about this book and its companion Web site, as did longtime charter industry experts Agnes Howard, Capt. John Terrill, Diane Fraser, Liz Howard, Alev Karagulle, and Cindy Brown. To them all, I say thank you for your honesty, expertise, and friendship.

Without the steady support of my parents, Marc and Donna Kavin, and my sister, Michelle Kavin, I would not be the journalist I am today. And without their phone numbers, I would have nobody to call when I need a break from writing.

Last on this list but first in my heart is Sean Toohey, who encouraged me to take on this project and always understood when I was still typing long past midnight. He is the partner of my dreams.

Introduction

A couple sat near me at the boarding gate in Miami International Airport, rummaging through their carry-ons and waiting for their row to be called. I tried to concentrate on reading my magazine, but the husband's disgruntled rant was even louder than the commotion his two young boys stirred up while they ran through the concourse.

"Ten!" he complained to his wife. "*Ten thousand dollars*! And the food wasn't even that good!"

From the bits and pieces I overheard of the raving monologue that followed, it seemed the family had just disembarked from a cruise ship somewhere in the tropics. The husband was particularly upset about having to eat fast food on deck simply to escape the overcrowded dining hall. He also, apparently, resented having to sit down with pre-assigned tablemates who constantly asked "to share" the wine he'd been pressured to buy in a package deal the first day he boarded the ship.

By the looks of his leather loafers, I think he could have easily afforded to spend three times as much on his family's vacation. The $10,000 wasn't the root of his problem. He was riled because he felt he hadn't gotten his money's worth, at any price.

I tried to keep my eyes politely on my own business, but another couple quickly chimed in, making the boarding lounge feel like an angry vacationers' support group meeting.

"That sounds like our last cruise," husband number two lamented. "We sat down to dinner the first night, and this couple comes over and realizes they're assigned to our table. The wife actually shrieks, like we're mass murderers or something. 'But I wanted to sit alone!' We were stuck with them the whole trip."

A few other airplane passengers, without looking up from their books and magazines, nodded with understanding.

"And the food," husband number two continued. "I hear what you're saying about the food. It's not very healthy." He grabbed his pot belly and squeezed it with disgust. "You know, you're on vacation. You just eat."

Husband number one then turned to his wife and declared, "I think we're done with cruise ships for a while."

At this point, I could no longer resist. I was flying home from a cruise in the islands, too, only mine had been part of an assignment for *Power & Motoryacht* magazine. I'd spent the previous four days onboard a private yacht, writing notes about the personalized service its ten charter guests enjoyed and taking photos of the secluded harbors where we'd anchored every night. I hadn't been crushed in a single crowd, my food had been exquisite, and even though I'd been working the whole time, I was more relaxed than these people who had paid to be on vacation.

I closed my magazine, turned to couple number one, and asked, "Have you ever thought about private yacht charter?"

They looked at me like I was Marie Antoinette telling their peasant family to eat cake.

"Too expensive," the husband grumbled.

"And too much work," his wife added. "I don't want to be Gilligan, running around with all those ropes. I just want to have a good time."

It was the same reaction I've heard countless times after suggesting the idea of private yacht charter, and it's unfortunate—because it's dead wrong.

I, too, used to think private yacht charter was only for the ultra-rich. I'm the daughter of two hardworking New Jersey public schoolteachers. When they took my younger sister and me on vacation, it was usually in the station wagon to places like Six Flags and Hershey Park. The couple of times we flew to Walt Disney World were a really big deal, especially the year we had a hotel room inside the park instead of a few miles away.

We took one cruise ship vacation during my entire childhood. I still remember my father's grimacing as the locals tried to bilk him for $5 shell necklaces at every single port. My parents finally decided that for middle- and upper-middle-class people like them and their friends, it was impossible to find an affordable and relaxing vacation on the water.

That was about 30 years ago. I never imagined back then that I would become an editor at a major boating magazine, or that I would be assigned to write stories about what is quickly becoming a global marketplace of private yacht charter. I had no inkling that I might ever get a chance to spend a vacation onboard a private yacht, but I was excited that through my work as an editor, I would at least get a peek at how modern-day Marie Antoinettes spend their vacations.

I quickly learned that some of the boats available for private charter are, indeed, just for the super-rich (with *weekly* rates of hundreds of thousands of dollars). But the more assignments I did over the years, the more I learned that there are a lot of private yachts out there that many people can afford, including the couples from the Miami airport who spent all that money on cruise vacations they ended up hating.

Today, I know that my baby boomer parents—who have since retired and started taking $10,000 cruises of their own—can afford some of the nicer, albeit smaller, private yachts with captains and chefs. If they spend just a little more, their level of luxury will rise substantially. Most exciting to me, though, is knowing that if they pool their $10,000 vacation budget with similar amounts their friends are spending on cruise ship suites, they can form a group of four or five couples who truly enjoy one another's company—and charter one of the bigger luxury yachts with a full crew and gourmet chef all to themselves.

I tried to explain this concept to the frustrated cruise-ship couples at the airport, but, like so many other people I've talked with over the years, they ended up thinking it all sounded too good to be true. Heck, their travel agent had never suggested private yacht charter. Who was I, this stranger at the boarding gate with a boating logo on my shirt? Was I some kind of saleswoman? What was my secret agenda?

I didn't have one then, and I don't have one now—except to help you and every other frustrated cruise ship passenger out there understand the world I've discovered, the world of private yacht charter vacations.

The yacht charter market is more complex than the cruise ship industry, in the same way a fine restaurant's a la carte offerings are more complex than a laminated menu at Applebee's. To enjoy private yacht charter, you have to learn to think about planning your vacation a bit differently than simply plucking a package deal from a list in a glossy brochure. You have to learn how to ask for what *you* want, as opposed to selecting among a bunch of prepackaged plans.

It can feel liberating when you realize that you no longer need to go along with the masses. However, you will face new challenges when it comes time to describe your ideal private yacht charter. You will have to admit the pitfalls of your previous cruises and learn to explain how you would have liked things to go differently. You will need to find and work directly with a specialized charter broker instead of calling your trusted travel agent, no matter how helpful she has been in the past. You will have to learn a little bit about yachts—not necessarily how to skipper them, but certainly which ones are designed in ways that best suit your cruising desires. You will need a new vocabulary to help you articulate the cruising vacation of your dreams, even though you've never before imagined many of the opportunities that await you.

Have the Whole Boat will teach you how to do all of that and more. The following chapters are organized to help you understand that when you charter a private yacht, you are reclaiming your at-sea vacation from the corporate cruise ship machine. Chartering a private yacht lets you regain control of your itinerary, your food choices, your budget, your daily schedule, and your ability to explore ashore in privacy. *Have the Whole Boat* will show you how to literally set your own course wherever, whenever, and however you wish.

Have the Whole Boat also will help you understand what to expect in terms of broker relationships, booking contracts and the onboard experience—which is likely to be dramatically different from your previous cruise vacations. In these pages, you will learn the names of people, companies and even specific yachts and crews that you can trust when you book your first charter.

This book also includes my personal observations from more than 30 private yacht charters I've experienced as a marine journalist around the world. I have cruised in popular locations like the Caribbean and the Mediterranean, in far-flung spots like Alaska and Fiji, and pretty much everywhere in between. You will benefit from the insider information I've gathered during each of those charters, along with additional knowledge I've gleaned from time spent onboard hundreds of other charter yachts at boat shows worldwide.

Finally, to make sure you don't feel like those couples in the Miami airport who feared I was running some kind of scam, I'm happy to tell you that the dozens of charter professionals quoted in *Have the Whole Boat* are not random sources I found in printed directories. Instead, they are reputable industry experts with whom I have developed personal relationships—and, in many cases, cruised onboard charter yachts—for a half-dozen years. I don't make a penny from any charter bookings they get from this book's readers, or from bookings they get anyplace else. I simply have come to trust them during my years of covering the charter business for major marine and luxury lifestyle magazines.

I hope that as you read, you will enjoy their insights and mine—and that you will make the most of our shared expertise when you decide to leave cruise ships for good and *Have the Whole Boat* for yourself.

Kim Kavin
Summer 2006

1

What Exactly Is *Yacht Charter?*

Loblolly trees and a lobsterman named Lowell—two things I didn't know existed until I visited an island called Anegada. I cruised there during my first private yacht charter, onboard the 65-foot sailing catamaran *Angel Glow* in the summer of 2000. I suppose I shouldn't have been all that surprised about discovering such new things, seeing as how up until the captain dropped anchor there, I didn't know Anegada existed, either. I'd heard only of other islands in the Virgins chain, like St. Thomas, St. John, and Tortola. You know, the spots most tourists visit.

Anegada, you see, is far from the international airports and sky-high resorts. The island is a dozen miles wide, has about 250 residents, and harbors a fledgling tourism seed that is unlikely ever to grow. Anegada's small air strip is equipped to receive just sporadic hopper flights, and coral heads—part of the second-largest barrier reef in the world—block virtually every approach from the sea. More than 300 ships have been wrecked trying to get into shore, and today, few commercial captains try the trip at all. Cruise ships certainly want no part of the gauntlet. Even if they did find a route to the beach, they would leave their passengers searching hopelessly for anything more than a single T-shirt shop that sells a few pieces of handmade jewelry.

I got to visit Anegada during my private yacht charter because *Angel Glow* is a beautiful, 65-foot-long boat with twin pontoons that are big enough to hold sleeping cabins, but that don't hang too far below the water's surface like single-hulled sailing yacht keels. Instead, the catamaran's draft (or depth below the water) is shallow enough to cross over Anegada's reefs, which makes *Angel Glow* one of the few boats that can get to the island in one piece. That fact, along with Capt. Greg Urlwin's extensive knowledge of the islands, made Anegada one of his favorite places to visit with newcomers. He liked to introduce his guests to the private world that yacht charter can offer, even in places as crowded as the Virgin Islands.

And so it was that I came to learn about the loblolly trees and the lobsterman named Lowell, two things you definitely won't find time to ponder during any cruise ship's group tour on any other island. The trees, which twist with knotty arms toward the sky, are made of pretty tough timber, their roots digging for water through limestone and sand. Lowell's arms certainly weren't knotty when I met him, but his fingertips were callused from all the effort he'd made to plant his own roots in the challenging landscape. He built and ran one of the island's only restaurants—an oasis of humanity in the wild that still offers a tiki-hut bar and a few well-used barbecues for cooking the day's catch—until he died a few years ago in a tragic welding accident. Today, his son does as Lowell used to do, taking reservations by VHF radio, a communication device that every yacht has onboard. Only when the boaters call in does the restaurant know how many lobsters the locals need to catch in time to serve that night.

We'd hailed Lowell using *Angel Glow*'s VHF radio when we were about a mile off Anegada's coast, to place our dinner order for a half-dozen crustaceans. They were broiling by the time we made it ashore. I savored every butter-slathered bite as I cracked open the red shells with my fingers, and I loved being on Anegada, so far from civilization that it was impossible *not* to slow down and relax. I had no deadline for rushing back to a ship or seeing a show, no crowds to battle in my search for a quiet corner of paradise, no need to even wear shoes as I stepped from our yacht's private dinghy onto the restaurant's beach.

If we liked it on Anegada, Capt. Urlwin explained, we could stay at anchor there all week. If we wanted to spend one more night and then cruise on in search of other little-known nooks he'd found throughout the years, that was a fine option, too. He could also get us back to the tourist areas, he said, if we'd rather party with the cruise-ship throngs. It was our itinerary to choose.

I couldn't imagine, at that moment, ever going back to *live* among the throngs, let alone share my vacation cruise with them. And I'd never felt that way before, so solitary and special—not in a resort, on a cruise ship, or during any other type of vacation.

It was liberating and frustrating at the same time. How could I have come so far in life, spent so much money on other vacations, talked to so many travel agents, and never even realized the option of private yacht charter was available to me?

Instead of staying at Anegada, we decided to set off the next day and go exploring. Yet the farther away we sailed from the island, the more I thought about the things I'd discovered there. I realized that the loblolly trees and the lobsterman named Lowell had a few things in common: They're unique, they're wonderful, and they're fairly hard to find unless you know where to look.

I soon realized that *Angel Glow*, the boat that had taken me to them, was much the same. Had I not known where to look for private yacht charter, I probably never would have found it. The only cruises I'd ever been offered as vacation options were onboard big ships with a thousand other people at a time. Private yacht charter was a phrase I'd never even heard.

If you're in the same situation now that I was in back then, you might do well to think of private yacht charter as a brand-new vacation idea that somehow feels like Anegada—a quiet, little-known haven you've been seeking your entire life without ever knowing you were looking for it, or that it even existed.

It's a fascinating option, really, especially given that just 50 years ago, there was barely a private yacht charter industry at all.

Wild West at Sea

Think, for a moment, about the cruise ship industry: Its boats are built as parts of fleets that global corporations own and control. These cruise ship companies offer you vacation packages that stay about the same from ship to ship, whose itineraries use the same ports, whose cabins look similar no matter which ship you climb aboard, and whose prices are usually non-negotiable. All the ships, itineraries, and prices are described in one glossy booklet that is distributed to you, the cruiser, by a single company.

With yacht charter, it's a far different story. While there are some big companies that help yacht owners manage the day-to-day affairs of their boats, the individual charter vacation bookings are usually accepted or declined not by the company, but by the individual yacht owners or their captains. The destinations available for charter are determined by where the yacht owners want to take their boats during any given season. The cabins onboard are decorated with the boat owners' tastes in mind, not for the comfort of the masses. Prices for charters, in some cases, can be negotiated depending on the yacht owner's whims.

Try to imagine every cruise ship on the world's waters being owned by a different person with his own quirks and demands, and you'll start to understand the world of private yacht charter.

Sounds crazy, right? Indeed, many newcomers to yacht charter often find this situation off-putting. Compared with leafing through a glossy cruise ship brochure's printed rates and itineraries, trying to book a private yacht charter vacation can feel a lot like the Wild West of pricing and negotiations. And the only help available to you is from charter brokers you've never met or even heard of, all of whom claim to know what's best for you—though different brokers may give you different advice.

Even worse, there is relatively little independent information out there for you to check if you want to do your own research. There are no reputable magazines that discuss the ins and outs of yacht charter on a monthly basis, no third-party databases that you can search for reviews like *Consumer Reports* online. And, unlike with cruise ships, you often can't ask your friends how they enjoyed their last private yacht charter. In many cases, they've never experienced one, either.

The good news that I've discovered during my years of covering the charter industry as a writer, editor, and photographer is that there *is* a structure at work beneath the seeming chaos—if you know where to look. Yes, private yachts are as different from cruise ships as the solitary island of Anegada is from the bustling tourist mecca of St. Thomas, but if you learn a bit about how the charter industry came to be, then you will have a much easier time understanding the way private yacht vacations are organized and booked. You'll also quickly see why you've never heard much about the industry before and how it has managed to blossom like a hidden-away garden in the broader landscape of vacation travel.

A good person to help explain why is Ted Rowe. He was there to witness the yacht charter industry being born, and he has grown up with it to become one of today's most prominent charter brokers.

Birth of an Industry

"In the old days, the way chartering worked back in the late 1950s and early '60s was that people who were interested in boating would charter boats through their friends. Somebody knew somebody who knew somebody who was a member of a yacht club and had a sailboat somewhere. That was basically it."

So says Rowe, now the owner of Ted Rowe Yacht Charters in Fort Lauderdale, Florida, and president of the Charter Yacht Brokers Association, a leading worldwide professional group. The 62-year-old Rowe has been around boating and charter his whole life, having started out working summers aboard a schooner on the Chesapeake Bay and in New England. By 1968 he was working aboard motoryachts, and he eventually earned the rank of captain.

His promotion happened to come right around the time the real excitement in charter was beginning.

"In the late '60s, there were some tax incentives that made owning yachts quite lucrative—especially if you put them into charter, because it then became a business," Rowe recalls. More and more wealthy people started buying more and more expensive boats, and they all wanted to rent them out for charter in order to reap the tax benefits.

All too quickly, charter was no longer about a single member of a yacht club who had a sailboat somewhere and was willing to let his friends use it. There were hundreds of wealthy men looking to get into the charter game so they could off-set the costs of owning yachts of their own.

"That's when Bill Whittamore and Robin Diston formed a company," Rowe recalls. "Bill was one of the young, up-and-coming, smartest guys on Madison Avenue, and one day he just went home to Darien [Connecticut] and said he'd had enough. He took all his suits, put them in the backyard, threw a can of gaso-line on them, set them on fire, and decided to go boating. He was independently wealthy by then, and he could afford to do something a little different."

The different concept Whittamore and Diston envisioned was a company called Yacht Management, a firm that oversaw everything that needed overseeing aboard yachts—from hiring crew to stocking spare parts to helping the chefs get provisions such as food and wine in various ports. These were things that wealthy men buying yachts for tax breaks didn't know about, things for which they would be willing to pay a flat, monthly fee to a company like Yacht Management. And with more and more wealthy men buying yachts, Whittamore and Diston fig-ured, it was a niche that was bound to grow.

It was a watershed, as Rowe sees the evolution of the charter industry, for two reasons.

First, people who had until that point made their livings as yacht bro-kers—taking a commission for selling one or two sailing yachts a year—suddenly could become part of a business plan that included collecting monthly fees from yacht owners whether their boats were for sale or not. These brokers wanted steadier incomes, which meant that they wanted more companies like Yacht Management to be created, which of course happened as other businessmen saw the same potential windfall.

Second, the more private yachts that signed on with the new companies, the more those companies became centralized locations where someone looking to charter a yacht could find available boats. A broker who had been helping a client book charters from time to time aboard one or two boats he knew at a yacht club could all of a sudden call a company like Yacht Management and ask about a dozen or more charter boats that were all seeking customers simultaneously.

A broker with that kind of access to information suddenly had an inventory of charter yachts that was much bigger than whatever handful of yacht club members' boats he'd known in the past. This meant he could serve more charter clients, like a travel agent serves clients needing airfares and hotels today. The yacht broker didn't even have to sell boats anymore to earn a living. He could focus exclusively on chartering them and have a steady income.

"This was the beginning of the charter broker, the specialist," Rowe says. "There were people like Jo Bliss in those days. She was one of the Fearsome Foursome: four ladies who created and ran this industry for some time. Lynne Jachney, Lenore Muncie, and Evelyn Whitney were the others. They were the first ones who sort of moved into the industry and said, 'We are charter brokers, we are not yacht brokers.' They didn't care about selling boats. They saw the handwriting on the wall."

These women who led the charge in the 1970s realized—after working, in some cases, as secretaries for yacht sales brokers in the newly created management companies—that selling yachts once or twice a year wasn't the best way to make a steady income. They decided to focus exclusively on chartering the yachts month after month after month, and they gave rise to the title "charter broker" as opposed to "yacht broker."

These charter brokers soon left the management companies to become independent businesspeople of their own. "The management companies were looked down on by the charter brokers," Rowe says. "'Oh, they're going to steal our clients.' I cannot tell you how many times I heard that story. 'I'm not going to book a boat through Bill Whittamore—he'll know my client's name, telephone number, address.' Then they discovered it was a lot easier to pick up the phone and call one place and say, 'I've got a client with six people on these dates in the Caribbean. What boats have you got?'"

There were, of course, other developments along the way—other people who played key roles in giving rise to the charter industry worldwide. Desmond Nicholson, for one, started offering charters around the Caribbean island of Antigua in the 1950s onboard his father's schooner, later helping to rebuild an old naval fort into what is today a major charter hub called Nelson's Dockyard. In the Mediterranean, too, there have been countless individuals who started small businesses that have since grown.

All of these people's efforts soon coalesced with the emerging marketplace of yacht management companies and the newly defined role of charter brokers.

An industry was born, and it was about to explode.

Bareboat Fleets

By the 1970s, the idea of centralized yacht management had taken firm hold among wealthy owners of large, private yachts. But the concept also had begun to entrench itself among entrepreneurs who envisioned owning entire fleets of smaller boats in major charter destinations—kind of like car-rental companies today that own fleets of Toyotas in airport hub cities.

These charter boat entrepreneurs figured that there was an entire other category of potential charter clients out there, people who were willing to do a bit of the sailing and cooking onboard themselves in exchange for paying a far lower price for their charter vacation, a price that was possible to offer if the boats were all kept in one easily accessible place, like the Virgin Islands, as part of a fleet.

So began the concept of bareboat charter, which is much different from the crewed charter that was going on aboard the bigger boats at companies like Yacht Management.

With bareboating, charter customers are offered the bare bones in terms of onboard help—you act as your own captain, cook, deckhand, stewardess, and engineer—but the cruising vacation is still onboard a private boat and at a fraction of the cost of the charter yachts that come with a full crew. Sometimes, a family's week aboard a bareboat costs even less than a week aboard a cruise ship (which you'll learn more about in Chapter Eight).

In many parts of the world today, bareboating is still a mom-and-pop business. A couple or a family will own one or two yachts that they make available for charter through brokers or directly to vacationers like you.

There are, however, several larger companies that have fleets of bareboats, power and sail alike, all over the world. Two of the biggest companies, Sunsail and The Moorings, recently joined forces under the parent company First Choice Marine and now book nearly 30 percent of the estimated quarter-million bareboat charters that vacationers take each year.

Lex Raas, the president of First Choice Marine, believes bareboating started evolving into a high-growth-potential vacation industry as recently as the early 1990s. He attributes the increase in bareboat demand to two key factors: better boats and better access.

"In terms of complexity, boats are now much easier to use," he explains. "Reliability, too, is improved. It's grown out of the user-friendliness of boats. Twenty years ago, there weren't a whole lot of options out there for production boatbuilders. Not many people could mass produce yachts at realistic prices, which would allow people to build fleets and then let people pay for bareboat charters.

Bareboat bases typically have a mix of powerboats and sailboats at a
marina dock. This is the kind of place where you would pick up and drop
off your bareboat.

"The whole other thing is accessibility to destinations," he continues. "Years
ago, the British Virgin Islands, it was quite a sweat just to get down there. Now,
you fly to San Juan and you can pretty much get anywhere. Places like Tonga
that are more remote, they'll come up [in bareboating popularity] when accessibility improves, too."

Raas also believes the style and design of newer bareboats is helping the industry continue to grow, with more and more companies bringing powerboats—and, particularly, power catamarans—into their fleets. You need not
know how to work winches and sails to operate them, you can drive them much
like you would drive a car, and their layouts and design (which you'll learn more
about in Chapter Three) are far more comfortable and spacious than traditional
sailboats.

"Catamarans have a lot of growth," Raas says. "Just in the past five years or so,
the real growth has occurred. About 35 percent of the Moorings sailing fleet is
catamarans now. Sunsail, they're at about 18 to 20 percent. The issue is ease of
sailing. People can take novices out without them having to worry about heeling

over, the kids being safe. The layout of the boats are just a lot more private. There's a lot more space that people can share."

In a further effort to make bareboating easier—to introduce more and more people like you to private yacht charter vacations—some bareboat companies now also offer a hybrid of the crewed and bareboating experience, called a skippered charter. In this case, you and your friends help out with the task of boating during the cruise but pay an extra fee to have a captain and sometimes even a chef at your disposal. They take care of actually running the yacht and help point you in the right direction when it comes to assisting with docking and navigating.

It's all part of the industry's continuing evolution toward making itself a better vacation option.

Boats, Boats Everywhere

The crewed-yacht management houses and bareboat fleets were well-established by the time the 1980s rolled around—along with a surge in the U.S. economy. As more and more people got rich, more and more people bought yachts, which meant that more and more yachts found their way into crewed and bareboat charter. Now there was real competition for charter bookings, and prices for even the fanciest of crewed yachts had to adjust.

In fact, there got to be so many large, individually owned yachts out there waiting to be chartered that a woman named Joyce MacMullen came up with the idea of creating a database to keep track of them all. MacMullen, who today owns Windward Mark Yacht Charters in Tequesta, Florida, was at the time a home-maker whose husband owned a boatyard in Maine. She had been booking a few charters here and there for clients she met through her husband's work—as did many of the women who were among the first true charter brokers—and eventually MacMullen decided that her side job would be easier if she had a database of every charter yacht's size, captain's name, number of crew, sailing area, and weekly rate.

"My husband and I saw a hole in the industry, that I needed a master list," MacMullen recalls. "We came up with the concept, and I went around to the management companies that were in existence at that time, like Bill Whittamore. I went to Antigua, Greece, England, Turkey, just to see if the idea would work, because at the time, this was 1982, and programming all of that information into a computer was a very big deal. We used the one that my husband had at the shipyard."

MacMullen turned her information into printed and bound copies, stamped the name Charter Databank International on them, and gave each booklet a bright orange cover so charter brokers could find it quickly on their desks. If a potential client called and said he wanted to cruise in Antigua aboard a sailing yacht that holds six people, the charter broker would simply flip to the "Antigua/ Sailboats" section of the CDI guide and discuss the available yachts.

With a tool like the CDI guide available, the job of being a charter broker became that much more attractive. Dozens of people from all corners of the boating industry—the vast majority of those people being women—found their way into acting as charter brokers. Some started out working as stewardesses onboard the yachts, while others gravitated from existing yacht management companies. "There were people like Missy Harvey at Destination Charters, she started out as a travel agent," Ted Rowe recalls. "Because she was booking [airfare for] all the crew flying back and forth to boats everywhere, she knew all the captains and, eventually, half the [boat] owners."

Soon it was the 1990s, and the Internet boom had made millionaires out of countless people who wanted not only to own yachts, but also to book them for charter vacations. Money was everywhere to be made whether you owned a bareboat fleet, a management house, or an independent charter broker agency. Bigger companies started to gobble up the smaller ones, creating today's yacht-management and charter-booking powerhouses like Camper & Nicholsons International. Today, in addition to the independent charter broker businesses that are still thriving, the big-name companies have entire staffs of charter brokers working in-house.

"The Camper & Nicholsons, all the major European management companies, they're all an outgrowth of finding and seeing this new profit center," Rowe explains. "In the old days, if you wanted to charter a boat, you'd better know the owner and have his home number and his office number because you had to go find him and the captain, and you didn't know where they were. The day that they put together this concept that there was a charter book, and you called one place, and they knew how to get hold of the owner, and you could deal with another broker instead of the owner—it was great."

Today's Best Brokers

By the late 1990s, the boats available for charter had begun to change, too. The economic boom years in America led to what some people call the Second Golden Age of Yachting—a return to the likes of 1920s "robber baron" wealth and the desire to flaunt it in ever bigger and better ways. You could book everything from a 25-foot sailing yacht to a 150-foot motoryacht for charter, and all of the boats had different features with different crew onboard. Unlike in Rowe's early days, when a captain worked for an owner his entire lifetime, crew began to move from smaller charter yachts to bigger charter yachts, much like other businesspeople move from small companies to big companies throughout their careers. Yacht charter was a true industry.

And within that industry, a good charter broker who could help you book the right vacation for your needs was now a far cry from being somebody who knew somebody who had a boat, or even somebody who used the CDI guide to keep track of all the boats and crews.

Instead, a good charter broker had become a person whose job required touring hundreds of yachts each year to learn what made them different in terms of cabin space and other features. A good charter broker had to keep track of which captains and crew were working aboard which yachts—and how their personalities were likely to interact with different types of vacationers. A good charter broker had to know about destinations, too, as more and more boats started cruising to new and different places that cruise ships would never even consider going—places that all have different rules, taxes, and regulations concerning private yachts. A good charter broker had to know such minute details as which 60-foot motoryachts had shaded top decks as opposed to open areas, for clients who preferred to cruise without getting sunburns. A good charter broker had to know which boats were built with safety features that families with small children would need during their charters, as opposed to which boats had the biggest, fanciest bars onboard for couples looking to party their vacations away.

Such is the job of a charter broker today, a complex mix of knowledgeable boater, world traveler, crew and client psychologist, yacht design expert, and highly organized planner.

And yet that job of helping you plan your private yacht charter vacation is showing signs of evolving again, along with the industry itself.

Teach Me, Captain

As more and more wealthy people bought luxury yachts, more and more of them decided that they needed to know how to drive them. (Thank goodness!) These folks started looking to "old salts"—licensed captains who had plenty of experience at the helm and were willing to take on private students. So began the first instructional cruises, back in the late 1960s and early 1970s. The "cruises" were as short as an afternoon spent boating near a wealthy yacht owner's office, teaching him how to steer and adjust the sails to make his boat go.

By the 1980s, the concept of instructional cruises had become a serious business idea—and was beginning to catch the attention of the entrepreneurs who owned bareboat fleets. These businessmen, who perhaps had a dozen or so do-it-yourself smaller yachts available for charter in the Virgin Islands, realized that in addition to their existing clientele of boaters from all over the world, they could appeal to many vacationers who had no boating experience at all, if only they could teach them the basics of cruising.

Think of the concept the way you think of driver's education. The more that car companies help to fund driving schools, the more drivers there will be and the more cars the companies can ultimately sell.

So it is with instructional yacht charters, which are cruising experiences in which you have a captain onboard teaching you to sail or operate a powerboat. They're not exactly vacations, per se, though they do combine the vacation element with the instructional goals.

Some schools are extremely orderly, with only students allowed onboard, while in other cases, your family can go along for the week and relax while you take lessons at the helm. Many schools will allow couples, families, or groups of friends to learn all at once, thus enhancing your fun and helping you to prepare for bareboating with the same group in the future. At least one bareboat/instructional company, called Sunsail, has land-based resorts where part of the family can enjoy a "regular" vacation while other members of the family take bareboating classes onboard yachts at the resort's marina.

Instructional charters can be as enjoyable as any other bareboat charter, provided you're interested in learning as much as you are in sightseeing. You'll have homework, for instance. It's nothing like cramming for final exams, but it will cut into your time ashore at night in restaurants and tiki bars. Some of the lessons are done in workbooks while the boat is at anchor, while other lessons are hands-on at the helm, on the boat's deck, and in the engine room. You aren't likely to cover as much cruising area as a regular bareboater would, but make no mistake: You will be underway, and you will be acting as the skipper or first mate more often than not.

The whole goal is to help you feel comfortably in control of a yacht so that you can become a repeat client for bareboat companies worldwide.

One of the pioneers in this branch of the yacht charter industry is Steve Colgate, who, with his wife, Doris, continues to operate the Offshore Sailing School from its home base in Fort Myers, Florida. The company—which he originally conceived at a cocktail party in the 1960s—was growing seriously by the 1980s. It is now affiliated with The Moorings, one of the biggest bareboat charter companies in the world.

"We teach on 26-foot sailboats," Doris explains. "You take a course to get to the intermediate level, and at the end of that course, the instructor gets off the boat and the students sail our $40,000 boat without the instructor onboard. The bareboat companies want people to learn so they can easily put them into the charter business. For us, our graduates get a 15-percent discount at The Moorings, and they tend to stay with it. There's a zillion different places you can go."

About 2,500 people learn to cruise each year through Offshore Sailing School, and Doris estimates that as many as 10,000 students are graduating annually from boating schools worldwide. Most of those schools still focus on sailing, though more and more are moving into powerboat instruction, too, as the demand for engine-driven bareboats increases.

"We're doing [a course called] Fast Track to Power Cruising now, too," Doris says, referring to a course that became available in June 2006. "We're working with The Moorings on their NauticBlue 46 powercats. It'll be a five-day course, board on Monday morning and the instructor gets off around noon on Friday. The students take the boat for a mini-cruise Friday afternoon, then bring it back Saturday afternoon."

Today, through Offshore Sailing School and other companies, you can book an instructional charter anywhere from the Chesapeake Bay to Alaska to the Caribbean, thus adding scenery to your experience. You can even book women's-only instructional charters in which you live aboard a yacht for a week and learn from other women at the helm along the way.

I did one of these women's-only courses back in 2000 with a St. Petersburg, Florida-based company called Sea Sense. I learned everything from driving and docking to checking the engine's oil and hailing the Coast Guard on the VHF radio, all from a salty female captain who had about four decades' experience at the helm. After my week aboard with Sea Sense—with no prior experience beyond driving small ski boats at my grandfather's lake house—I felt comfortable navigating, docking, and troubleshooting engine-room problems aboard a 42-foot trawler yacht. Even better, along the way, I got to see beautiful Gulf Coast sunsets and dine at fantastic waterfront restaurants.

Sea Sense still offers the kind of course that I took on Florida's West Coast, and the company has since branched out to offer additional vacation-style instruction everywhere from the Pacific Northwest to Southern Italy.

Again, it's the continuing evolution of the industry.

The World Is Yours

Just as the options are continuing to expand for people who want to book vacations onboard bareboats, so, too, are the choices for people who want to vacation onboard fully crewed yachts—and there are a lot of people out there who fit that category. Although there are no statistics on the number of worldwide charter bookings for crewed yachts, a good guess is that about 50,000 weeks of crewed charter get booked every year, with the yachts themselves ranging from about 60 feet long to much, much longer.

A 60-foot sailing yacht, once considered a jaw-dropping sight, is today a yacht of average or even smallish size on the world's waters. The wealthy men buying yachts as we approach the year 2010 typically start out shopping for boats that are at least 125 feet long. The biggest yacht available for charter in the world today is more than 400 feet long—a whopping 40 stories tall if stood on its stern.

This astounding movement toward bigger and bigger private yachts affects your charter choices at the top end of the price spectrum. Bigger boats have bigger engines, bigger sails, and bigger fuel reserves—which means they can cruise farther and to more places than ever before. When Ted Rowe started working in the business back in the 1960s, he remembers charter taking place only in New England, the Caribbean, and the Mediterranean. "I can remember when there was no such thing as a yacht going to Alaska," he recalls, adding that today, charter yachts go there and beyond to the South Pacific, the Galapagos Islands, and even Indochina. "It's absolutely an established international industry. It's not worldwide—yet. But it's fast becoming worldwide as the yachts get bigger and people want to go more places and do more things."

Just how far charter yachts go on private vacations these days became apparent in 1997, when a broker named Jo Russell was asked to put together a nearly year-long charter. One of her clients, a real estate developer from Newport Beach, California, wanted to sail around the world without buying a boat of his own. Russell worked with Nicholson Yachts of Newport to arrange the trip aboard a 110-foot sailing yacht called *Vairea*, which cost more than $100,000 a month. After two years of planning, Russell's clients set off aboard *Vairea* from Tahiti in the winter of 1999, worked their way through the South Pacific, Thailand, the Maldives, the Red Sea, and the Mediterranean, and ended in Antibes, France, in June 2000.

"That was the first big one that I know of," Rowe recalls. There have since been several other "worldwide charters," including a hugely successful 'round-the-world booking for a couple and their young daughter aboard the 108-foot motoryacht Askari, organized by Debra Blackburn at Fraser Yachts Worldwide.

Some of the larger, more expensive charter yachts are leaving traditional
Caribbean and Mediterranean cruising grounds and heading for new
destinations, such as the Seychelles, shown here.

As the new millennium progresses, she and other charter brokers are hearing
more and more requests from people who want to charter in new and exciting
places around the globe—which, in turn, is beginning to spark a new business
idea in the minds of the men who own yachts big enough to explore new
grounds. The concept is simple: A megayacht owner can have his captain coordinate a worldwide cruise and then fly in to visit his yacht in far-flung destinations
for a few weeks at a time. During the weeks when the owner is not using his
yacht, he can allow charter brokers to place clients aboard, thus helping to defray
the yacht's operating expenses on such an expensive journey—and in the process
opening up new markets for charter by people like you.

Only a few megayachts have left the typically requested charter grounds in the
Caribbean and Mediterranean to try this business adventure. The early adopters
include the 152-foot motoryacht *Montigne* and the 184-foot motoryacht *Pangaea,* both of which went around the world with great business success. *Pangaea,*
in fact, is being promoted by its management company, The Sacks Group, as
entering the 2006/2007 winter charter season with a 100-percent repeat charter

rate—which means every single charter client booked another cruise onboard—in the South Pacific, specifically in and around Tahiti.

As more and more yachts like these cruise to new places, more and more captains and brokers are getting to know those places and are becoming able to help people like you plan vacations there. This concept of opening new markets to charter already has the attention of at least one major charter company manager: David LeGrand at Fraser Yachts Worldwide. He told me in a recent, private conversation that he sees destinations like China—until now not even a thought when planning charters—opening up to just that possibility as soon as the year 2010. As wealth grows there, and in places like Russia and India, the elite businesspeople who live there will buy yachts and build marinas to house them. If companies like Fraser can then sign those yachts into their charter fleets, they can begin to promote those destinations for charter right alongside promotions for yachts in the Caribbean and Mediterranean.

All of which means ever more vacation options for you aboard fully crewed charter yachts. And, as happened in the past, the bareboat segment of the industry is continuing to follow the more expensive crewed yachts geographically.

For instance, NauticBlue, a company that offers powerboats for bareboat charters, is based in the well-traveled charter destination of the Caribbean Sea—but recently opened an office with a small fleet in Greece. Its sister company, The Moorings, has bareboat sailboats available everywhere from the Indian Ocean to the South Pacific, in addition to the more popular Caribbean. All of this, and other options from other companies like Sunsail, means you can work with worldwide organizations to experience all the fun of yachting in an exotic, emerging charter ground, and that you can do so for the low cost of a bareboat charter, which in many cases is even less than a cruise ship trip.

"The world of yachting continues to grow," as Ted Rowe puts it. It started as a group of wealthy buddies letting their friends use their sailboats in the 1960s. "Now, we're heading into new and emerging markets."

How to Choose?

Now that you understand the evolution of the private yacht charter industry, it's easier to see why it functions much differently from the world of cruise ships. Individual people owning unique boats, or even small fleets of unique boats, and taking them anywhere they choose is a far cry from global cruise-ship corporations with massive marketing budgets that operate sisterships cruising back and forth among the same commercial ports. The only way you would even hear about the insulated world of yacht charter vacations is through a charter broker, who, until now, you probably didn't even know existed.

Hopefully, your new knowledge of the yacht charter industry's foundation will help you see its booking challenges more along the lines of vacation opportunities. No, there are not glossy cruise-ship-style booklets that detail itineraries down to the minute, but that's because with yacht charter, you can literally go anywhere at any time. Yes, you will have to rely on a charter broker more so than you might a travel agent, but that's because the charter broker is an expert in this one, specific kind of cruising vacation as opposed to many kinds of vacations on land and at sea. Yes, the owners of the private yachts control their charter prices and can change them at any time, but worldwide competition has an impact, and there is room in some cases for negotiation.

The way you choose the right private yacht charter vacation is by figuring out what you want and then knowing how to work with a knowledgeable charter broker to get it. You can request an off-the-beaten-path journey through the loblolly trees with a captain like the one who took me to Anegada onboard the catamaran *Angel Glow*, or you can go off in your own direction, cruising anywhere and in any way that suits your idea of an ideal vacation.

You can cruise aboard a bareboat alone with your friends or family, aboard an instructional bareboat with a captain, aboard a skippered bareboat with a captain and chef, or aboard a fully crewed yacht with a team dedicated to serving you. Even better, you can choose any of those styles of charter from the Caribbean to the Mediterranean and beyond.

The history you learned in this chapter is your first step toward getting there, introducing you to the inner workings of a vacation industry unlike any other. Your next step begins with Chapter Two, which will give you a general overview of the ways that all types of private yacht charter differ from the cruise ship vacations you know.

2

Yachts vs. Cruise Ships

In the summer of 2005, I found myself aboard two very different cruise vacations. In mid-August, I helped to celebrate my grandfather's 90th birthday with 16 of my aunts, uncles, and cousins—and about 2,000 other people—onboard a 700-foot-long Royal Caribbean ship bound for Key West and Cozumel. The very next week, I helped to celebrate my father's 58th birthday aboard a private 60-foot yacht on the Chesapeake Bay, with just my parents and sister onboard.

These cruises were not Pepsi versus Coke. They were more like soda pop versus chardonnay: both in the same genre, but meant for entirely different audiences with completely different tastes.

Now, I like a cool, refreshing soda pop once in a while, and I have to say, I enjoyed a lot of things aboard that Royal Caribbean cruise ship. Given our large group's widely varied ages and interests, the cruise ship was ideal, offering lots of activities and adequate (though downright ugly) interior cabins for everyone at a total cost of around $1,000 per person, including excursions, liquor, and gratuities. My twentysomething cousins had pretty girls to chase, my aunts and uncles shopped at the onboard art auctions, I got to do some scuba diving, and my grandfather played his favorite games in the card room until his fingers hurt. Our extended family had plenty to discuss each night over dinner—pretty much the only time I saw most of my relatives during the trip. Which was good, in this case, because some of my relatives can't stand much more of one another's company. A smaller boat where we were together constantly would have been a disaster on the social front.

The cruise ship was definitely a success, especially in the eyes of my grandfather, who enjoyed having his family all around him at a price most cruise vacationers would consider a decent bargain. But I must admit that when we returned home, the rest of us were all exhausted from our "vacation." My father, for one, said he couldn't believe he was going on *another* boat in just a few days.

Yet there we were the following weekend, my parents, my sister, and me, sitting on our private deck aboard the 60-foot motoryacht *Irony*, enjoying our last bites of freshly prepared lobster ravioli as the sun set in magnificent reds and yellows. There was not another family—or even another boat—in sight. It was just the four of us, sipping every glass of chardonnay the crew poured for us, awaiting a sugar-free dessert that chef Libby Cole was preparing especially for my diabetic dad. Later, we would retire to our cabins, which were easily twice the size of the ones we'd had aboard the cruise ship and certainly decorated more elegantly. Mine was lined with rich mahogany planks, and the bathroom had a beautiful marble shower. Mom and Dad's cabin was similar, but with the addition of French doors that opened onto a private deck. From there, they could step ashore or enjoy the scenery as they pleased.

Up on the deck where we had just eaten dinner, Dad leaned back in his chair in a way I hadn't noticed in a while. He wasn't thinking about the fact that this cruise cost about the same amount per person as the week aboard the cruise ship. Nor was Dad thinking about what time he'd have to wake up in order to join a group for an onshore excursion. There were no groups, and we could decide on the excursions whenever the mood struck us.

Instead, Dad was simply leaning back in his chair, letting his supper settle, and not thinking at all.

That's when Capt. Dan Cole popped his head out onto the boat's deck and casually asked, "What time do you want to head out in the morning?"

"What time do we have to leave?" Dad answered, still in the cruise-ship mode of pre-planned itineraries.

"We can leave whenever you want," the captain replied. "We're on your schedule. If you like it here, we'll have a leisurely breakfast. If you're ready to go, we'll get moving early."

It was the antithesis to the previous week's cruise ship experience, and Dad articulated the moment beautifully.

"It's different," he said of the private yacht charter vacation. "The cruise ships, they offer something for everybody to *do*. This is more about just *being*. One's not better than the other. They're just different."

My dad's a pretty smart guy. And his conclusion is true not just when comparing cruise ships to private yachts, but also when comparing private yachts among themselves.

Styles of Charter

There is a tendency with vacations to think that just because one is more expensive than another, it is by definition better. A $10,000 cruise, we tell ourselves, is vastly better than a $1,000 cruise. There can't possibly be any comparison. After all, why would people pay ten times as much if they really were both the same?

I agree that a $10,000 trip is likely to be far *different* from a $1,000 one, but I don't buy into the idea that the more expensive vacation is necessarily *better*. I've been aboard big ships and private yachts that range in price from $1,000 to $1 million a week—yes, a million smackers a week when all the extras are factored in—and I've honestly found that each cruise had wonderful attributes the others lacked.

When comparing private yacht vacations, I tend to think the way my father does when comparing cruise ships to private yachts. Different prices simply equal different experiences.

In the case of a cruise ship, a higher cost typically means bowtie-wearing waiters serving tea to well-heeled grandparents who enjoy playing bridge. That's perfectly lovely if you're a silver fox with a thick money clip, but it would be the worst vacation in the world for a young couple with small children who scream like banshees unless they get to eat hot dogs with actors dressed as cartoon characters. For them, the less-expensive cruise is probably far closer to paradise.

With yacht charter, you have to think in those same terms. The most expensive cruises are not necessarily the best *for you*. I know several men who own some of the world's biggest, most expensive, most luxurious private motoryachts. Do you know what they do once or twice a year for fun? They charter 40-foot bareboats that they can skipper themselves, without captains and crews getting in the way of their setting a course toward the sunset. Yes, they enjoy the pampering they receive during fully crewed megayacht cruises, but from time to time, they just want to have a different vacation experience.

In fact, I once heard that Princess Diana liked to charter not the fanciest, most expensive megayachts, but "smaller" motoryachts in the 80- to 100-foot size range. That way, she could enjoy a fully crewed, highly pampered vacation without attracting the attention of the paparazzi.

Which, when you think about it, makes the richest vacationers in the world no different from you and me when it comes to choosing a yacht charter: We all want what is best for our personal needs. If you picked up *Have the Whole Boat* in the first place, you've probably taken a few cruises aboard big ships with the masses and are looking for a new kind of experience. The biggest mistake you could make as you learn about private yachts is limiting yourself by believing the most expensive charter out there is automatically the best one for you.

Instead of thinking about private yacht charter in terms of cost, you should think about it in terms of style. As you learned in Chapter One, there are crewed styles, bareboat styles, instructional styles, hybrids that combine more than one style—you can find pretty much any style of charter, in pretty much any price range, in the world of private yacht charter.

Just as yacht charter itself is different from cruise ship vacations, so each particular yacht charter is different from the next.

Bareboats and Instructional Yachts

Bareboats, as you recall from Chapter One, are the do-it-yourself version of yacht charter. They are for people who already know enough about boating that they can act as their own skipper, mate, chef, deckhand, stewardess, and dinghy driver. If you own your own 35-foot boat in, say, Massachusetts but you want to experience a private yacht cruise in, say, St. Thomas, bareboating could be an option for you.

Bareboating also might be an option if you have some experience aboard smaller boats, such as Hobie Cat sailboats or lake-going powerboats. In some cases, you can apply your small-boat experience to bigger yacht operations after a few days of lessons. A family I used to watch sailing 18-foot Hobie Cats and one-person Sunfish sailboats during the 1970s and '80s on New Jersey's Culver Lake now use their skills during weeklong bareboat vacations onboard 45-foot catamarans in the Virgin Islands. "This November, I'm going to go for my ninth time," Allen Bentson told me in the summer of 2005. "Two years ago was the first time I took my kids down there, two boys, 26 and 24. For all those years of teaching them on the Sunfish and the Hobie, it just opened up their eyes to the fun that you can have. You learn how to sail, and the same principles apply."

Because many people cruising onboard bareboats are this brand of once-in-awhile cruisers—and because many bareboat fleets use those same boats for instructional charters with first-timers learning to sail or drive a powerboat—the boats themselves tend to be older and in less than pristine condition. Folks who don't cruise all the time bump into things like dock pilings and underwater hazards, and they tend to care for their chartered boats in about the same way you might take care of a rental car. Nobody who charters a bareboat wants to leave the thing in complete disarray, but scrapes and scratches are likely to be part of the cruise. Hence the lower cost of a bareboat charter when compared with a fully crewed luxury yacht—you're likely to have a lot of fun, but you won't have silk draperies and marble bathrooms.

The yachts in bareboat fleets tend to be anywhere from 25 to 60 feet long (give or take a few feet), easily handled by and comfortable to cruise aboard for a couple, a foursome or even a group of six or eight people. You can bareboat aboard a sailing yacht, a powerboat, or a catamaran depending on your budget. In the vast majority of cases, a bareboat will cost you less than or the same amount per person as a low- to mid-range cruise ship, with the price rising slightly if you add a captain's weekly pay for an instructional or skippered charter.

The 36-foot *Blue Note* is an example of a typical instructional or bareboat trawler yacht. *Blue Note* has two cabins with private bathrooms inside, plus a galley and dining area.

Some of the larger bareboat companies offer the option of letting you cruise in a *flotilla*—a group of bareboaters moving together along a pre-determined itinerary. This takes away your independence in terms of destination planning, but offers you a way to take the helm without being entirely on your own. It's often a good first solo charter for novice bareboaters who want the privacy of their own yacht as well as experienced help nearby should the need arise.

Your cabins, in many cases, will be as big as or bigger than the lowest-priced interior cabins aboard cruise ships. At least one cabin usually has a private bathroom that's about the same size as those aboard cruise ships, while in some cases (particularly aboard catamarans) all the cabins have en suite facilities. In still other cases, the smaller-cabin bathrooms may be the type where a shower and toilet are in the same compartment, shared via separate entrances by the people sleeping in two adjacent cabins. (Remember: You always book the whole bareboat, not by the cabin, so anybody sharing a bathroom will be your friends or family.)

Reputable bareboat companies take great pains to ensure their bareboats and instructional yachts are clean, have working navigation equipment, and have proper safety gear onboard—even if the exterior paint jobs aren't perfect and the galley cupboards are a bit scratched up from improperly stowed pots and pans banging around. Think of some bareboats like the older vessels in a cruise ship company's fleet, and you'll get the idea.

Whether you plan to book a bareboat or instructional charter aboard a sailboat, powerboat, or catamaran, you need to think about the whole boat as opposed to just the cabins.

"Your average charterer thinks newer is better, always," explains Barney Crook, a 25-year veteran of the bareboat business who owns TMM Yacht Charters, with sailboat and powerboat bases in the British Virgin Islands, Belize, and the Grenadines. "In general, if people [narrow their choices to] four boats of the same type that are all a little bit different, they'll nearly always book the newest boat first. But the people who have chartered before, they don't do it that way. They know we maintain our boats, and they know how certain boats handle, what they like, which layouts work for them, and they book those boats. In our case, we have a fairly diverse fleet, but each boat in the fleet has its own page on our Web site, and people can see what each boat's got. They select boats by name, not by type.

"That varies from company to company, of course," he adds—and it's a point well worth taking. With a less-reputable company that does less maintenance, an older bareboat indeed might be a rundown bag of bolts that you wouldn't want to get near with a ten-foot boathook.

Sea Sense, the company I mentioned in Chapter One when discussing women's-only instructional charters, takes good care of the boats it offers even though many of them are older. I remember my week aboard that 42-foot Grand Banks trawler yacht as being perfectly comfortable, though not exactly luxurious (the same way I felt aboard Royal Caribbean's older ship *Empress of the Seas*). I did my best aboard the trawler yacht to keep the decks dry as juice dripped from a mango I was eating, but I knew it wouldn't have been the end of the world had a few sugary droplets collided with the teak below.

My carefree attitude changed—in some cases more than others—aboard the skippered and crewed yacht charters I have enjoyed.

Skippered Bareboats

A lot of bareboat companies offer skippered charters aboard the same yachts they make available to bareboaters and instructional cruisers. As explained earlier, with a skippered charter you pay extra for a captain to do the majority of the work involved with running the boat, and you help out as needed instead of paying for a full crew. In most cases, you can add a captain to your bareboat vacation for $200 to $300 a day in addition to the yacht's weekly rate. Chefs are also sometimes available at similar day rates.

With skippered bareboat vacations, you'll still get to sleep in the biggest, most comfortable cabins onboard your private yacht, though the boat itself may be somewhat dinged up from previous bareboat cruises where no captain was hired. And, with a captain and chef aboard a bareboat, you're likely to help out with only basic tasks such as anchoring and tying lines to the dock. These things aren't hard to do—the captain will show you how—and can even be a lot of fun if you've ever wanted to try sailing without the responsibility of being in command of a boat. Kids, in particular, *love* to help out with the basics.

Without question, adding a captain and chef to a bareboat charter is the least-expensive way to enjoy a partially crewed yacht vacation. Yet there is another option for partially crewed charters, one that enhances both your surroundings and your service.

Higher-End Partially Crewed

In some cases, a husband-and-wife team will act as your captain and chef on a single yacht they own and live aboard or on a yacht that has a single owner instead of being part of a fleet. The husband and wife do virtually all of the work aboard, while occasionally asking you to lend a hand with smaller tasks that require a third set of hands. We're talking two or three things the entire week, not two or three things each day. You still sleep in the nicest cabins, while the two crewmembers sleep in the crew's quarters—even if they own the yacht.

The work you'll be asked to do is no harder than what you'd do on a bareboat with a captain and chef—in most cases, you won't be asked to do much at all—but with the husband-and-wife teams working aboard single yachts that they call home, your yacht itself is likely to be far nicer in terms of upkeep. Plus, the couple serving you are likely to offer superior service to what a bareboat captain brought on for a week might provide, since the liveaboard couple usually see themselves as hosts instead of hired hands.

The captain and chef who took care of my family during my father's birthday cruise aboard the 60-foot motoryacht *Irony* are an example of this style of higher-end partially crewed charter. The boat they work aboard is a stunning, mahogany-filled vacation getaway owned by an American businessman. Where a fully crewed yacht the size of *Irony* might have three crew tending to guests in other cases, this particular yacht has just two, a husband and wife who used to work aboard fully crewed yachts twice *Irony*'s size. They provide excellent service and gourmet meals—the kind found onboard the 120-foot megayachts where they used to work—and they handle all the major boating requirements, too, perhaps once in a while asking a guest to add an extra set of hands for tying off the lines during docking. I think I helped with that task twice during our entire cruise, and only after I volunteered. My parents and sister weren't asked to help with anything at all, and we truly felt as though "their" yacht was our own for the entire vacation.

Another example of this higher-end style of partially crewed charter is the one offered by folks like Al and Jane Castleman, a married couple who built the yacht of their dreams so they could retire aboard and cruise around the world. I met the Castlemans in Rhode Island's Newport Harbor in the summer of 2004, when they were working with Tom Rowe of Newport Yacht Management to book charters onboard their 57-foot, $1.4-million motoryacht, *Fine Romance*. Al was prepared to serve as captain, with his wife, Jane, serving as chef and stewardess. They offered one couple per week the master stateroom aboard for an all-inclusive rate (even wine and liquor) of $8,500.

That's more than a couple would pay for most skippered bareboats, but it's still well in line with what a couple would spend for a week aboard a nicer cruise ship in an ocean-view cabin—and you do get your own luxury yacht going wherever you choose, along with a personal chef.

"Our long-term goal is to circumnavigate," Al told me at the time. "I would love to develop a clientele of 15 or 20 couples that really like us, and we really like them, and they sign up for different legs of the trip." Again, that's not exactly like picking a destination out of a glossy cruise-ship brochure, but it shows you just one of the many options that are out there in the world of yacht charter.

There aren't nearly as many high-end partially crewed yachts as there are fleets of skippered bareboats, but if you work with a charter broker, you can find the more luxurious smaller yachts—the *Ironys* and the *Fine Romances*—in many parts of the world.

Fully Crewed Yachts

Yachts with full crews are the most expensive charter vacations available. In some cases, the cost breaks down, per person, to what you might pay aboard a mid-range to high-end cruise ship. In other cases, particularly when the yachts are bigger than 125 feet long, the cost is well into six and sometimes even seven figures for a single week onboard.

The yachts themselves can be impressive in all size ranges, even when they're in the 60- to 80-foot-long range, but even in terms of the biggest, fanciest, most expensively built megayachts, what you are really paying for onboard fully crewed yachts is the service.

"You will be impressed," explains Catherine Ambrogi, who works from Antibes, France, as the head of charter for Yachting Partners International. "You will be onboard a $30-million yacht in some cases, but it's the crew that makes the difference. Whether you're on a 150-foot yacht or a 60-foot yacht, as soon as you are onboard, you are considered the owner of the yacht by the crew. Whatever you want to do, wherever you want to go, it's your yacht. The crew on the yacht, whatever the size of the yacht or the price or the value of the yacht, the crew will be there for you and your guests 24 hours a day, only for you. They will remember what you like each day, and you will never have to ask again for a glass of whiskey or whatever it is that you prefer. They will simply have it ready for you. If you want formal service, you have formal service. If you want informal service—still being totally looked after—you will have it. You have superb service, however you want it."

Prices for fully crewed yachts reflect many things, primarily the size of the boat and the number of crew. At the lower end of the scale are yachts like the 68-foot motoryacht *High Energy*, which I cruised aboard during the summer of 2004 from Southampton, England, to the Isle of Wight. It was a sleek, fast motoryacht with a luscious, glossy-wood interior and wide-open deck for sunbathing. I stayed in *High Energy*'s second-best cabin, which had a queen-size bed, a private bathroom, and a glass hatch above the bed that let in bright sunshine every morning like a skylight. The best cabin aboard the $4.5-million yacht was even bigger and more luxurious, with a private bathroom separated from the sleeping area by frosted-glass French doors.

This was nothing like a bareboat, or even a partially crewed private yacht. This was high-end luxury, albeit on a smaller scale than many of the world's larger, fully crewed yachts.

Stefan Wertans and David Ward, the owners of Sunseeker Charters, happened to be staying in the master cabin and acting as my hosts onboard *High Energy*. It is their personal yacht, and it is just one of the dozen or so Sunseekers that are owned by other private individuals but that Wertans and Ward oversee as part of the Sunseeker Charters fleet that extends from Britain to Malta, Greece, Mexico, Spain, Croatia, Italy, and the United States. If you want to book a charter aboard a Sunseeker-brand motoryacht, they're the guys to call. "We can make it anything they want," Wertans explains. "What we want to do is try to have personal packages."

The smallest yacht in the Sunseeker Charters fleet is a 46-footer that takes four guests for a weekly base rate of about $21,500, or about $6,700 per person with average additional expenses factored into the cost. That may sound a bit high to you—indeed, there are less-expensive crewed yachts out there in the same size range—but keep in mind that Sunseeker Charters is based in England, so its prices must be converted from British pounds. (The exchange rate to U.S. dollars was high at the time of this printing.) The largest yacht in the Sunseeker Charters fleet is currently a 105-footer that takes eight or ten guests for a base rate as high as $98,000 per week, or about $12,250 per person with expenses. Ward says the company expects to add a 121-footer to the charter fleet in early 2007, with prices yet to be announced.

At any size, a yacht's rate includes the highly personalized service on which Sunseeker Charters prides itself. "Anything can be arranged," says Jackie Phillipson, the marketing agent for Sunseeker Charters. "If somebody wants a celebrity chef, we know them. We're building relationships with golf clubs, hotels, everything so there will be elite options. Maybe you want to learn how to cook Italian food while your husband plays golf on the other side of Sardinia. Say you're a clay shooter and you want to go from Heathrow [airport] straight to [the high-end gun-maker] Purdy. We can do that through our contacts."

They knew I was a fan of the theater, for instance, and so scored us director's seats for a sold-out performance in the best venue in Southampton, where we happened to dock the charter yacht one night. These are the kinds of options you typically will not find aboard bareboats or even many partially crewed private yachts, where you're sometimes making your own dinner reservations ashore and planning your own excursions using guidebooks (with advice from your captain, if you have one).

The service aboard fully crewed yachts does come at a price, but the service is personalized and unparalleled—even when compared with what you get for tens of thousands of dollars a week aboard the world's most expensive cruise ships.

$7,500 Per Person, Per Week

I spent a week in 2004 cruising from Georgetown to Nassau, through the Exumas part of the Bahamas chain, onboard the 120-foot motoryacht *Joanne*. That yacht—which was originally built for King Juan Carlos of Spain—charters for a base rate of $45,000 per week plus expenses like fuel, food, and dockage, making the total cost of a week aboard for eight guests somewhere in the neighborhood of $55,000 to $65,000, or about $7,500 per person, per week. That's certainly well into the asking price for some of the world's most expensive cruise ships, but still in line when you add in the cost of cruise ship excursions, wines and liquors, and other extras.

My cruise was arranged by Shannon Webster, a longtime independent charter broker whose husband, Dan, is *Joanne*'s captain. The yacht is unique in that it was built to cruise about twice as fast as other yachts the same size. The Spanish king had a pair of military engines put onboard at a reported cost of about $5 million for the machinery alone, giving *Joanne* a top speed of 42 knots—faster than many patrol boats. Capt. Webster used that speed advantage during our weeklong charter to help us spend minimal time under way and maximum time exploring little-known islands such as Allan and Sampson Cays. I'd say we spent about 85 percent of our time at our actual destinations, as opposed to the 50 or 60 percent of time I typically get to spend at destinations on cruise ship itineraries.

No matter where we found ourselves, *Joanne*'s crew launched the yacht's kayaks, Jet Skis, and other water toys before the other guests and I were even ready to go play onshore (a far different experience than waiting in line to board a cruise ship excursion, then waiting in another line to actually climb aboard a water toy). And when *Joanne*'s guests and I did finally make it ashore, the crew encouraged us to stay as long as we liked. On one particularly sunny afternoon when we had an entire secluded sandy stretch to ourselves, Capt. Webster had his team set up a full-on beach barbecue complete with chicken, ribs, and s'mores so we wouldn't have to go back to the yacht at all. They even brought custom-embroidered crew jackets back to the beach for us to wear if our newfound suntans gave us a chill while we toasted marshmallows at dusk.

When we'd at last had our fill, the crew helped us aboard our private dinghy for the short hop back to *Joanne*, where staterooms bigger than some studio apartments awaited us, en suite facilities included. We took high-pressure hot showers before meandering up to the top-deck hot tub, where we let the bubbles massage our feet while the crew brought us the cocktails of our choice. We mulled what we wanted to do during our next day aboard as we watched the sun set on the horizon. The itinerary was ours to choose. We simply had to let the captain know our wishes come morning.

Top of the Line

The most sumptuous stateroom I've ever slept in was aboard the 171-foot motor-yacht *Solemates*. My cruise was in the summer of 2002, and even back then, the rate for ten guests to enjoy a week aboard was $245,000 plus expenses like fuel, food, and dockage. All said and done, a single week aboard that yacht would cost about $32,000 per person—well more than all but the most expensive cruise-ship penthouse suites in exotic destinations.

During my week aboard *Solemates*, we cruised from Antibes, France, to Portofino, Italy, on an itinerary suggested by Rupert Connor, president of Luxury Yacht Group. It was a stunning cruise, highlighting all of the fineries for which southern Europe's best ports are known, but what went on aboard the yacht truly highlighted the reason she commanded such a high charter rate.

For starters, there were the living spaces. Their décor rivaled what you might find in the most expensive mansions. The entry foyer alone was a two-story affair made of limestone that reportedly took craftsmen more than two years to carve by hand. The sky lounge, which is like a casual sitting room in a house, boasted a wall-to-wall theater screen, a drop-from-the-ceiling projection system, and surround-sound speakers that nearly blew out my eardrums when we loaded up *The Matrix*. Most of the staterooms, including mine, had king-size beds and marble-covered bathrooms bigger than the ones you'd find in most four-bedroom Colonial houses. Heck, even the powder room on the main deck featured a sink basin that had been dipped in gold.

And as awesome as the yacht was, the service was even better—if you prefer formality to beach barbecues. *Solemates* carried 13 crewmembers to tend to every need and whim of the ten guests onboard—better than one-on-one service, something no cruise ship in the world can offer. The stewardesses, who serve meals and make up the rooms, did their several daily cleanings not with rags, but with Q-Tips. They spoke to me only after I spoke to them, otherwise respecting my privacy. The French chef's most basic meals were astoundingly good, including the orange sponge cake muffin bottoms served with poached pears baked right on top, served with freshly ground coffee for breakfast. The sight was nearly as beautiful as all of Portofino as I munched on bites while overlooking the harbor from the yacht's top deck.

The top decks, or sundecks, onboard fully crewed motoryachts are usually pleasure paradises. Hot tubs and wet bars are common finds, as are barbecue grills and sunbathing areas.

I stepped off around midday to wander through the shops and cafes, and though I was carrying several cameras and a notebook—and wearing a hat that read *Yachting Magazine*—one tourist on the dock pulled me gently aside and asked, in a stunned whisper, whether *Solemates* was my boat.

"I'm just a writer doing a story about the boat," I told her, pointing to my hat as if it were a card identifying me as "one of us regular folk."

She nodded in silence, and then asked, "Who rides on boats like this?"

"The last guests I heard of," I answered, "were Kenneth Lay and his wife. You know, the guy from Enron."

Such is the impressive level of exclusivity that top-dollar private yacht charter can buy, an experience well beyond anything you will find on even the finest of cruise ships. Personalized service, gorgeous accommodations and the envy of everyone ashore are the hallmarks of many a big-money private charter booking.

Remember Yourself

As glamorous as the most expensive charter yachts in the world may be, it's important to remember that a formal, fully crewed yacht charter might not be the right experience *for you*. Remember what you learned in the beginning of this chapter: As different as cruise ships are from private yachts, so each private yacht is different from the next. *Irony, High Energy, Joanne,* and *Solemates* are but four of the thousands of yachts available for charter today. Every single one of them stands apart, offering experiences that combine with and add in countless ways to the ones I've described in this chapter.

Sure, it's jaw-dropping to hang out in a limestone foyer where only the world's wealthiest people ever step foot, but is your vacation goal to walk around agog all day dodging the paparazzi onshore? If yes, then a big-money charter is exactly what you should book. If no, then it's a waste of your vacation dollars, just like high-end cruise ships can be a waste of money for couples traveling with hot dog-eating kids.

This may shock you, but it's true: As much as my time aboard *Solemates* impressed me, if I were forced to choose a trip to take again, I'd head back to the Bahamas aboard the far less expensive *Joanne*. I'm just not as into wearing diamonds and having speechless, uniformed servants as I am into being towed on water skis behind a fun-loving captain wearing a polo shirt while driving a dinghy.

Would I go back if invited aboard the 171-foot *Solemates* to write another magazine article? Of course. Or any megayacht like her. It is, after all, a stunning experience. But if I had all the money in the world to spend on my own private charter vacation, I'd book the 120-foot *Joanne*, where I felt more at home given my personality. Heck, I already explained to you at the beginning of this chapter that for my father's 58th birthday, I went even less expensive and booked the partially crewed 60-footer *Irony*. It was one of the best family vacations we've ever had in 30 some odd years, and I hope to go back again soon. I happen to be like those billionaire yacht owners who truly enjoy helping out with the lines aboard smaller boats. Doing so makes me feel like I'm boating instead of floating around on a moving hotel, and I simply enjoy the fun of it.

So you see, private yacht charter in all its forms—bareboat, skippered, instructional, partially crewed, fully crewed—is far different from cruise ship vacations at any price. But every yacht charter is also unique in and of itself, and it's up to you to figure out which style and budget suits you best.

If you can develop a basic vocabulary about what you envision as your perfect charter vacation, then you can work with a knowledgeable broker to find what literally may be your dream boat.

A good place to start is with the size of the cabins, the layouts, and the general amenities typically found onboard certain kinds of yachts. That's what Chapter Three will explain: exactly how different the insides of each yacht can be.

3

Boat Basics

If you've been aboard a cruise ship, then you know the drill. You enter into a grand foyer with a bank of elevators near a front desk. The buffet restaurant is on the top deck near the main pool, and the theater is down near the ship's bow, past the main dining hall. If there is an art gallery, it's somewhere in the middle of the ship, probably near the card room and library. "Mr. Sexy Legs" contests are held on the Lido Deck, and the photo shop is along the main concourse. Bars are strategically placed in between all of these destinations, in case you want to buy a $12 pina colada to quench your thirst as you make your way around.

True, some higher-end cruise ships have more intimate layouts that include private restaurants and cigar bars, but for the most part, all cruise ships are designed in a similar fashion—because they all have to move masses of people around efficiently. The décor may change from ship to ship, but the general layout tends to stay the same. The cabins are aligned in rows, identical within their decks and often quite cramped. You don't see many cruise ships with sails or with intimate tables for two inside the galley.

Charter yachts are a different story. Some of them do have sails, and intimate tables for two inside the galley, and all kinds of other features that make each boat unique. Some have indoor bars, some have outdoor bars, some have hot tubs where others have sunbathing areas, some have workout rooms, some have kids' playrooms, some have master cabins on the bottom deck while others have master cabins on the main deck, some have surround-sound theater systems, some have aquariums for viewing, some have wide swim platforms for getting in and out of the water, some have narrow passarelles for walking over the water and right onto shore in formal dinner attire, at least one yacht I've been aboard has an arcade—and the list goes on and on.

Why? Because each yacht is owned by an individual person with individual tastes. Where one yacht owner might see a spare cabin where his children can sleep, another yacht owner might see a stowage area for his extensive wine collection. Yachts are built to suit their owners' desires, not the requirements of the masses. They are built to keep a half-dozen or a dozen people comfortable from time to time, not a stream of thousands content for months and months on end. Some are built for owners who like to go from port to port, exploring the shops and restaurants on land. Others are built for owners who like to spearfish and scuba dive, with lots of ocean access and watersports gear stowage compartments.

Keeping in mind those differences—which a good charter broker can help you sift through—you can begin to form a picture of the general arrangements aboard different kinds of yachts. Powerboats shorter than 80 feet, for instance, tend to have different layouts than bigger motoryachts. Sailboats shorter than 80 feet typically feel more like, well, sailboats than bigger sailing yachts, which can feel like motoryachts once you get inside their cabins. Catamarans, whether they are powered by sails or engines, tend to have entertaining areas far bigger than those aboard most "regular" powerboats and sailboats. Luxury charter barges typically have more intimate areas onboard, while super-size megayachts, which carry as many as 36 charter guests at a time, feel like small cruise ships in many respects.

The way a yacht is designed will have a great impact on the mood and comfort of your charter vacation. If you like to be in the sun, for instance, one style of yacht will be better for you than another. If you like to sit in the shade while cruising in between ports, a different kind of yacht may suit you best. If you like to go fast and visit as many island bars as possible, you'll want a certain kind of powerboat. If you like to meander slowly while reading a book in the breeze, a sailboat or slow-moving trawler motoryacht might be better for you.

While every yacht is different, there are generalities that hold true for powerboats shorter than 80 feet, motoryachts longer than 80 feet, sailboats of different sizes, and the like. Understanding the differences is like moving from theater to theater along Broadway in Manhattan, which each venue playing a role in the feel of the production itself.

Powerboats to 80 Feet

Let's start with powerboats up to 80 feet long. The reason for choosing that length is that after 80 feet long, powerboats tend to be built with crew quarters. At 80 feet or smaller, a powerboat usually can be skippered by one or two people—a couple, as the boat manufacturers see things. These are your bareboats, your instructional boats, your partially crewed powerboats, and a handful of your fully crewed powerboats at the lower end of the price scale.

There are five basic kinds of powerboats up to 80 feet long that you can usually find for charter: trawler yachts, express cruisers, motoryachts, classic motoryachts, and wild cards. Each has pros and cons, and all offer unique elements that can add to different charter experiences.

Trawler Yachts

Trawler yachts are common in bareboat and instructional fleets. Trawlers take their name from commercial vessels that are designed to cruise thousands of miles in search of fish. (Remember *The Perfect Storm*? The *Andrea Gail* was a fishing trawler.) It's more important that trawlers be stable than fast, since rough seas are a concern to offshore fishermen. It's also important that they have enclosed areas for sitting and eating, as opposed to open decks for sunbathing. And, they must be built solidly, to take the beating that comes with hauling in big catch.

Now, trawler yachts built for pleasure cruising are far nicer inside and out than commercial fishing trawlers, and they make excellent bareboats and instructional boats because they have a lot of the same performance characteristics as their commercial siblings: They move slowly, they're more stable than other kinds of boats, and they can handle being knocked accidentally into a piling at a dock. These attributes also make trawlers comfortable choices for first-timers seeking a partially crewed or fully crewed charter because the boats stay steady in the water and are generally comfortable onboard when you are under way.

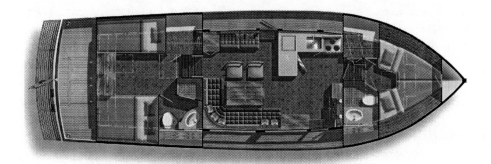

This accommodations plan shows the inside of a Grand Banks 42 Classic, a trawler yacht often found in bareboat fleets. This plan shows the optional layout that the builder offers, with a second bed in the master cabin toward the back of the boat. The table in the galley lowers and holds a mattress pad as well, creating a third area for sleeping.

One of my recent trawler charters was an instructional cruise aboard the 36-foot *Blue Note*. The boat is owned by Southwest Florida Yachts in Ft. Myers, and courses are offered through a sister company called Florida Sailing and Cruising School. We had two cabins on our boat, one with a double-size bed in the bow and the other with a queen-size bed as well as a twin-size bed in the stern. Each cabin had its own bathroom with shower. I was aboard for a week, sharing the aft cabin with a female co-worker. A male co-worker took the forward, smaller cabin, and our instructor, also a man, slept in the main living space—which included a galley and a table that lowered to convert into a double-size bed with a mattress insert.

We had plenty of room and never felt cramped. Truth be told, we spent most of our time on the top deck, watching dolphins swim in our bow wake. *Blue Note* cruised at about six knots—which is quite slow—but that was exactly what we needed, since my co-workers were learning to drive for the first time. Other trawlers can go faster, but even the fastest are still considered some of the slowest powerboats on the water.

Express Cruisers

Express cruisers are an entirely different kind of small powerboat. They're designed with sun, fun, and speed in mind. *High Energy*, which I described in Chapter Two, is an example of an express cruiser. It's sleek-looking instead of boxy (like a trawler yacht is) and tends to have entertaining and water sports in mind more so than sightseeing over long distances at a slow pace. Express cruisers typically have lots of sunbathing areas along with wet bars and cocktail tables on both their top and bottom decks. And they move quickly—at least three or four times as fast as trawlers—meaning that the majority of your charter time is spent onshore at Points A and B, instead of cruising from Point A to Point B.

It can be a challenge to find an express cruiser in a bareboat fleet because most companies (rightly) want occasional and novice skippers moving as slowly through the water as possible. However, you can find some express cruisers available for skippered charters and partially crewed charters.

If you do choose an express cruiser, keep in mind that high-speed boating comes at a price. The faster your yacht moves through the water, the more fuel you are likely to burn—and the more you will have to pay in terms of expenses. (We'll look at expenses in more detail in Chapter Eight.) Also note that express cruisers tend to have fewer shaded areas than trawlers or motoryachts. If you're a sun worshipper, that's great, but if you're leery of skin cancer, a trawler yacht or motoryacht might be a better choice.

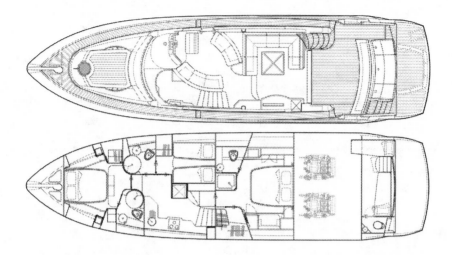

This accommodations plan shows the layout of a Sunseeker Manhattan 60, which is an express cruiser. Notice how the top deck has lots of seating for conversation and sunbathing, plus access to a good size swim platform for getting into and out of the water.

Motoryachts

The term motoryacht can be used to describe powerboats shorter than 80 feet long. It is not to be confused with the term megayacht, which typically refers to powerboats more than 80 or 100 feet long. Motoryachts tend to combine the attributes of trawlers and express cruisers, with an added dash of luxury that can be similar to what is found onboard megayachts.

A good example is the Horizon 76 motoryacht that I toured in early 2005. It has all the sunbathing and water sports areas that you would expect to find aboard an express cruiser, plus all of the stability and comfort of a trawler, *plus* some of the elegant touches that you usually find only aboard larger megayachts.

For instance, the headroom inside the boat was nearly seven feet—far higher than aboard many express cruisers. The countertops were covered in granite instead of Corian, there were plasma-screen televisions where an older trawler might have boxy sets (that can fall over in rough waters if not secured), and the cabins were as roomy as my guest bedrooms at home. In addition, there were dedicated crew quarters near the motoryacht's engine room, meaning that the yacht was designed to keep crew and guests separated when privacy is important.

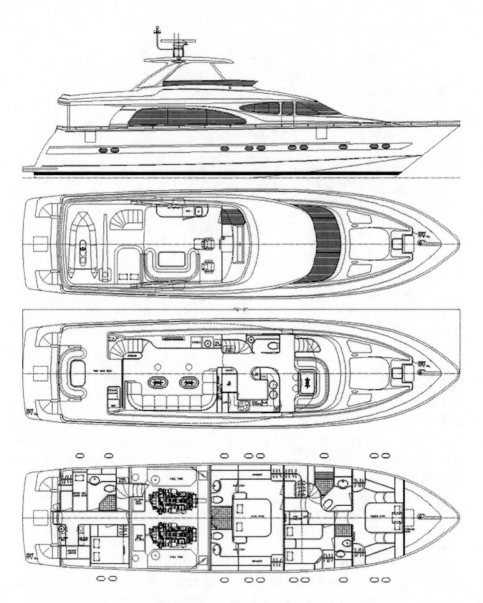

This accommodations plan shows the layout of a Horizon 76 Motoryacht. The three guest cabins are toward the front of the boat, while the crew quarters are in the back, behind the engine room. The middle and top decks are full of relaxation and entertainment areas.

Classic Motoryachts

Classic motoryachts are similar to regular motoryachts, except that because of their age—built from the 1920s onward—they tend to have features more in line with what people used to do aboard yachts before the invention of Jet Skis and other modern toys.

A good example is the 81-foot motoryacht *Lady Elizabeth*, which I cruised aboard from Mystic, Connecticut, to the Hamptons on New York's Long Island in 2003. (I know she's 81 feet instead of 80, like this section's headline says, but trust me, the extra foot doesn't matter in this context!) *Lady Elizabeth* was built in 1971, when yachting on motoryachts in New England consisted mostly of having friends aboard for dinner and watching the local sailboat races. To that end, she has a lovely enclosed aft deck where we could sit in the shade, untouched by the wind unless we wanted to feel the breeze, and look out over every harbor we found. I felt almost like a Rockefeller aboard that yacht, and when we cruised into Mystic Seaport and docked among the "historic" boats, several tourists actually asked Capt. Mike Nesbitt for a quick look around because they thought *Lady Elizabeth* was part of the display. It was great fun.

On the other hand, I know enough about boats to know that had I been aboard *Lady Elizabeth* down in the Caribbean, even with the same great captain, the experience might not have been so magical. In a destination like that, easy access to the water is key for swimming, kayaking, and other fun activities with modern-day water toys, and older motoryachts like this one can have steep, narrow ladders leading to their swim platforms instead of wide steps with railings, like newer motoryachts.

This doesn't mean there's anything wrong with a classic motoryacht like *Lady Elizabeth*—hey, I had a great time aboard in New England—but the layout and design of the boat will definitely affect the way you interact with your destination.

Wild Cards

The last style of powerboat shorter than 80 feet is a category I like to call wild cards. These are yachts that don't fit neatly into another category, but likely have attributes that fit into several. In many cases, these wild cards are custom-built yachts—designed not for a factory line, like a housing development, but for a single individual, like a custom-built log cabin. As such, they can be even quirkier than other charter yachts in a wide variety of ways.

If your charter broker asks you to consider a "wild card" yacht, don't worry. These boats are no better or worse than any other kinds of boats, and your broker may simply realize that the yacht owner's quirks are similar to your own—making it the perfect charter boat for you.

The 60-foot *Irony* is a "wild card" that looks different from most charter yachts, but don't hold that stout exterior against her. She has a mahogany interior just as beautiful as the ones onboard sleeker boats, taller ceilings with more headroom than most other yachts her size, and a hull that provides safe, steady cruising.

Sailboats to 80 Feet

Smaller charter sailboats are much easier to understand than smaller powerboats for the simple reason that no matter how many masts and sails you put on them, they basically have the same hull shape and purpose—to *sail*. You could drive yourself crazy learning the differences between yawls, ketches, and other kinds of sailboats, but for the purpose of charter, all you really need to know is how a sailboat that's 80 feet or shorter compares with a powerboat of similar size.

A good person to trust on this issue is Tina Hinckley, a longtime independent charter broker whose husband, Bob, owned and operated The Hinckley Company for many years. Based in Maine with additional offices in Rhode Island, Maryland, Georgia, Michigan, and Florida, The Hinckley Company has historically been one of the world's preeminent builders of sailing yachts. And Tina, for much of that time, has been booking charters aboard those and other companies' larger, fully crewed sailboats through her company, Hinckley Yacht Charters.

"First-time charterers usually will charter a smaller sailboat, 50 or 60 feet," she explains. "Partly, it takes time for them to get used to the price, and partly, it's because usually just the husband or just the wife has sailed before, and they don't want to spend a large amount of money on something they don't know if everybody else in the family is going to like.

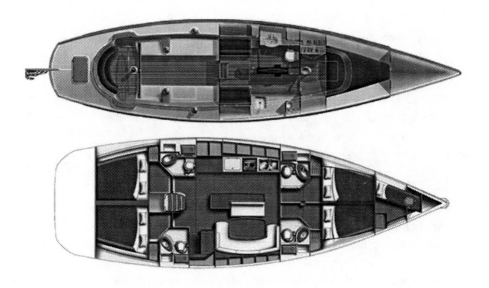

Boats that are similar in size can have quite different interior layouts. The top sailboat here is the Hinckley DS42, which is meant to hold a few couples during the day but only one overnight. Note the long, lightly colored seating area near the helm toward the back of the boat, but only one sleeping space, the dark V-shape in the boat's front. The bottom sailboat shown here is the Moorings 51.5, which is just ten feet longer than the Hinckley but advertised as having five cabins. Notice how four are similar in size, with one smaller cabin tucked inside the yacht's bow.

"The difference with a 60-foot sailboat from a 60-foot powerboat," she continues, "is that the powerboat is going to be a lot more expensive, and a lot of people just have the sailing dream. A lot of people who sailed as children, they want to introduce other people to sailing. And these sailboats, even at the smaller sizes, they have engines, air conditioning—a lot of the features of the powerboats, but you can go sailing, too. I think the word luxury applies to all these boats in this size range. If you have a crew working for you, it's pretty great no matter how big the yacht is."

Tina and I cruised together in Maine back in 2002 onboard *Azzura*, a 96-foot sailing yacht. (I know, I know, again a few feet too big for this section, but please just go with me on this.) Our experience, organized perfectly by Cox Marine in Newport, Rhode Island, was far different from any charter I've done on a motoryacht of any size. While we did have an auxiliary engine for motoring around (as all sailboats do), much of each day was devoted simply to sailing—not to getting somewhere and going ashore, or to holding cocktail parties onboard, or to lounging on a sunpad next to a hot tub, but instead to sitting back, letting the wind blow through our hair, and listening to the rhythm of the water as *Azzura*'s bow cut a path toward the horizon.

The sightseeing aspect made our *Azzura* charter feel kind of like being onboard a trawler yacht, only we were working with nature to create motion instead of barreling through with noisy, diesel-powered engines—and we were moving a heck of a lot faster than your average trawler's top speed. We also were tipped sideways much of the time with the wind in our sails—or heeled over, as yachties like to say—as opposed to remaining upright as we would have aboard a powerboat or catamaran. Some people find the heeling a bit unsettling, but I thoroughly enjoyed the excitement of it.

This experience is the essence of what makes a sailboat charter different from a powerboat charter aboard boats in the 80-foot-and-smaller size range.

Catamarans of All Sizes

Catamarans get their own section in this chapter because, whether they are sail- or engine-powered, they typically have the same kinds of layouts—and those layouts are much different from traditional powerboats and sailing yachts.

Whereas most powerboats and sailboats have a single hull (and are called *monohulls* within the industry), catamarans have two hulls connected by a rectangular deck. The boats originated with early sailors attempting to lash two tree trunks together via a tarp in between them that served as a seat. Today, the "logs" are long fiberglass pontoons big enough to hold full-size sleeping cabins and bathrooms. The "tarp" in the middle is a full-blown covered yacht interior that can encase a master cabin, sitting area, and galley—all as elegantly decorated as any traditional, monohull sailboat or powerboat.

Angel Glow, the boat I discussed cruising aboard to Anegada in Chapter One, is an example of a sailing catamaran. And though we did sail quite a bit on that trip, I must say that it was a different feeling than I described earlier in this chapter, of sailing aboard the monohull sailboat *Azzura*. Aboard *Angel Glow*, even when we were moving fast with the wind, both of the boat's pontoons stayed on the water's surface. We never once heeled over the way we did aboard *Azzura*, and the steadiness of the catamaran made it easier to relax, since I didn't have to brace my feet against anything—though true "old salt" sailors will tell you this is one of the things they most *dislike* about sailing catamarans.

We also had more room to spread out aboard *Angel Glow* because of the way catamarans are designed. On a monohull sailboat, if you want to be up on deck (out in the fresh air), you basically have two choices: You can sit in the cockpit where everyone else is sitting, near the boat's skipper, or you can walk all the way forward and sit near the bow. When you've got six or eight people aboard, you're always going to be sitting with somebody else. By contrast, catamarans (both power and sail) typically have multiple seating areas on deck. There's the main area in the middle where the skipper is driving, plus areas on each side above the pontoons to stretch out, plus a hammock-like netting in between the front ends of the pontoons. Three couples aboard a catamaran could sail all day and never exchange a single word. I slept for about two hours while we were underway, right there on deck in the warm sun, and didn't hear a word from anybody else.

"The family or the couples that have never considered doing a yacht vacation really would be most attracted to the catamaran layout just because it is stable," says Carol Kent, a reputable charter broker based in Boston, Massachusetts. "People have a fear of heeling over. They see all those racing pictures and say, 'My God, I can't do that!' Catamarans can also get into shallow places where a monohull can't even get close. Certainly, the configuration of the berths, more times than not you've got equal accommodations. For families, too, people need their space. There's more of it. You've got so many places to escape to just within the boat itself, just to be away from the cockpit where people are talking.

"As a price point, too, they're great," she continues. "A sailing catamaran will be less than a motoryacht, but with a lot of the same attributes. And they carry so many more toys than the monohull [sailboats] because they have more space. They're perfect boats for scuba diving and snorkeling, too, because the water access is so much easier than on a monohull. A lot of men can get their wives to say yes to a catamaran where they'd say no to a monohull."

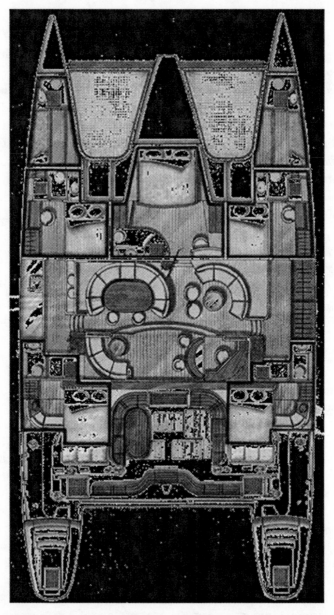

Catamarans typically have a master cabin in the middle of the boat plus guest cabins in the pontoons. This accommodations plan is for the 65-foot *Angel Glow*, which is part of the fleet at Nicholson Yachts of Newport. She has five guest cabins plus extra sleeping spaces far forward (at the top of the page) for the crew.

Catamarans without sails are typically called powercats, and they have all the same design features as the sailing catamarans described above (except, of course, for the sails). More and more bareboat companies are adding powercats to their fleets because first-time cruisers seem to prefer the expansive space they offer when compared with the adequately sized interiors aboard regular powerboats.

A remaining challenge, whether you charter a bareboat catamaran or one with a full crew, is that catamarans are much wider than monohull powerboats and sailboats—and therefore take up far more space at marina docks. Many marinas still have only a few slips that can actually hold the wider catamarans, since historically, monohulls have dominated boating. Thus, when you charter a catamaran, you're likely to spend more of your nights on anchor in a harbor or cove (which I actually prefer) instead of at a marina dock, as you would have the option of doing onboard a monohull. This may change as marinas adapt to catamarans' growing popularity, but expect the pace of that costly change in dock configurations to be slow.

Power and sailing cats are becoming more established at the top end of the charter marketplace as well. In 2004, I cruised aboard an 81-foot powercat called *Spirit* in New Zealand. The cruise was organized by Allan Jouning, an extremely knowledgeable captain-turned-broker with Fraser Yachts Worldwide. He introduced me to *Spirit*'s owner, who told me he'd bought the boat because his wife would no longer cruise with him aboard monohulls. She was willing to sail only if she could have the comforts this luxury catamaran offered, including a hot tub on deck and a sprawling master cabin complete with a king-size bed and desk—the kind of cabin usually found only aboard megayachts.

Perhaps the best-known luxury catamaran available for charter is *Douce France*, a 138-footer that oozes the same kind of opulence on an even bigger scale. This sailing cat has six guest cabins, each with en suite bathrooms, and an interior luscious with mahogany and rosewood furniture. Sitting inside her feels like sitting in a proper yacht club, with service to match. You pay for it, with an all-inclusive rate of $85,000 per week, or about $7,100 per person, but that's still far less than you'd pay for some fully crewed motoryachts with similar interior spaces—or for a top-notch suite on a cruise ship where you have to share the crew with hundreds or even thousands of other people.

Barges

You might not think of a river barge as a form of yacht charter, but then you'd miss out on some wonderful inland cruising opportunities. Barges, particularly in

Europe, are readily available for charters along rivers everywhere from Ireland's green hills to France's wine country.

They're actually a good way to learn bareboating, since you really can't go too far off course when you're cruising up the middle of a river. And in regions like the border between the United States and Canada, you can charter 32- to 45-foot bareboat barges and learn how to cruise through locks along the Champlain and Erie Canals.

At the top end of the luxury scale where the charters are fully crewed, barges that compare with high-end yachts are fewer and farther between. What passes for "luxury" in barge-company brochures is not usually in keeping with what you will get aboard top-dollar seagoing charter yachts.

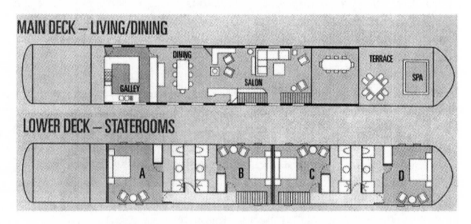

This accommodations plan is for *La Bonne Humeur*, a 126-foot barge available for yacht-style charter in France. All of the labeled areas are for guest use, with crew sleeping elsewhere.

"There are some very high-end barges, and they're in the more expensive category," explains Jody Lexow, a longtime broker who owns Jody Lexow Yacht Charters in Newport, Rhode Island. She books all kinds of yachts but is well known in the industry as an expert on barges, too. "There are the self-drive barges, equal to bareboats, and then there are hotel barges, comparable to the crewed yachts. It's the same concept: The broker is matching people with people, taking into account the accommodations and the cruising area. I know France backwards and forwards, so my forte would be firsthand knowledge of matching people with barges there.

"You pay for what you get," she continues. "That doesn't mean the less-expensive barges are unacceptable, but you need the broker's knowledge of each product and where it might fit with each client. There are two or three, with maybe more coming, barges that have been restored and made into charter barges by yacht crew. They bought the hull, they redid it in the manner in which a private yacht is done, and they are offering charters like private yacht charters on the canals. It's a work of love, and the owner and captain must do a really good job in restoring the barges to make them on par with the yachts. There's even one now in France that has an elevator. I've got some fabulous barges that can take four couples in equal staterooms, six-night trip, seven days, picked up in Paris, a luxury air-conditioned minivan that takes you around to the sites, and you'll pay $40,000 or $50,000 total. That's $10,000 a couple."

Barges aren't yachting in the truest sense, but they do offer an alternative if you want to try a charter but aren't yet ready to sail from island to island through wind and waves. The desire to stay inland would be a key factor in choosing a barge for your charter vacation.

Megayachts 80 to 250 Feet

True boating enthusiasts will tell you that there's a heck of a difference between an 80-foot sailing yacht and a 180-foot power-driven megayacht—and they'd be right. But for the purposes of your introduction to yacht charter, I've lumped all boats 80 feet and larger, sail and power alike, into the category of megayachts.

Why? Because at this size, most yachts are fully crewed, and at the bigger end of the spectrum, the interiors aboard sailing yachts can be difficult to distinguish from those aboard megayachts. That gives these yachts a heck of a lot in common as relates to charter, even if the vacations themselves are as different as hanging out in T-shirts in the Bahamas versus turning heads like movie stars in Italian harbors.

"If you've been on a high-end cruise ship, with these large yachts, you're going to get much higher quality of furnishings," explains Tim Nelson, a broker with Seven Seas Charters in Nokomis, Florida. He specializes in booking charters onboard yachts 100 feet and larger. "You'll have as many or more crewmembers as you have guests onboard the yachts. Everything is customized to your wishes, where when you're on the cruise ship, you have to eat the food and do the activities that they've got onboard along with everybody else on the ship. With the yachts, you go where you want to go and you can have seafood every meal if you want it, prepared however you want it."

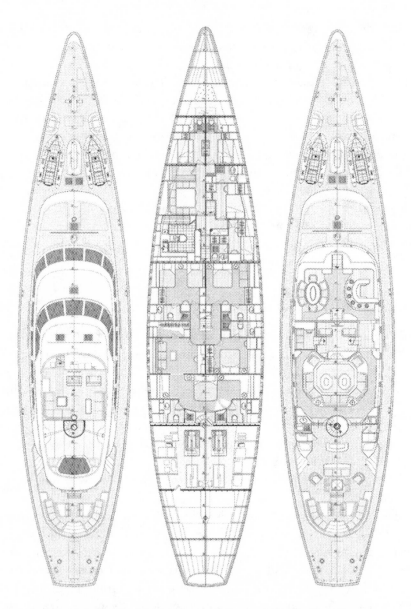

Andromeda la Dea is a 154-foot luxury sailing yacht in the Nigel Burgess charter fleet. Notice how the crew sleep in bunk beds in the bow, far from the guest areas. Also note how much of the main deck (at far right) is devoted entirely to guest relaxation and entertainment space.

There are differences between sailing yachts and power-driven megayachts, of course, but most of them are more in terms of space and performance, as opposed to the quality of the amenities and service.

"A displacement motoryacht is going to be slower, generally, than a planing motoryacht, but they'll usually be more stable and a more comfortable ride in high seas," Nelson says. "The faster planing motoryachts are lighter, and the hull is not meant for heavier seas. On the one hand, you've got a yacht that's slower but will ride better, and on the other hand you're going to get to where you want to go faster.

"Most sailing yachts, except for catamarans, are a displacement-type yacht," he says. "They have a good ride to them. The typical sailing yacht is more for someone who has grown up sailing and likes that whole atmosphere. Even the big catamarans like *Douce France* are more for people who are not quite as heavy into sailing, but they just want to try something different. The Perini Navi [brand name] sailing yachts, they're almost like motorsailers. Great sailing, but with the kinds of accommodations you would find on a top-notch megayacht."

Some of those accommodations and amenities at this level of charter are pretty darn spectacular. One of my favorite megayachts is the 197-foot *Paraffin*, which takes 12 guests at a whopping rate of $450,000 per week plus expenses like fuel and food. *Paraffin*'s owners are very much into creating a first-rate ambience, so much so that they had the shipyard forgo alarm clocks in the master suite and instead install time-sensitive draperies. If you're sleeping in the king-size master bed, you will be gently awakened in the morning by curtains set to infuse the room with sunshine at the hour of your choice. You also won't be disturbed by any noise coming from *Paraffin*'s galley. The shipyard built the doorway from the crew serving area to the main dining room so that when the door opens—say, with a stewardess carrying a tray of caviar—all of the galley lights and radios automatically turn off, leaving the dinner party to continue their conversation in the low lighting they prefer.

Those kinds of luxuries can also be found onboard the world's finest luxury sailing charter yachts, including *Mirabella V*, which is managed by Jacqui Beadon Yachts. At 245 feet long, *Mirabella V* is the world's tallest sailing yacht—with a mast that towers 289 feet into the sky. Her weekly charter rate for 12 guests is $300,000 plus expenses, with onboard amenities including a 20-person hot tub, an on-deck movie screen, a 21-foot swimming pool, and a complete wine cellar.

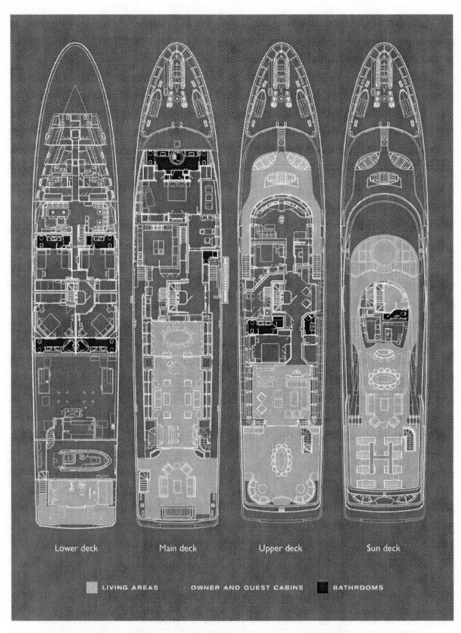

Lower deck   Main deck   Upper deck   Sun deck

LIVING AREAS   OWNER AND GUEST CABINS   BATHROOMS

Ability is a 177-foot motoryacht that is part of the Nigel Burgess charter
fleet. Starting at far left, you can see the guest cabins in the middle of
the bottom deck, then the master suite on the main deck all the way
forward. Also notice all the different light-gray areas throughout the
yacht for guest relaxation and entertainment.

The point is that with these top-dollar, fully crewed yachts, you really can expect the best of amenities and style whether you select a yacht with sails or large engines.

"It depends on what you want to try," Nelson says. "It's just a matter of whether you want to be onboard a sailing yacht or a motoryacht."

Super-Size Megayachts

There is one other category of charter yacht that is becoming more common on the world's waters. These boats are technically called megayachts, just like the boats in the previous section of this chapter, but for the purposes of distinguishing them as charter vessels, I like to call them super-size megayachts. Sometimes, you'll see them referred to as gigayachts or even mini-cruise ships.

A super-size megayacht is a boat that carries more than the 12 guests, or six passenger cabins, allowed by international statutes. These super-sizers adhere to special safety and construction rules that force them to look a bit more commercial in some respects, but that allow them to carry as many as 36 charter guests at one time.

An example of a super-size megayacht is *Christina O*, a 325-footer that used to be the private vessel of Aristotle Onassis. I've been aboard *Christina O* a few times, and I can say firsthand that her general décor is lovely, but no more striking than many other top-rate "regular-size" megayachts that are available for charter. *Christina O* does have unique features that only a yacht of her size can offer—such as a mosaic-lined swimming pool that converts to a dance floor on her aft deck—but what truly sets her apart in terms of charter is her layout.

A typical megayacht's formal dining room may seat a dozen people, but it still feels like an intimate eating space. Aboard *Christina O* (as with other super-size megayachts), the dining area has several long tables to accommodate several dozen guests, making the space feel more like a hall than a room. And, speaking of halls, the way cabins are laid out on super-size megayachts like *Christina O* represent another distinguishing factor from "regular" megayachts. Whereas on a ten-guest yacht, you might find an owner's suite on the main deck and four guest cabins below, super-size yachts like *Christina O* have rows of a dozen or more cabins along various hallways, just as cruise ships do. The cabins are all spacious with marble en suite bathrooms, but for the most part, they're no bigger than what you'd find aboard a "regular" megayacht.

"By and large, with the size and category of these boats, you're looking at [charter] parties with a large entourage," explains Alev Karagulle, who spent 22 years as a charter broker before becoming the marketing director for Nigel Burgess in London. "It was very difficult in the past. You had people who had an entourage, or a large family group, or several families coming together, or a special celebration charter. The maximum six staterooms [onboard "regular" charter yachts] were a nightmare, because you had to put them on several yachts. Inevitably, none of those yachts can host a sit-down meal for the entire group. It's a disjointed way to run a charter. Now, with these larger gigayachts, mini-cruise liners, whatever you want to call them, it's fantastic."

The base rates these super-size yachts command are also fit for the celebrities with entourages, corporate CEOs, and royal families who charter them. *Christina O*, for instance, reportedly uses her historical significance to command rates from $540,000 to well over $1 million for a week, for 12 to 25 guests. That's in the neighborhood of $30,000 to $40,000 per person, per week.

Other super-size charter yachts are a comparative discount, such as the word can be used when talking about massive sums of money. For instance, the recently restored 257-foot *Delphine*—former private yacht of automobile magnate Horace Dodge—takes 28 charter guests a week at a base rate of about $300,000, or just shy of $11,000 per person, per week.

"These large parties, these large groups can all be together on one yacht, having meals together and cruising exactly at the same pace all on one vessel," Karagulle says. "They've been a huge success."

Form Equals Function

The point to keep in mind when considering different yacht layouts—big versus small, power versus sail—is that they have a great effect on the type of charter you will experience. That's true whether you're a bareboater onboard a trawler yacht or a Hollywood hotshot booking a super-size megayacht.

Sailing may be just the thing for you, or you may turn out to love cruising under power all the time. Sitting in the sun may be your only desire, or you may want easy ocean access aboard a yacht that carries plenty of water toys. You may want an intimate yacht with one main cabin where you can rekindle ties among your immediate family, or you may require a big-money megayacht with sprawling decks for hosting blowout parties.

The basic terminology you learned for describing boats in this chapter will help you articulate your general yacht-layout needs to everyone from budget bareboat operators to top-dollar charter brokers. If you think you might like to go slowly under power, you now know to ask first for a trawler yacht. If you want to feel the wind on your face and feel like a racer, you'll think first to talk about chartering a monohull sailboat. If you want to try hands-on boating but are nervous about leaving inland waters, you'll look to a barge instead of a powerboat or sailboat at all. And so on.

Next, in Chapter Four, you'll learn how yachts can differ in terms of the onboard experience they offer—giving you an even broader vocabulary for finding the best charter yacht to meet your needs.

4

The Onboard Experience

By now, you've grasped the primary point about private yacht charter: Every boat is different. To say that all yachts offer even similar vacation experiences would be like saying that all cheddar cheeses taste the same. In truth, the variations may be subtle or spectacular, but the differences are very real. With or without crew, any given three yachts of the same size and style are likely to offer three entirely different vacations. Change the sizes and styles of the boats, not to mention the destination where the charter takes place, and even more options present themselves.

This makes it quite challenging for me to tell you about a "typical" onboard experience. I've cruised aboard nearly three dozen charter yachts and have spent time aboard hundreds more, and I could write an entire chapter about the onboard experience that I found with each one. They're simply all different, an amalgam of ambience, design, service, food, and more that can be difficult to compare. Again, it's not like cruise ships, where the same themes and styles tend to show up aboard multiple vessels in the same fleet. Each yacht has an individual owner with unique tastes, which makes for personal onboard choices that charter guests may or may not like.

For this reason, I've broken this chapter into general headings that describe things you'll encounter onboard every charter yacht: cabins, menus, shore excursions, and the like. Then, where necessary beneath each of those headings, I've broken the descriptions into sections labeled "bareboat" and "fully crewed." You already know that all bareboats are not alike and that all fully crewed yachts differ, too, but my hope is that these general overviews will help you understand what *types* of things you should expect to experience onboard a bareboat or fully crewed charter yacht.

I've left out special headings for instructional, skippered, and partially crewed charters because, as you've already learned, those types of vacations tend to be offered aboard bareboats or yachts that are quite similar to fully crewed boats.

You'll also notice that itineraries are omitted from this chapter. While they do play a key role in determining what kind of onboard experience you'll have, I believe they merit entire chapters of their own. We'll get to itinerary choices later in *Have the Whole Boat.*

For now, your goal should be to understand the primary factors that contribute to the general onboard experience, and to learn a few terms that will help you during the booking process when you need to explain what appeals to you.

Cabin Choices

Whether you're aboard a bareboat or a fully crewed yacht, cabins are going to be described the same way.

The nicest cabin aboard a yacht is called the *master*. It almost always has an en suite (connected) bathroom, and it usually has the biggest bed and closets. The second-nicest cabin aboard a yacht is called the *VIP*, and it typically is the second-largest space, often with its own bathroom as well. Aboard some boats, the VIP can rival the master in terms of space and amenities.

A guest cabin may be called just that, or may be referred to as a *double* or *twin*—which refers to the size of the bed(s) in the cabin. Sometimes two twin beds can be locked together to form a double. Twin cabins also sometimes include a *pullman*, which is a fold-down twin bed that functions like the top section of a bunk bed.

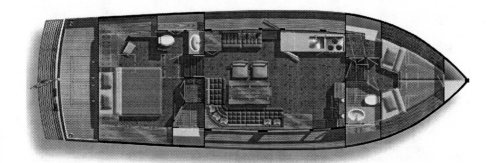

This accommodations plan shows the standard layout for the Grand Banks 42 Classic, with one bed in the master cabin toward the back of the boat plus one bed in the VIP cabin toward the front of the boat. Adults can share a VIP cabin like this, which has a V-berth (named for the bed's shape), but if you have one couple and two children traveling together, the adults would be more comfortable in the master.

Beds are typically placed *on centerline* aboard yachts, which means the head and foot of the bed are parallel to the front and back of the boat. There is a reason for this: Most boats, either when moving or at anchor, tend to roll slightly with the waves, from side to side. If you're lying in bed on centerline, that motion will feel almost like being rocked to sleep in a cradle.

On the other hand, some yachts have one or two beds placed *athwartships*, meaning that the head and foot of the bed are parallel to the sides of the boat. I once tried to sleep in an athwartships berth, and I had a terrible time because as the boat rolled from side to side, my head and feet went up and down as if on a see-saw. I much prefer beds that are on centerline, as do most boaters—which is why athwartships berths are, thankfully, rare.

Most cabins, even the smallest ones made for children, have a source of natural light and sometimes fresh air as well. These may be called windows, *hatches*, *portlights*, or *portholes*. The more, the better, no matter what size or style of yacht you choose.

All of the terms described thus far apply to bareboats and fully crewed yachts alike. But that's where the similarities in cabin choices end.

Bareboat Cabins

Bareboats are usually one-half or even one-third the size of fully crewed yachts. As such, even their biggest, fanciest cabins are going to offer fewer amenities than the master cabins aboard larger, more luxurious yachts. There's simply less space to work with onboard most bareboats, so fewer features can be included.

A master cabin aboard a typical bareboat is likely to have a queen-size or full-size bed. It may be a *walkaround berth*, which means the head of the bed is adjacent to a wall and the other three sides are open to the room. It also may be a *step-up island berth*, which means the head of the bed is adjacent to a wall, the foot of the bed is open to the room, and the sides of the bed connect to platforms that you can step up while climbing into the bed. There is no difference between the mattress sleeping area with walkaround or step-up island berths, but taller people may prefer walkarounds, since step-ups can force you to crouch with your head closer to the ceiling when getting into and out of the bed. The step-ups are simply a function of some boat hull designs.

The closet in a bareboat's master cabin may be full-length, able to accommodate a dress, or it may be half-length, more the size of a man's sport jacket. Either is fine if you're cruising in the Caribbean, where the fanciest restaurants you're likely to encounter are beachfront lobster eateries where formal gowns would be horridly out of place. If you're cruising in the Mediterranean, though, you might look for a bareboat with a full-length closet in the master cabin. Europeans tend to dress up for dinner, and you'll occasionally stick out as a "yachtie" if you show up in a T-shirt and sarong.

In the twin cabins aboard bareboats, the ceiling height above the sleeping areas may be far lower than normal. Some twin cabins are suitable only for children, who will be able to touch the ceiling over their heads after climbing into the beds. I've slept in a few of these cabins, and at first, I felt a bit claustrophobic. I did feel reasonably comfortable after I got used to the space—and remembered not to sit straight up and bang my head when getting out of bed.

Another twin-cabin design element to watch out for is the placement of the beds themselves, which you can see on accommodations plans like the ones shown in Chapter Three. In some cases, the foot of a twin bed is open to the rest of the cabin, meaning that taller people can stretch out their legs, albeit with their feet hanging off the end of the bed. In other cases, the foot of the twin bed abuts a wall, meaning that taller people will have to sleep with their knees bent at all times.

Closets are typically smaller in bareboat guest cabins than they are in masters and VIPs, and drawer space is proportionally limited as well. Two adults can often share a guest cabin aboard a bareboat quite comfortably, but they should be light packers and good friends, as the space will likely be tight.

Bareboats also may have spaces that convert to form extra beds, such as a dining table that lowers to become even with the bench seating around it. A mattress insert is then placed atop the table, forming a double- or twin-size bed. These kinds of spaces—often called *convertible berths*—are adequate for children or overnight guests, but don't count on adults tolerating them for an entire week aboard. They have no separate bathrooms, have no closet or drawer space, and are in the middle of public areas with limited privacy.

Fully Crewed Yacht Cabins

Onboard yachts that are 80 feet or longer, the cabins are much more spacious—and in some cases are downright decadent when you're talking about master cabins. Some of the bigger crewed yachts even have masters with 180-degree views out panoramic rows of windows, gigantic plasma-screen televisions that pop up out of the furniture at the push of a button, and his-and-her marble bathrooms with hot tubs for two.

"My favorite is on *Aquasition*, a 147-foot Intermarine megayacht," explains Nicole Caulfield, a charter broker in Fort Lauderdale, Florida, with Robert J. Cury and Associates. "It's got the master cabin on the main-level deck, forward of the main saloon. So you've got privacy from the other guests, whose cabins are all down below. It's got an office/lounge area, and then the his-and-hers head, which is a huge luxurious bathroom with a Jacuzzi tub and big, separate shower.

"In the 150-foot range, most of the master cabins are on the main deck like that," Caulfield continues. "When you go into the 100- or 120-foot motoryacht range, a lot of the masters are down below, with the rest of the cabins. They're more of a master cabin, as opposed to a suite, which you get on the 150-footers and bigger, where you have an attached office or lounge area. They're becoming more popular, as more and more people decide they want to work on vacation."

King- or queen-size beds are the norm in master cabins aboard fully crewed yachts, and full-length, cedar-lined closets are also a common find, many of them walk-in size. Some master cabins have vanity areas for putting on makeup, in addition to the office space for keeping in touch with business from afar. Large televisions and even surround-sound systems are often found in master cabins, which can rival or even surpass the size of master bedrooms in most houses.

VIP and guest cabins aboard fully crewed yachts are usually on the bottom deck, on either side of a foyer that leads to a guest-use-only staircase (or to an elevator aboard some 150-foot and larger motoryachts). These cabins typically have double- or twin-bed configurations, though you can find guest cabins with king- or queen-size beds, especially on larger and newer builds. Twin cabins aboard fully crewed megayachts can often be quite comfortable for two unrelated adults, a fact to which I can personally attest, having spent my share of cruises in twin-bed cabins with fellow female industry professionals.

Full-length closets are the norm, and most guest cabins aboard fully crewed yachts have televisions and entertainment systems as well. The décor in these cabins is often quite beautiful, to boot.

Bathrooms

The bathrooms aboard bareboats are typically small, sometimes as small as the ones you'll find in the lowest-priced cabins aboard cruise ships. While bigger bareboats may have bathrooms with separate toilet and shower compartments, smaller bareboats will have one compartment with both the toilet and shower inside. I've used these kinds of dual-purpose compartments many times, with no problems at all. Taller men may have to crouch a bit, though, which is something to ask the bareboat company or charter broker about when booking your yacht.

Most bareboats (and many fully crewed yachts) have toilets called MSDs, which stands for *marine sanitation devices*. MSDs work just like regular toilets, except you push a button instead of a short handle when it's time to flush. Older bareboats may have pump toilets, with foot pedals and long handles attached to the bottom of the bowl section. You flush these by standing up, pressing down a foot pedal to let in salt water, and then pumping the long handle to suck the salt water and toilet paper down and out of the bowl. I've encountered pump toilets only once, aboard a very old trawler yacht, and I must admit I found them a bit disgusting. You have to face the bowl in order to pump out its contents. They were not difficult to use, though, and I don't think I'd let their presence dissuade me from chartering a boat that suited the rest of my needs perfectly.

Aboard fully crewed megayachts, the bathrooms rival what you would find in a nice home. Most of them have Corian, marble, or granite countertops, toilets that are separate from the showers, and in some cases, bathtubs with whirlpool jets. Guest cabins usually have showers instead of tubs, and aboard older megayachts, the showers can be a tight fit for bigger, taller men. Good charter brokers actually climb inside showers during yacht tours and note the dimensions, so they can direct taller clients toward yachts with bigger facilities.

Many fully crewed megayachts also have a *day head*—a nicely decorated bathroom with toilet and sink only, located on the yacht's main or upper deck. The concept is the same as having a half-bath near the living room of a house, a facility to use when you don't want to go all the way back to your cabin.

Yacht Décor

When you imagine being onboard a yacht, you probably envision a traditional décor: lots of richly stained wood, brass lamps and fixtures, with nautical flags and oil paintings of sailors adding a seagoing character to the whole place.

This may be true aboard some classic yachts, but it is not usually true of newer bareboats or fully crewed yachts. Today's boats are decorated in ways that mimic vacation homes, with everything that concept implies about varying tastes, tones, and styles.

Bareboat trawlers and sailboats may look like the classic picture in your mind, but bareboat catamarans or express cruisers are likely to have a more modern ambience. Lighter tones, colorful fabrics, and even tropical decorations are often part of the décor scheme, creating the vibe of a Mediterranean villa or a Caribbean getaway.

Larger sailing yachts and power-driven megayachts typically contain exquisite woodwork, but even aboard those boats, the woodwork ranges from light pine to medium cherry to dark mahogany (with burled and rare woods thrown into the mix as well). Some woodwork even includes hand-carved details that add to the yacht's charm. Different colored marbles and granites are usually chosen to match fine fabrics and leathers, with furniture aboard power-driven motoryachts and large sailboats alike running the gamut from modern minimalist to royally opulent.

Guest and Crew Spaces

Capt. Dave Laird, with whom I cruised aboard the motoryacht *Princess Marcie,* has a saying that bears repeating: When the boat is 85 feet long, you're never going to be more than 85 feet away from anybody else onboard.

It's an important point as you consider which yacht you want to charter, because the way those 85 feet of space are laid out will affect how much space is allotted to you versus how much space is reserved for the crew. (We're talking only about crewed yachts here, since bareboats, by definition, have no crew.)

The way the space is designed also will affect how you interact with other people onboard. If you choose a power-driven megayacht with three separate eating areas, you can have group or intimate meals as the mood strikes you. By contrast, if you choose a medium-sized sailing yacht, you likely will have one main outdoor dining area and a smaller indoor eating space to be used only in inclement weather. In some cases, the secondary eating area aboard a motoryacht or a sailing yacht will be in the galley, where the chef is working. Again, all boats are different—and these are the sorts of details good charter brokers can explain to you when comparing one yacht to another.

In general, though, aboard most sailing and motoryachts, crew spaces are in two places on the bottom deck: far forward, where the bow of the boat gets narrow and only bunk beds will fit, and near the engine room, where the engineer needs to be in case of an emergency. These are parts of the boat where you really should have no need to go, thus helping to keep the guest areas separate from the crew's.

Aboard some power-driven megayachts, there also may be a captain's cabin behind the helm, for proximity in case something goes awry. This cabin usually has a separate entrance on the side of the boat that's opposite the guest passageways, making it a space you should have little need to encounter.

Also aboard large sailing and megayachts, there is usually a crew lounge where deckhands and stewardesses can congregate out of your way during their break times. This lounge is usually on the bottom deck all the way forward, near the crew cabins, down a separate staircase than the one that leads to the guest cabins.

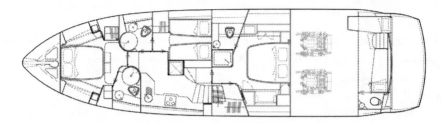

Take another look at the sleeping quarters for the Sunseeker Manhattan 60, an express cruiser. Notice how the crew quarters are all the way in the back of the boat, in a small space behind the engine room. The layout affords guests a good deal of privacy.

Most of the space that remains on a yacht, sailing or power, will be devoted to guest use. The interior guest spaces typically include some combination of cabins, a formal dining area, and a *main saloon* (a formal living room). Depending on the size and style of yacht, you also may have an interior *sky lounge* (a secondary entertaining room), a *country kitchen-style galley* (an eat-in kitchen), a bridge seating area (for watching the captain drive the boat), and an office.

In terms of the outside spaces, the only area traditionally reserved for crew use is far forward on the bow, where the anchor and related equipment are kept. On sailing yachts, the main outdoor guest area is the *cockpit*—a large seating area with a table near the boat's steering wheel. Onboard power-driven megayachts, the outdoor guest areas usually include the *aft deck* (a dining and sitting area at the back of the main deck), the *boat deck* (a similar space one level up), and the *flying bridge* (the very top deck). Some flying bridges have secondary helm stations all the way forward, where the captain sometimes drives. Other flying bridges are entirely reserved for guest use, in which case they may be called *sundecks*.

In general, onboard yachts of all shapes and sizes, guests stick to guest areas and crew stick to crew areas. Yes, you intermingle and always have access to a crewmember should you need something, but they do their best to stay out of your way and to keep their cleaning and maintenance tools out of sight. In some cases, the yacht's design actually helps them maintain your privacy. One of my favorite yacht features, *walkaround side decks*, allow the crew to move all the way from the bow to the stern of the yacht without stepping foot inside, should you be dining there or watching a movie while they need to do the work of moving the boat to your next destination.

You will interact with the yacht's crew during every day of your vacation, but rest assured that they do go out of their way to stay out of yours.

Onboard Entertainment

The entertainment aboard private yachts is far different from what you're used to experiencing aboard cruise ships. There are no showgirls doing fan kicks on a stage, no art auctions where you can bid, and no organized activities like Hula Hoop contests at high noon.

Instead, the boating experience itself becomes your main source of onboard entertainment—sailing, swimming, snorkeling, napping, conversing with friends, and more. I can honestly say that in most cases, I rarely look to even turn on a television while cruising. The view from the yacht's deck is usually far superior to anything on the boob tube.

Still, you can rest assured that there will be things onboard for you to do should the weather turn ugly and you find yourself stuck inside.

Bareboat Entertainment

As with most things in bareboating, you will be responsible for making your own fun. Usually, this is as simple as bringing aboard a deck of cards or a favorite board game to play over a bottle of wine after sunset. Most bareboats have CD players in their main living spaces, so you can bring your favorite tunes to liven up the mood. DVD players are sometimes onboard as well, but be sure to ask before you cart your favorite movies down in your suitcase for the week. Books, too, are sometimes provided, but don't count on current bestsellers from *The New York Times* being stacked in your shelves.

A lot of people enjoy using the cruising guides and nautical charts aboard bareboats as a source of entertainment. Planning your next day's journey is a great way to get your entire group or family involved in the charter, and it makes everyone feel as if they are somewhat in control of their destiny—a hallmark of the charter experience. Reading through cruising guides also can give you a sense of the geographical and historical importance of whatever area you happen to be heading toward. This makes getting there all the better and far more memorable in the long run.

Another waterborne source of fun is using fish and reef identification books to learn what new species you saw during your day's swimming and snorkeling adventures. You'll be surprised at how quickly an hour can pass when you're flipping through a book about fish, looking at all the photographs and trying to figure out which one looks most like the silver-and-yellow swimmer you crossed paths with earlier in the day.

	Cruise Ship	Private Yacht
Shore Excursions	Organized in advance, with no changes to departure or return times. Usually include at least a dozen people, with other passengers who are strangers to you.	Whenever you wish, with total flexibility on departure and return times. Go ashore in your own yacht's private dinghy, with no strangers onboard.
Dining	At a predetermined time on some ships, at your leisure on others. Inside large dining halls or, for an extra fee, in smaller restaurants. Menu for the masses.	Whenever you like, on your yacht or at a restaurant onshore. Cook for yourself while bareboating, or have a chef on a crewed yacht create a menu to your taste.
Water Sports	An extra expense, except for onboard swimming pool. Timing determined in advance, like shore excursions, with no changes for weather or mood.	Whenever you like, for free on crewed yachts (except scuba). On bareboats, rent your gear for the week and use it again and again, or bring your own gear for free.
Shows and Activities	Free shows and games including musicals that you see with hundreds of other people. Predetermined by the cruise ship, no alternatives.	Onshore theaters, eateries, and bars, depending on cruising area. Onboard cards, conversation, or midnight swimming, as the mood strikes.
Crew	Like hotel staff, hourly workers tending to countless families and couples simultaneously.	Tend to your group exclusively. Yacht owner's personal staff, sometimes one-on-one service.

Most of all, a lot of bareboaters discover that other bareboaters can be a fantastic source of fun. In at least one cove, you'll typically find yourself making new friends, sharing stories and exchanging addresses so that you can keep in touch when you get back home.

Fully Crewed Yacht Entertainment

The bigger yachts typically have CD and DVD players in both the main living areas and in all the cabins, and in many cases on-demand satellite television will be included in your charter rate. Onboard some yachts, there is one satellite receiver, which means that every television will show the same programming (unless DVDs are playing in various cabins). Onboard other yachts, each cabin and the main living space all have separate receivers, so people in different rooms can watch different satellite programs at the same time. Good charter brokers can tell you which setups are aboard the yachts you are considering.

Even better, a lot of the bigger yachts also have at least one surround-sound theater setup in a main gathering area, such as the main saloon or sky lounge. Sometimes this includes large plasma-screen televisions, while in other cases, pull-down screens show movies from a projector that drops out of the ceiling. At least one sailing yacht I've been aboard, the 177-foot *Parsifal III*, even has a built-in bowl the size of a coffee table that sits in the middle of its arc-shaped main saloon sofas, ready to be filled with popcorn for movie-time munching.

You can bring your own CDs and DVDs aboard the bigger yachts, but you aren't likely to need them. Most of the bigger boats have extensive onboard collections from which you can choose, in some cases simply by pushing a button on a remote control. I've been aboard yachts that carry literally 300 different DVDs, organized alphabetically and again by genre on printed menus, so that you can quickly find a title you may have missed in the theaters.

Some fully crewed yachts carry XBoxes, Sony PlayStations, Nintendo Game Cubes, and other video-game systems with countless cartridges for adults and kids alike. Virtually every large yacht has a cache of cards, board games and books at the ready if there's a lull in the action or a spate of inclement weather.

Aboard the biggest yachts, you also can find a few unique onboard entertainment areas. The 173-foot megayacht *Passion*, for instance, carries a couple of old-style, stand-up arcade games including every golfer's favorite, Golden Tee. Some large sailing and power-driven megayachts have game tables for playing favorites like chess, checkers, and backgammon, while a handful of others have gaming areas for playing blackjack.

Calling and E-Mailing Home

In many cases, your cellular telephone or Blackberry will not work during a charter yacht vacation. If you have a triband setup with global access, you may get a signal, but cruising areas are notoriously deficient when it comes to cellular towers. An island may have one or two towers—but perhaps on the other side of a volcanic peak from where your yacht is docked. This has happened to me many times, especially on more remote islands without resorts and shops, and I've had to make due with whatever communications equipment was onboard the boat.

Aboard bareboats, your choices are going to be limited. In most cases, your only means of communication will be your VHF radio, which allows you to hail other boats, marinas, some restaurants, and the Coast Guard (or other local authorities). You can often leave your bareboat company's main telephone number with friends back home in case of an emergency, and the company's operator will hail you on the VHF to relay the message.

In some ports—but not to be counted on—you will be able to find Internet cafes for checking e-mail. You can bring your laptop onboard a bareboat, but as with the cellular situation, you shouldn't count on having a wireless network available. Some marinas have them, but outside of that, you'll be out of luck.

Larger, fully crewed yachts are a different story. They have satellite communication systems that can send and receive ship-to-shore calls, e-mail messages, and even faxes in some cases. Most larger yachts have computers onboard, too—at least one for the crew's use and perhaps another in the guest office area (if there is one).

Making calls and using e-mail will likely cost you an extra fee—usually calculated in per-minute satellite usage time—but unless you are constantly in touch with home, the cost should be negligible in relation to the overall expense of a crewed yacht charter. Checking in for five minutes once each night with the baby-sitter isn't going to break the bank.

Service

This section relates only to crewed yachts, as bareboats obviously have no crew aboard to offer you service.

Aboard a fully or partially crewed yacht, the service you receive should be second to none. Whether the captain and crew wear colorful polo shirts or starchy white collars, you should want for nothing and feel completely pampered. You should be offered a drink before you even realize you're thirsty, be handed a dry towel before you finish climbing up the swim platform, and be served your favorite wines without having to tell the crew, more than once, which vineyards you prefer.

Agnes Howard, a straight-shooting crewed yacht charter broker with Camper & Nicholsons International in Fort Lauderdale, Florida, knows quite a bit about proper onboard service. She worked as a stewardess aboard charter yachts for several years before becoming a broker, and her husband, John Terrill, has served as captain aboard prestigious boats including the presidential motoryacht *Sequoia*.

"The big buzzword is discreet," Howard explains. "We also talk a lot about crew anticipating your every need. I do think those are accurate. Generally, most of the crew on these yachts have at least a four-year college degree. These are people who are multinational—they have a certain personality other than a nationality. They are very keen about travel, fun, healthy lifestyle. Even if they're a little bit older, in their mid-40s, they still tend to be healthy and wholesome people. They're the kind of people that you want to be around. By the time you're done with your charter, you're looking for a position in your company so you can hire them. It used to happen to me all the time. The Hollywood people would say, 'Come ashore. We'll create a position for you.'

"These people have the wherewithal to stay away from you, even when there is one crewmember for every guest," she continues. "You use buzzers and bells. They find out what you want to drink, and they'll stock a small fridge on the top deck. They'll say, 'I'm here to serve you, but if you want to be left alone, here's everything you've said you like. I'll leave it for you, but I'm always available.'"

Aboard smaller yachts with only two or three crew, each crewmember may do multiple jobs every day. (Some captains refer to themselves as chief bottle washers.) Aboard large sailing yachts and power-driven megayachts, there are entire departments devoted to interior jobs, on-deck jobs, engineering jobs, cooking duties, and more, with crew who have specialized training in each area.

"You should expect top-notch service no matter what kind of crewed yacht it is," Howard says. "The level of service is not directly related to what you're paying for the boat. There are husband-and-wife teams that continue to prove themselves onboard an 80-foot yacht, who very often have been trained working as a head stewardess and first mate onboard a 180-foot yacht. They just downsized. So your expectation of excellent service should be met, no matter the size of the crewed yacht. It's an underlying pride that we have in the yachting industry. It's almost like a competition among the boats."

Menus and Meals

My favorite story about dining onboard a yacht comes from a cruise I did in 2003 through Greece's Aegean Islands aboard the fully crewed 85-foot motor-yacht *Oh Que Luna*. After a few days of gorging on feta cheese, fresh octopus, and every other local delicacy the yacht's chef put on a plate before me, I asked him if we could please take things down a belt size by having a simple, hors d'oeuvres-only supper. He responded in the only way he knew how: by preparing a smorgasbord of finger foods that covered an entire tabletop. He simply could not imagine failing to offer charter guests anything less than their wildest imagination could conjure, and he wanted to make sure my imagination was as satisfied as my belly.

That's not to say that every charter yacht chef will stuff you silly. On the contrary, some pay close attention to how much food is left on different guests' plates the first night or two of a cruise, and then adjust the following evenings' portion sizes accordingly. They'll even begin to season your meal differently from the other guests' if they notice, say, that you prefer an extra dash of salt.

My point is that aboard yachts with chefs, you can literally have whatever your stomach desires.

The way yachts prepare for your vacation is by provisioning, or stocking their galleys with whatever you request. If you're aboard a bareboat you can do your own provisioning (thus saving a few dollars at the local grocery store), or you can fill out a form and have the bareboat company provision the boat for you before you arrive, for an additional fee. Either way, you'll have all of your favorite foods and drinks onboard, ready to prepare, serve, and eat however you like.

Fully crewed yachts also ask you to fill out a provisioning form, but they call it a *preference sheet*. On this sheet, you'll be asked to list not just the foods, drinks, and alcoholic beverages that you prefer, but also your style of eating: big breakfasts, light lunches, buffet-style dinners, formal sit-down affairs, and so on. The crew's goal with this preference sheet is to get a feel not just for what you like to eat, but also how you like to be served.

Your preference sheet will also ask you about food allergies, conditions such as diabetes, and anything else that might affect your meals and menus onboard. The more honest you are on your preference sheet, the better the yacht's crew will be able to tailor your vacation to your personality.

A fully crewed yacht's chef will outline a general menu for the week after reviewing your preference sheets, in some cases organizing so that he can cook two or three separate dishes per mealtime for guests whose tastes don't always agree. Many yacht chefs have trained at the world's finest culinary institutes and can offer a wide repertoire of everything from classic French to avant-garde cuisine. If you prefer to eat fish but your spouse will only have beef, the chef can accommodate that with two deliciously different plates served simultaneously. In most cases, you can request vegetarian, low-cholesterol, low-fat, low-calorie spa, Atkins, South Beach, and other diet-oriented meals as well.

The best part about dining aboard charter yachts—bareboat or crewed—is the ability to integrate the day's activities into the evening's meals. I've eaten everything from mahi-mahi caught off the back of the yacht to shrimp purchased from a commercial trawler making its way across our yacht's path from offshore. Seafood just doesn't get any fresher. Lobsters and conch are bound to pop up on most Caribbean cruises, while if you're cruising up north in colder climes, you may luck out with some salmon, halibut, or king crab.

In many cases, the crewed yachts will even incorporate themes into the evening's meals. When children are onboard, for instance, crew may put together a "pirate night" complete with treasure maps and troves of gold-covered chocolate coins. The crew dress up in pirate garb, decorate the dining area with skulls and crossbones, and even sing pirate songs if the mood is right.

For more mature crowds, the dinner themes may be appropriately tailored, such as the one I experienced in 2003 aboard the 120-foot megayacht *Kayana*. During that Alaska charter, which was beautifully organized by CEO Expeditions, we happened to come upon an iceberg. Its tip jutted out of the water like a sparkling sapphire, and the crew took us up close enough to touch it in the yacht's dinghy. While we were there, mesmerized by the sight, the crew chipped off a large, round chunk of the crystal-clear, thousand-year-old glacial ice. It resurfaced that night over dinner, both as cubes in our drinks and as a fabulous table centerpiece holding a tall, flickering candle.

Shore Excursions

Going ashore from a private yacht is far different than going ashore from a cruise ship. For starters, cruise ships pull in at big, often ugly, commercial docks, while charter yachts either dock at privately owned marinas or stay on anchor in a natural setting, say just offshore of a beach in a quiet cove. With a private yacht, you go ashore whenever you're ready—not at a predetermined time—and you go with only the people from your boat instead of with dozens of strangers who happen to be with you aboard a big ship. Can your group go ashore to a crowded bar, restaurant, or shopping area to socialize? Of course. But you're just as free to go ashore to walk along a secluded trail on an uninhabited island if you'd prefer an evening unto yourselves.

Whether you're aboard a bareboat or a fully crewed yacht, you have two choices when it comes to shore excursions. You can either step off the yacht directly onto a dock or beach, or you can ride in the yacht's *dinghy*. Generally speaking, a dinghy is a rigid-bottom boat with inflatable tubes for its sides that you can sit on, along with regular cushioned seats inside the dinghy itself. Dinghies are usually no bigger than 16 or 18 feet long, and you will find them even aboard the very large megayachts and sailing yachts, which also sometimes have *tenders*. A tender can be anything from a 25-foot speedboat to a 35-foot sportfishing boat. Some yachts are big enough to carry these larger tenders on deck alongside dinghies, while other yachts tow the larger tenders from port to port.

A fully crewed yacht will have at least one inflatable-style dinghy, like the one shown in this photograph's foreground. Some large yachts also carry or tow a fishing-style tender, like the one with the pointy bow in the top of this photograph. The yacht's deck crew, called deckhands or mates, will be at your service for shore excursions, water sports, and anything else you desire.

At any size, dinghies and tenders are perfectly safe and comfortable to ride aboard. Your only problem is likely to be people onshore who watch you come in from the yacht, thinking you might be rich or famous. As you step out of the dinghy and head toward the local shops or restaurants, you might get a few more stares than you're used to!

Shore excursions themselves are also different from what you find aboard cruise ships, since they are never tours with other groups. In some cases, they are not even pre-planned guided outings. You can enjoy those types of excursions if that's what you prefer, but you also can choose to go ashore to shop far from the cruise-ship docks, to try quaint little restaurants, to play a round of golf, to visit a spa, or to sip rum punch at a two-stool beach bar.

A comparison that illustrates this point is between a cruise-ship excursion many people have experienced—visiting a turtle farm—and a memory I have of going ashore during a charter in Costa Rica aboard the 125-foot megayacht *Centurion*.

At the cruise-ship turtle-farm excursion, I basically was herded through narrow alleyways so that I could look at turtles trapped in cages. I was surrounded by dozens of other people, I couldn't hear anything the tour guide said above the din of the crowd, and I was on a strict schedule that had to be met lest we miss our bus back to the ship in time for dinner.

Aboard *Centurion* in Costa Rica, I went onshore with a half-dozen other guests from the yacht and a private guide whose exclusive services our captain had prearranged. We entered a nature preserve that was filled with everything from alligators to capuchin monkeys, all of them living free and in the wild. I could hike along whichever trails I wanted, for however long I wanted—with the guide pointing out three-toed sloths and exotic birds along the way—and the yacht wasn't going anywhere until I'd had my fill, even if it took a few days. Dinner would wait until my return, with the chef keeping tabs on our return time by talking on the VHF radio with the deckhand who was with us, carrying a cooler of cold water bottles should we become thirsty.

This is the essence of all shore excursions during private yacht charters. You get to do whatever you want, whenever you want, for however long you want, on whatever day you want, with only the people of your choosing. There are no crowds (unless you set out to find them), and there are no deadlines for finishing up onshore and racing back to the boat.

It's simply the most relaxing, most interesting, and most liberating way to explore ashore, anywhere in the world.

Water Sports and Toys

I can't remember ever having been aboard a yacht without a single water toy. From water skis to Jet Skis, kayaks to mini-sailboats, snorkeling gear to fishing poles, virtually all yachts carry some sort of gear to help make your days at sea a whole lot of fun.

Bareboats may carry a dinghy and a kayak, or perhaps a dinghy and a set of water skis. You can also rent kayaks, snorkeling and scuba gear, and even water tubes or wakeboards at or near most bareboat fleet hubs.

Crewed yachts carry all of that and more, sometimes offering toys that you can't find anywhere else. They are almost always included in the price of your charter, and you can use them as many times as you like, morning, noon, and night.

"Typically, it will be dictated by what area of the world you're cruising in," explains Robin O'Brien, an extremely friendly crewed yacht charter broker with Fraser Yachts Worldwide in Fort Lauderdale, Florida. "What you'll find, primarily in the Bahamas and the Caribbean more so than in the Mediterranean, is great snorkeling and diving, so you'll have that equipment on most boats if not all of them. In the Bahamas, you'll also have Wave Runners. Most of the Caribbean and New England, they have very strict rules about Wave Runners. It's soon to come that they'll be altogether outlawed. If you absolutely want them, the Bahamas are the place to go. But every time I book a charter, I look to see if the laws have changed.

"Water skiing is almost always offered, and many boats are adding things like kite surfing," O'Brien continues. "The chef on one of my charters recently was a professional kite surfer, and he gave two of the children a free week of instruction. That was a unique situation, but typically, all of the water toys are included in the price of the boat. That includes kayaks, and if they don't have kayaks, they'll have a canoe. A lot of the larger poweryachts are carrying Lasers, which are small sailboats. Anybody can get on them and use them. Some yachts still offer Windsurfers, but they seem to be less popular. And then of course there are all the floating toys that get pulled behind the tender, like hot dogs and tubes. If you're a little more athletic, there are kneeboards and skurfboards. Kneeboards, you kneel on it and strap in at a crouched position. A skurfboard, you stand up and hold on, just like a kneeboard but you're standing up. It's a board, like a short surfboard with fins, but designed to be pulled behind a tender."

O'Brien and I cruised together in Fiji onboard the 115-foot motoryacht *Surprise*, which is one of the rare megayachts that offers scuba diving right off the boat. Most megayachts, because of liability and insurance, will arrange for scuba enthusiasts to rendezvous with local dive companies instead of diving with the yacht crew. But *Surprise*, being out in the middle of the South Pacific, had its own operation run by local crew.

They led O'Brien and me to everything from exotic fish to coral heads the size of Volkswagens—just the two of us, with no other groups of divers to worry about in our midst. We dove right from the yacht's dinghy, setting out whenever we wanted before or after lunch. We not only went hour after hour underwater without seeing another diver, we went all week without seeing another dive boat. It was an unbelievable, highly personalized experience that would be impossible to repeat on a cruise ship or at a shore-based resort. This crew knew parts of the ocean landscape, simply from their cruising experience, that no other land-based divers could ever find.

"The beauty of charter is that the crew who work on deck are really, really good at these things, and they'll spend all day teaching you how to do water sports if that's what you want," O'Brien adds. "Scuba diving, those yachts that offer it are very good at it, and they have either a dive master or dive instructor onboard. If it's a dive master, you have to be certified to dive. Typically, the boat will have equipment and a compressor for refilling your tanks. Often, a yacht crewmember will go with you as a buddy if they can."

Unique Every Time

The point of all this—as with pretty much everything else you've learned about yachts so far—is that your onboard experience with one yacht will differ from your onboard experience with the next.

Some bareboats will have one kind of cabin and one kind of entertainment systems, while other bareboats will be set up in a completely opposite fashion. One fully crewed yacht will have a surround-sound theater system and a scuba-diving compressor, while another will have a wine bar and a large outdoor dining area instead. And all of these differences will be in addition to the unique general styles of the powerboat, sailboat, or catamaran designs that you learned about in Chapter Three.

Indeed, options onboard yachts are as endless as the places those yachts can take you—which is the next major factor you should consider when choosing a charter vacation. Once you've figured out what style of boat might be best for you and what kinds of onboard experiences you'd like to have, it's time to decide where in the world you'd like to cruise. Chapters Five, Six and Seven will help you do just that.

5

Destinations

I could be at a cocktail party, or a family reunion, or sitting at a train station chatting with a strangely outgoing stranger. No matter the setting, the scenario is the same. People ask me what I do for a living, I tell them I write about boating vacations, and they ask me—with great anticipation—where they should take their next cruise.

Now, I know Miss Manners would slap my tongue for answering a question with a question, but I always do. It's simple, really: Just because I cruise onboard a lot of charter yachts in a great variety of destinations doesn't mean I know which boat and place are best for everybody. So my reply to the question of where other people should go cruising, each and every time, is, "That depends. What do you like to do?"

At this point, the inquisitive would-be cruiser tends to develop a twitch in their brow, kind of like a puzzled puppy trying to figure out exactly what trick I want it to perform so that it will get the reward I'm withholding. But I'm not hiding any magic treats; I'm simply trying to get the person to articulate their idea of a dream vacation, so that I can tell them which style of yacht they might enjoy in which kind of cruising destination.

This is when they really start to lose their minds, so I offer up a few examples while they nod along, making mental notes.

Without question, the best charter I've done amid quiet coves, snorkeling reefs, and pristine beaches was aboard the 120-foot megayacht *Joanne* in the Exumas chain in the Bahamas. I know people think of the Caribbean first when they want to escape to the tropics, but I've yet to find waters as clear and paths as untraveled as the ones Capt. Dan Webster showed me in the Exumas.

That cruise was the complete opposite of the charter I did aboard the 180-foot megayacht *Revelation* with Venture Pacific Marine in the Galapagos Islands. There, about 600 miles west of Ecuador and literally atop the equator, I saw the same species of finches, marine iguanas, and giant tortoises that inspired Charles

Darwin—and I engrossed my mind in one of the most substantial ecological adventures of my life.

Yet as great as that charter was, it differed tremendously from the one Nigel Burgess invited me to do aboard the 137-foot sailing yacht *Infatuation* off the western coast of Italy. We moved spectacularly with the wind by day, spent our afternoons climbing through the remains of walled cities onshore, and then gorged on the chef's delicious meals each night while watching the sun set over buildings more colorful than my grandmother's rouge collection.

Oh, and did I forget to mention the hands-on cruise I did up New York's Hudson River? I was onboard the Nordic Tug 42 trawler yacht *Wilde One* with Bill Boyer and Ben Wilde from Wilde Yacht Sales in Connecticut, and I thoroughly enjoyed taking the helm as the bright sunshine beamed down over the Catskills—almost as much as I enjoyed getting to my final destination, the riverfront region that served as inspiration for Thomas Cole, Frederic Edwin Church, and the other great painters who introduced New England's beauty to the world nearly two centuries ago.

Truth be told, this is about the time I really start to gab about just how unique every yacht charter experience can be, given the different styles of yachts and all the different destinations where they offer cruises. I'm usually about to launch into my story about getting to touch the actual tip of an iceberg while on charter in Alaska aboard the 120-foot motoryacht *Kayana* when the inquisitive would-be cruiser smiles politely and wanders off, somewhat sickened that I earn a paycheck while participating in such grand escapades.

But my point, as you no doubt have figured out by now, is that each destination can be as different as the yachts based there—and that your itinerary will have a great deal to do with the kind of charter vacation you end up experiencing, no matter what style of boat you choose.

What's Your Dream?

You've already learned that charter yachts allow you to choose your itinerary, in many ways, on the fly. If you like a particular harbor or island, you can stay there as long as you like, changing your mood with the weather. If you get to a place you thought you would enjoy but realize it's just not all you imagined, you can pull up anchor and set a course for another port without wasting a second of your vacation time. You and your captain (or you alone, if you're bareboating) can decide these things day by day, hour by hour, and even minute by minute.

However, you will have to select a general itinerary before setting sail so that your captain or bareboat company can pre-arrange provisioning shipments, marina dock space, and the like. The yacht needs to know where to pick you up and drop you off, for instance, in keeping with your commercial or private airline reservations.

With bareboats, you'll almost always start and end your cruise at the company's hub marina, where it keeps its fleet. With fully crewed yachts, though, you can start in one place and end in another if you prefer a one-way cruise that covers more territory than a round-trip course.

The trick when planning your itinerary is to ask yourself what you really, truly want to do during your yacht charter—to put into words what you envision as your dream vacation. Do you want to see as many tourist-friendly islands as possible? Or would you prefer to hopscotch around with the wind, discovering little-known sand spits and two-stool bars? Would you like to see and be seen in the most luxurious marinas on the Côte d'Azur? Or are you interested in cruising outside the regular ports to an up-and-coming coastline like Croatia's? Will you be happy in a well-known destination like the Virgin Islands? Or have you been there a few times already, leaving you longing for a more exotic locale like the South Pacific? Do you want to be in warmer climes in a bathing suit? Or would you rather don a sweater and cruise among the glaciers in Alaska?

These are the kinds of questions you should think through before booking a yacht charter of any style. Once you have a general idea about the kind of experience you're after—say, bareboating in the Caribbean versus a fully crewed charter in the Mediterranean—you can work with the bareboat company or a good charter broker to set a basic itinerary for your cruise.

Seasonal Hot Spots

Cruise ships go to the Caribbean year-round, even under the blustery threat of hurricane season. They go the Mediterranean year-round, too, even though half of Europe is covered with snow during the winter months.

Private yachts are different. While bareboats that are part of fleets may stay at their hub marinas year-round—as do some fully crewed yachts—the majority of boats available for charter move from region to region with the seasons.

Why? One major reason is that most yachts are literally built to be used in warm weather, when their owners are on vacation. The boats may have air conditioning, but they aren't likely to have heat. It's a waste of money for most owners to install a heating system aboard their yachts unless they plan to cruise in places like Scandinavia, Alaska, or southern New Zealand. The yachts that go to those places have special features—like heat—that make them appropriately outfitted for their environments.

Another reason why charter yachts typically move with the seasons is that cruising can be downright uncomfortable in some places during off-season months. Remember, yachts are much smaller than cruise ships. Nasty swells and looming hurricanes are not worth battling in a private boat.

This seasonal pattern affects your charter vacation because if you want to cruise in a particular region, then going there during the correct cruising months will guarantee you the largest number of possible boats from which to choose. While you may find cruise ships in Alaska during February, for instance, you're not going to find a single charter yacht up there in the frigid dead of winter. There isn't a single marina open to tend to the boats. During that time of year, most charter yachts will be based at marinas stretching from Florida to the southern Caribbean, where it's warm.

In fact, to make your planning easier, you can break the world's most popular charter regions down to just a handful of seasonal locales. If you know you want to visit one of the following regions, you should plan on doing so during the appropriate time of year.

Summer Hot Spots

From late May through early October, most charter yachts are either in the Mediterranean, New England, or Alaska. This also is the time of year to look for the handful of charters available in Bermuda, along the U.S. East Coast, on the Great Lakes, and out west in the San Juan Islands near Seattle and Vancouver.

Winter Hot Spots

From mid-December through early April, most charter yachts are in the Caribbean, including the U.S. and British Virgin Islands. However, this is also the warmest time of year to look for the handful of charters available in the South Pacific and along the western coast of Mexico.

Year-Round Availability

Many yachts stay year-round in Florida and the Bahamas, and you can book charters in either location most of the time. Based on my experience, though, the cruising in both regions tends to be the most comfortable during late spring and early summer, say May through July. I suggest steering clear of these regions between August and November, when hurricanes tend to barrel through. March, too, can be tough in the Bahamas because of gale-force winds that sometimes blow for days at a time.

Zeroing In

Once you determine the region where you want to cruise during any given season, it's time to decide on a general itinerary. In the case of a Caribbean charter, this means selecting specific islands you think might be worth visiting. If you're looking into the Mediterranean, you might decide which cities from Palma to Portofino excite you the most. If you're considering New England, you might have a mix in your mind that includes cities like Boston and islands such as Nantucket.

Here, as with everything involving yacht charter, you will find that you have to think differently than you might when choosing a cruise-ship vacation. Yacht charters are much more compact in terms of distance. The boats are smaller, they carry less fuel (or rely on sails), and they typically stay at anchor or in a marina instead of cruising overnight—all of which means your charter yacht will cover far less distance in a week than a typical cruise ship.

For instance, if you want to charter a yacht for a week in the Mediterranean, you might focus solely on exploring the western coast of Italy—as opposed to a cruise-ship itinerary that would make one stop in Italy in between visits to Spain, France, and Greece. By the same token, a weeklong cruise-ship itinerary in the Caribbean may include St. Thomas, St. Lucia, and Cozumel, literally crisscrossing the entirety of the Caribbean Sea, while a yacht charter that starts in St. Thomas is likely to spend the rest of the week within the borders of the Virgin Islands.

In my experience, this is a very good thing. Instead of having less than a day at any given port to rush ashore and find a T-shirt shop, a yacht charter gives me all the time I need to slow down and really get to know a place. I always have time to wander way, *way* off the streets lined with trinket shops and rip-off souvenirs, and I never fail to find a cute little watering hole or luncheonette where a local person befriends me and points me toward the destination's lesser-known treasures—the stuff I'd never find on a five-hour cruise ship excursion before rushing back to my cabin.

"I lived in St. Thomas for ten years," explains Ann Landry, a well-respected, longtime crewed yacht charter broker in Fort Lauderdale who left the big management companies to form Ann Landry Yachting in early 2006. "I would see the cruise ships come in and disgorge passengers. There would be a line of taxis waiting on the quay. Some would go on the open-air transports, some of them went downtown to shop, others would go diving, and so forth. But basically, the boat is there for six, maybe eight hours, and everybody runs around and does these things quickly and then gets back on the boat. Because the food is included, they don't sample the local restaurants.

Cruise Ship vs. Private Yacht Itineraries

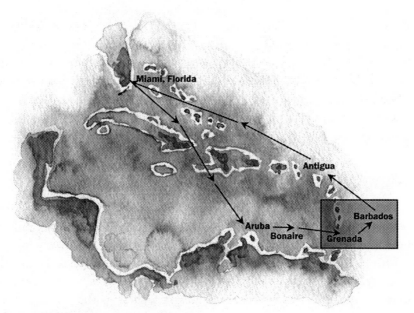

A typical weeklong cruise ship itinerary (above) may cover the entire Caribbean Sea, while a typical yacht charter focuses on one area, such as the Windward Islands (above shaded box, enlarged at right).

Practically speaking, this means you spend far more time exploring your destination onboard a yacht, poking around in secluded harbors and exploring ashore on smaller, unmapped islets. The cruise ship, meanwhile, must keep moving on schedule from port to commercial port, as the arrows indicate.

"They really aren't interacting with the local community as they would on a private yacht," she continues. "You get more of a feeling for the culture when you go on a private yacht, more of a flavor for the island. The crew on the yacht act like a personal concierge. It's their job to know the place like the back of their hand. It's not just an overview. They know the very best people to call for any service. You don't have to wait until a van is full and wait to stop off at five or six places."

The point is that even though you are likely to visit fewer islands or locales during any given yacht charter, you will definitely get to know each one better than you ever possibly could on a cruise-ship vacation.

In terms of planning your private yacht charter vacation, then, your goal is to determine not only what region you'd like to explore, but also what your must-see destinations are within that region versus the "nearby" stops you are willing to forgo should the weather or your mood change. This is true whether you're considering a yacht in a geographical charter hub or an emerging market.

Geographic Hubs

Geographic hubs are the main areas where charter yachts tend to be available during a given season. They are the hot spots—primarily the Caribbean during the winter months and the Mediterranean during the summer months.

What makes a place a geographic hub for yacht charter is infrastructure, things like marinas, crew placement services, stores where crewmembers can get supplies and tools, fueling locations, yacht repair services, specialty shops where chefs can provision the finest foods and wines, easy access to airports and hotels for charter guests, and the like. All of these things make your charter better, such as getting you to your yacht easily and allowing the crew to stock anything you desire onboard. In many ways, the existence of these yacht charter infrastructures saves you money, too, since pretty much everything a yacht could need for your charter is available locally.

That's not to say that these charter hub regions are as built-up as cruise-ship hubs. On the contrary: If you visit the Virgin Islands on a cruise ship, and then you visit it again onboard a charter yacht, you will find two vastly different places. The cruise ship will tie up at a large, commercial dock near lots of stores and restaurants and activities, while your charter yacht will likely anchor out in the middle of a quiet cove, where you can wake up the next morning and go snorkeling all alone with the sunrise before breakfast.

In a geographic hub, you'll simply be closer to civilization when the time comes for cruising to your charter's end point and hopping on an airplane, perhaps for a direct flight home. Your yacht's crew will also be closer to the supplies and services they may need to easily meet your last-minute requests and expectations.

Emerging Markets

The opposite of a geographic charter hub is an emerging market—places like Croatia, the South Pacific, and South America where more charter yachts are now beginning to cruise, but where the infrastructure to support dozens of charter yachts does not yet exist. There's absolutely no reason to forgo a yacht charter in an emerging market, as long as you understand that there will likely be additional costs and, perhaps, a compromise or two.

For instance, if you want the finest French wines in a place like Fiji, they will have to be flown in at your expense because there are no fine wine bistros on most of the islands in that region. You may have to sit in a car for a half-hour or hour to get from the airport to your yacht, instead of making a ten-minute trip in a geographic hub where the pickup points and marinas are more centrally located. Of course, your bareboat company or crewed yacht team will work hard to give you everything you want with a personalized touch in an emerging market, but they may not be able to make, say, a case of something so specific as s'mores-flavored Atkins bars appear out of nowhere on a half-hour's notice. The emerging markets are, by definition, not yet fully developed in terms of the Western tourism idyll.

You also have to be prepared for potential problems in emerging markets. Two memories come to mind here. First, there was the time I was working as an editor and assigned a photographer to cover a yacht charter vacation in Fiji. Her camera broke somewhere along the 18-hour flight to the South Pacific, and she didn't realize it until she was onboard the yacht—well more than a day's journey from the nearest camera store. Luckily, one of the crewmembers was an avid photographer who had excellent equipment to share. Otherwise, so far from even a small town, the photojournalist would have been out of luck.

Another emerging-market memory comes from my first cruise to the Galapagos Islands, in 2001 aboard the 125-foot motoryacht *Parranda* as a guest of Quasar Nautica. There happened to be a man in his 70s aboard at the same time I was there. He'd recently had hip surgery and had been working his muscles back into form so that he could take this dream cruise of his life in a destination filled with hiking among wild animals. The problem occurred during one of the hikes, when the man overdid things a bit—despite crewmembers' warnings to slow down—and his hip popped out of its socket. We were two days' cruising away from the nearest medical facility, and he ended up having to be strapped to a long, wooden table in the yacht's main saloon for more than 24 hours. It was the only place on the main deck where he could be immobilized until we got to a doctor.

Now, both of these examples have something in common besides the fact that they happened in emerging markets: The people involved didn't do such a good job taking responsibility for themselves. That photojournalist should have had more than one camera, since she knew she was going to the end of the earth, and that 70-year-old man should've taken it easy while hiking around the volcanic trails in Galapagos just a few weeks after having hip surgery.

Still, we all make mistakes from time to time, and it's important that you realize how they can be amplified when you're cruising outside a geographic charter hub. I actually love to cruise in emerging markets—the excitement of it all is thrilling—but less-adventurous people (and many first-time charterers) prefer to cruise in geographic hubs where transportation, provisioning, and services are more readily available.

Inland Cruising

I mentioned briefly in Chapter Three that bareboats and fully crewed barges are charter options if you want to stay away from the ocean and instead cruise along inland rivers. This style of charter is particularly popular in Europe, where the bareboats far outnumber the fully crewed barges that are on par with fully crewed "regular" yachts.

"I had a recent charter, there were eight guests, and it was a wide range of ages, and they wanted to do a lot of walking and seeing the countryside instead of spending all of their time on the water," recalls Elaine Stewart, a charming independent broker who owns Elaine Stewart Yacht Charters in Roswell, Georgia. "They loved having the barge in France. They flew into Paris, then went down and picked up the barge. Basically, they used it as transportation. They found wonderful places to eat along the way, with all the convenience of unpacking just one time. And they loved going through the locks. It was really fun for them. They were not sailing people, and they had never done a yacht charter. For people who want to spend their time seeing the countryside instead of seeing what comes by as they're sailing from place to place, it's a good option. For non-sailors, I think it's a great thing."

The bareboats you will find along French waterways, as well as those in Germany, Ireland, and Belgium, are not always as up to date as those at the more globally oriented bareboat companies in the Caribbean and Mediterranean Sea. In some cases, you will have everything you need—as long as you don't need stylish accommodations or galley appliances newer than about 30 years old.

Another inland cruising option is in the United States and Canada, along the part of the "Great Loop" that includes the Mississippi River, the Great Lakes, and the St. Lawrence River. Often, boaters cruise these waterways on their way to or from the Intracoastal Waterway, a sort of boating highway that runs down the Eastern Seaboard. There are not a lot of bareboats to be found in these areas, but more and more fully crewed yachts are making the Great Loop trip and spending summers in the Great Lakes—meaning that you can often pick up a one-way charter in whichever direction a given yacht is already heading.

Good charter brokers will know which yachts are moving where and which ones are already making the Great Loop. In some cases, you can even book a charter like this at a discount, since the yacht is being moved along the inland waterways anyway, with or without you onboard.

Greece and Turkey

The Eastern Mediterranean countries Greece and Turkey are unusual when compared with their Western Mediterranean counterparts. As cruising grounds, they have a decidedly different European flair.

"The thing I would stress is not so much about the boats, but about the area," explains Rosemary Pavlatou, a crewed yacht charter broker with A1 Yacht Trade Consortium in Piraeus and Rhodes. Pavlatou is a British ex-pat who is now a naturalized Greek citizen, fluent in both English and Greek—and very well traveled. "The Western Mediterranean is much more formal, much more crowded. Chic in a way. Greece and Turkey are timeless. They're still not as busy and crowded. It's not as much see-and-be-seen. It's much more relaxed. If you want to get away from the crowds, really get away from it all, this is the place."

In the case of Greece, the boats themselves are different, too. Because of national laws that regulate what kinds of yachts can cruise inside its borders, Greece has what is essentially its own bareboat and fully crewed yacht fleets. Whereas in Turkey, just as in France or Italy, you could book a summertime charter aboard a yacht that spends winters in the Caribbean, that same yacht in most cases would not be allowed to book charters in Greece.

This situation has created what is essentially a Greek-owned fleet of charter yachts that will in most cases be your only choice for chartering in that country's waters. With few competing charter yachts coming in from other countries until the past few years, this Greek fleet has not been held to a standard of international competition. The boats may be a bit more run down than similar yachts elsewhere on the world's waters, and their crew may be less savvy when it comes to the fineries of, say, serving hot tea with a silver set.

"In Greece, you still have the closed market of boats," Pavlatou says, "but the quality is starting to come up. Not as quickly as I'd like, but it's happening."

The charter I did off the coast of Athens aboard the 85-foot motoryacht *Oh Que Luna* (remember the dinner of hors d'oeuvres?) was perfectly lovely—although the captain was one of only two crewmembers on the entire yacht who spoke English. Aboard every other similar-size motoryacht I've visited anywhere else in the world, basic or better English was spoken by the majority, if not all, of the crew.

The questionable condition of some Greek charter yachts, along with your need to have the best possible crew, make working with a good charter broker even more important when considering Greece for your vacation. Not all charter brokers attend the annual industry-only boat shows in Greece and Turkey, and many of the brokers have never cruised in these places at all. You need somebody who not only knows about the boats and places, but also can communicate in a place where everyone may literally be speaking Greek.

I was fortunate that Pavlatou acted as a personal guide after arranging my *Oh Que Luna* charter. I would turn without hesitation to her for a recommendation the next time I get the opportunity to charter a yacht in Greece or Turkey.

Hidden Costs

I know we haven't yet gotten to the chapter on pricing, but it's important to note here that if you're considering booking a yacht charter in an emerging destination, then you're likely to have to pay more expenses than you would when chartering in a geographic hub. Your hidden costs may even go beyond the financial, depending on how far off the beaten path you want to cruise.

Extra fees in emerging destinations are sometimes things that charter brokers don't like to discuss: overpriced fuel, super-inflated provisioning costs, even the occasional bribe. That kind of imagery doesn't make for very pretty charter sales presentations, but you need to be aware of what's happening. Remember, emerging destinations are just that; they haven't yet been brought completely into the worldwide tourism fold. If a charter yacht is going there at all, it's sometimes by way of a literally uncharted course.

Other hidden costs can include more standard things like delivery fees, in the case of fully crewed yachts. A delivery fee is the price a yacht's owner charges you to move his boat to the vacation area of your choice, if it's not the same as the place where the yacht is normally kept. "Generally, delivery fees for long hauls are more than four or five days," explains Chris Craven, a Monaco-based crewed yacht charter broker with Edmiston and Company. "You'll get [yacht] owners who want 50 percent of the charter fee, per day of delivery, plus fuel costs. The fuel, that's non-negotiable. That's the cost of getting the boat there. What is negotiable is payment for the time between Point A and Point B. One key is how long you want to be on the boat. If you're looking for a four-week charter, it's more worthwhile to the owner to move the boat on your terms.

"If you do a place like the Galapagos Islands or the Northwest Passage, you also have to have a guide onboard or a specific captain, and it's a hundred dollars a day for the guy," Craven says. "Sometimes in these kinds of places, you have to fly to the nearest airport and then get a helicopter to the nearest island where you can meet the boat. Make sure the broker explains any taxes that are involved locally, island to island. The broker also needs to know if the boat can legally be in some places. If it's an adventure charter into a place like the Amazon or the South China Sea or off of Hong Kong, you need to be aware of the possibility of piracy. We don't like to talk about it, but that's something to consider.

"The more adventurous you want to be, the more detailed the broker's work has to be," Craven says. "There are a lot of questions to be considered. You need a broker who knows more than just the regular yachts."

Delivery fees and pricey transportation might also be a factor in a geographic cruising hub, of course, if you're trying to get a particular yacht to go somewhere that it doesn't typically cruise. However, you are far less likely to run into the shadier sorts of extra costs in a geographic cruising hub than you are in some emerging destinations.

Event Charters

Sometimes, it's not a region you want to experience on a charter. Many, many people book private yacht vacations each year based on an event.

The biggest are typically the Cannes Film Festival and the Monaco Grand Prix, but other events draw heavy charter bookings, too, including the Newport Jazz Festival in Rhode Island, Antigua Race Week, July Fourth fireworks in New York City, and the America's Cup races (wherever they may be in the world). The idea is that instead of staying in a hotel onshore and having to watch the daily activities with all the crowds, you can be in the heart of the action onboard your own yacht, sitting on your private aft deck with a clear view and a stewardess bringing you refreshing drinks.

The downside to chartering during these types of events is that they garner top-dollar rates, with competition among vacationers not just to get the best boats for the occasion, but also to get the best marina slips and anchorages. Many of these events—especially in Cannes and Monaco—are see-and-be-seen paparazzi paradises that draw the rich and famous, and the people who own the yachts and marinas know it. The charter rates stay high, and there are rarely bargains to be had.

"I believe the dockage fee just for a week in Cannes or Monaco these days is somewhere around 30,000 or 40,000 euros," explains Steve Elario, who books high-end crewed yachts while serving as director of the charter division at International Yacht Collection in Fort Lauderdale, Florida. That, remember, is a cost that is added to the weekly base rate for the yacht itself—which in this case will be well into six figures.

If you want to enjoy an event charter without breaking the bank, you can of course book a smaller crewed yacht or even a bareboat, but dockage fees at the nearby marinas will still be a substantial expense, and the crowds will still be huge. It's for these reasons that many people choose to create their own "events," say a golf tournament charter, a scuba cruise, or a wine tasting week. These can be done anywhere, at any time, and can be tailored for whatever you want the highlight of the charter to be.

"We have anniversary parties," Elario says of some of his clients. "One charter on [the 280-foot megayacht] *Alysia* next year, I'm doing a big family get-together, a reunion. These are events, and people do that. Most people tend to want to just have a vacation. They don't want to be dealing with crowds."

Set Your Course

So you see, while you won't be able to mimic a cruise ship's path and visit seven countries in seven days aboard a private yacht, you will get to charter in whatever part of the waterfront world that is most exciting to you—and you'll get to know that place far better than you ever could during an eight-hour stopover with one onshore excursion.

Just as with the yachts themselves and the different experiences you can find onboard each of them, various cruising destinations hold countless opportunities for you to discover new experiences time and time again. You simply have to articulate the kind of vacation you're after, in what part of the world, and your bareboat fleet operator or professional charter broker will be able to pinpoint an itinerary that will work for you.

In many cases, you'll be able to follow a route that private yacht guests like you have enjoyed before. We'll take a look at a few of the most popular weeklong itineraries next, in Chapter Six.

6

Sample Itineraries: Classic Charter Grounds

Yacht charter itineraries may cover less geographical ground than cruise ship itineraries, but they offer far more opportunities for you to really get to know any given destination. Cruise ship passengers are fond of saying, "We *did* Mexico, we *did* Europe, we *did* the Caribbean," but usually, all they can tell you about is a fast-paced tour they took of a monument or landmark. The truth is, most cruise ship passengers are *introduced* to a destination. They rarely get an opportunity to spend quality time outside of touristy shopping areas, restaurants, and bars.

A yacht charter guest, on the other hand, is more apt to say something like this: "We spent a few days in this great little corner of an island, got to know the locals and the culture, wandered around on shore at our leisure, and snorkeled without another person in sight. I feel like I really got to know the place without having to rush around with lots of crowds."

The reason is the more compact itinerary onboard charter yachts. Covering less geographical ground in the same week's worth of time means a more in-depth experience. In fact, even when a yacht charter is for a fewer number of days than a cruise-ship journey to the same destination, you are likely to see as much if not more of the place during the yacht charter.

This chapter and the next one will introduce you to itineraries from charter vacations that I have experienced myself, or that are typically suggested by charter brokers and yacht captains alike. In this chapter, the focus will be on classic charter grounds—the regions of the world where there are lots of marinas, plenty of infrastructure to support charter, and, usually, the widest selection of charter yachts. In Chapter Seven, you'll learn about emerging charter grounds—places where some charter yachts are available, but where, for a variety of reasons, there typically are fewer boats available when compared with the classic charter grounds.

Bear in mind that you can work out any itinerary you'd like when you book your own charter yacht—and that you can change it along the way, whether you're onboard a bareboat or a fully crewed yacht. The examples in the rest of this chapter are simply intended to give you an idea of how much ground you can expect to cover during a week onboard a yacht in the world's most popular charter destinations.

Where noted in this chapter and the next, some itineraries are recommended by yacht management companies. If you'd like to get copies of the "charter annuals" or any other additional information these high-end, crewed charter companies offer, you can contact them directly: Camper & Nicholsons International *(www.cnconnect.com)*; CEO Expeditions *(www.CeoExpeditions.com)*; Fraser Yachts Worldwide *(www.FraserYachts.com)*; International Yacht Collection *(www.Yacht Collection.com)*; Merrill-Stevens Yachts *(www.MerrillStevens.com)*; Nigel Burgess *(www.nigelburgess.com)*; and Yachting Partners International *(www.ypi.co.uk)*.

Virgin Islands

The U.S. and British Virgin Islands are great places to begin discussing yacht charter itineraries because they are terrific places for first-time charterers—bareboat and crewed alike.

Bareboats probably outnumber fully crewed yachts in the Virgin Islands most days of the year, although some of the most luxurious megayachts in the world do visit the area annually. You can find virtually every kind of charter yacht in the Virgins, power or sail, monohull or catamaran, at pretty much every price point. The islands are close together, which means easy sailing, and the tropical environment is delightful for beachcombers, swimmers, and scuba divers alike.

"It's a short flight from the States, and it's also easy from Europe," says Alex Braden, managing director of Yachting Partners International in Monaco, where he specializes in crewed yachts. "The British Virgins are a beautiful circle of islands which, together with the reefs, provide protected water even when there's good wind. If you're in a sailing boat, you can sail quite fast without rough sea conditions. In a motoryacht, too, it's very easy water cruising. There are lots of anchorages, many of them very picturesque.

"The downside is that it can be a little bit busy because there are quite a lot of charter boats there," Braden continues. "In the high season, if you're on a big yacht, you don't have a lot of space [to anchor]. But that's a small disadvantage, especially if you're a first-time charterer. An hour or probably three is the maximum cruising between islands, which is very nice as a first-time charterer. There are lots of people around, you're not out in the far beyond somewhere. There are nice hotels there as well, where you can go ashore to restaurants and bars. You can't use Jet Skis—they're banned—so you're not being bothered by their buzzing all the time, and you're not in danger from them when you're swimming. The water is very clean; it's coming straight from the Atlantic, and it isn't polluted at all. The government is quite careful about the area, too. There's no vast development going on, in contrast to the U.S. Virgin Islands."

Braden also points out that he feels the British Virgins are more secure for cruising than the U.S. Virgins, with St. Thomas in particular being a questionable island in terms of yachting safety. "The BVIs, they are secure," he says. "If you take normal care, without your jewelry hanging out all over the place, you'll be fine. The people live off yachting. They value that kind of tourism."

My most recent trip to the Virgins was in early 2005, organized by The Sacks Group onboard the 156-foot motoryacht *D'Natalin II*. It was an abbreviated charter—four days instead of seven—that started and ended at a St. Thomas marina within sight, but not walking distance, of the massive cruise ship terminals and crowds. Without rushing from island to island during our four-day itinerary, we visited the duty-free shops on St. John, the Baths on Virgin Gorda, and the favorite local bar Pusser's. We even made time to visit the duty-free shops on St. Thomas, waiting to make our way downtown until *after* the cruise ship crowds had left for the night. I felt safe the entire time ashore, though never walked alone after dark.

The thing that stands out in my mind about the Virgins harks back to what Braden explained about activities in the area: It's a tropical place where you can always find something to do, be it lounging in the sunshine or spending your money. The shopping, especially for jewelry, really is quite good (I bought my white gold wedding band tax-free on St. John), and there are plenty of handmade, non-mass-produced crafts to be found if you wait to look for them on the less-visited islands like Virgin Gorda and Jost Van Dyke.

Snorkeling and swimming all around the Virgins is dynamite, with clear waters and lots of marine life. One caution: I think The Baths on Virgin Gorda are beginning to suffer from their world-famous reputation as a swimming and snorkeling paradise. I felt quite crowded on the day that we visited, and the local woman selling T-shirts from a clothesline foretold, no doubt, of an actual gift shop going up sometime in the future. *D'Natalin II*'s captain told me that he, too, thought the site was becoming too touristy, and that he brings guests there not because he recommends it, but because a lot of guests want to say they've "done" The Baths.

Outside of Anegada and the loblolly trees—none of which I got to visit during this most recent charter in the Virgins, because larger motoryachts can't get across Anegada's rings of coral reef—my favorite charter-friendly destination is the area is known as Soper's Hole. A handful of colorful shops sit right next to a well-kept dinghy dock, and the rum-infused Painkillers served at Pusser's are exactly what the body craves after a day of sunshine and water sports. Just across North Sound from Pusser's on the island Virgin Gorda is The Bitter End Yacht Club, which takes its name from the "bitter end" of a line, that last inch of rope a sailor can hold onto before losing his grip altogether. The notion is that the high-end (by tropical standards) yacht club is that last connection to civilization in paradise, with its private villas, restaurants, bars, and extensive watersports equipment rentals. It's a great place to get a good meal and a brand-name bottle of wine if you're bareboating without a chef, or simply to spend a few nights before or after a charter of any style if you want to combine your time at sea with some time on land.

Following is a weeklong charter itinerary that Camper & Nicholsons International recommends—one of several it lists as captains' favorites in the Virgins. You'll notice a few islands that, like my favorite Anegada, are probably new to you. That's because they are small, far too small for cruise ships to visit.

Day One: Charlotte Amalie, St. Thomas, and Hurricane Hole, St. John. The shopping in Charlotte Amalie is busy, but good. Hurricane Hole is surrounded by a national park.

Day Two: Trunk Bay, St. John, and Cane Garden Bay, Tortola. Trunk Bay features a snorkeling trail. Cane Garden Bay offers access to panoramic views from Mount Sage as well as to lively bars on shore.

Day Three: Soper's Hole, Tortola, and Norman Island. Soper's Hole is the place I described from my most recent Virgins charter, where Pusser's bar will serve you a Painkiller. Norman Island boasts caves that you can explore in your snorkeling fins.

Day Four: Peter Island. This is the place for lovers of water sports, with wide-open bays that are great for water skiing, wakeboarding, and all the swimming your body can handle.

Day Five: The Baths, Virgin Gorda. Like I said, I found far more crowds at The Baths than I care to see during a yacht charter, but the rock formations are pretty cool to look at and walk through. The snorkeling sites are just offshore and easily accessible, but again, I found them filled with lots of people.

Day Six: North Sound, Virgin Gorda. This is the home of many a yachtie's favorite destination, The Bitter End Yacht Club. It's a great opportunity to enjoy a delicious dinner on shore, followed by drinks overlooking the sunset.

The Virgin Islands

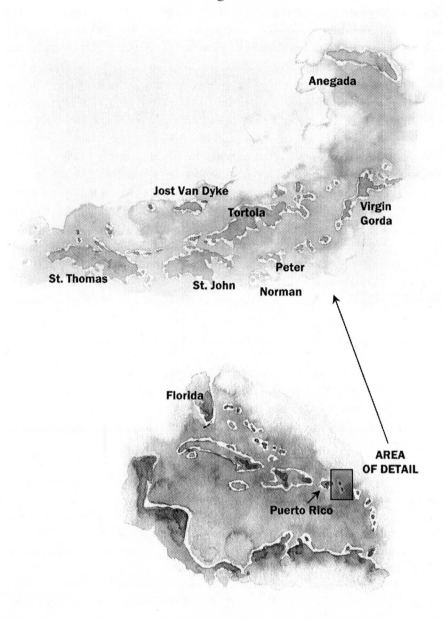

Day Seven: Jost Van Dyke. This is another of those islands that cruise ships haven't yet infiltrated. It has lots of terrific snorkeling reefs and white-sand beaches, and it is the home of Foxy's, a beach bar that's pretty much just for boaters. If you happen to be chartering near here during the winter holidays, plan to spend New Year's Eve at Foxy's. It's a heck of a party.

Day Eight: Back to St. Thomas for your flight home.

Northern Caribbean

In the language of yachting, the northern Caribbean is described as the Leeward Islands—comprising about 120 miles' worth of individual islands from Anguilla in the north to Dominica in the South. The Leewards are not as big a bareboating destination as the Virgins, but they are the home of St. Maarten, a hub for power-driven megayachts, and of Antigua, a home base for many fully crewed sailing yachts. If you want to charter a fully or partially crewed yacht during the winter months, the Leewards usually offer you the most choices.

In fact, each December there are industry-only charter yacht shows held on St. Maarten and Antigua. Charter brokers tour dozens upon dozens of yachts to see what kind of shape they're in, which crew have come and gone, and other details that they can later use to help you book the right boat for your needs. Because many yachts attend these boat shows and then stay in their slips at the marinas after the shows end, St. Maarten and Antigua are often recommended as beginning and/or ending points for charter vacations. The yachts are already there, and the supply infrastructure for food and fuel is well in place.

I've cruised around and near both islands, and my two most memorable experiences were in two opposite environments.

While onboard the 122-foot motoryacht *Bon Bon* as a guest of International Yacht Collection, I visited the island of Saba—a towering volcanic creation that has just one road (no joke, it's called The Road) and seven eco-zones, making it desert-like at the bottom and true tropical rainforest all the way at the top. I did a lot of terrific hiking on Saba and snacked on fruit that our guide helped us to pick fresh from the trees, though I didn't do the trail that runs straight up the island to the top of Mount Scenery. The 1,064 rock and concrete steps just didn't look like a good match for my flabby thighs. If you're more athletic than I am, you might give it a try. I hear it's a spectacular hike.

My other favorite memory of this region came during a different charter in the Leewards, organized by The Sacks Group aboard the 111-foot motoryacht *Strait Jacket*. I visited the island of Anguilla, home of The Dune. It's a bar unlike any other I've seen, with an upside-down boat hull for a ceiling and rum concoctions served out of a questionable-looking jug. I felt almost as if I were in a treehouse when the owner, Bankie Banx, took to the stage to perform his Bob Marley- and Bob Dylan-infused music. I was entranced, by both the drinks and his powerful voice, and I ended up buying a $20 CD that I still listen to today, more than three years later. My favorite song is Bankie's autobiographical *Busted in Barbados*. You get the picture, mon.

Following is an eight-day itinerary in the Leewards recommended by Nigel Burgess. As with the other sample itineraries in this chapter, it's one of many regional possibilities to keep in mind.

Day One: Antigua and Barbuda. Meet your charter yacht on Antigua, where you can explore Nelson's Dockyard, home of restored brick buildings that have welcomed sailors since the days of Admiral Lord Nelson himself. From there, it's a few hours' cruise to Barbuda, where you can explore pink-sand beaches and snorkel along reefs that most regular tourists will never find.

Day Two: Barbuda to Nevis. Again, you can explore beaches and do some snorkeling, or you can head up toward the top of the 3,232-foot Nevis Peak, surrounded by hills filled with monkeys.

Day Three: Nevis to St. Kitts. Scuba is a favorite activity here, if you're a certified diver. Or you can walk through lava formations that are both stunning in beauty and spectacular in revealing nature's raw power.

Day Four: St. Kitts to St. Barts. Properly called St. Barthelemy but known the world over as St. Barts, this is the place full of tony shops and restaurants made for seeing and being seen among the rich and famous. The beaches are great, too.

Day Five: St. Barts to Ile Fourche. This is another one of those places the cruise ships pass by, a completely uninhabited island where your yacht can anchor in a pristine cove. You won't believe how bright the stars look at night, without the glare of a single light coming from onshore.

Day Six: Ile Fourche to Tintamarre. The locals call this little gem Flat Island. It's a natural reserve where the reefs and marine life have been wonderfully protected—making for terrific snorkeling.

Day Seven: Tintamarre to Anguilla. You'll have lots to reminisce about by the time you get to Anguilla and grab a table at Bankie Banx's place, The Dune. There's also plenty of snorkeling and beautiful beaches to enjoy.

Day Eight: Anguilla to St. Maarten. Your cruise ends on the Dutch side of this half-French, half-Dutch island. Since your flight may not be until early afternoon, there may be time for a round of golf or some boutique shopping in Marigot.

Northern Caribbean

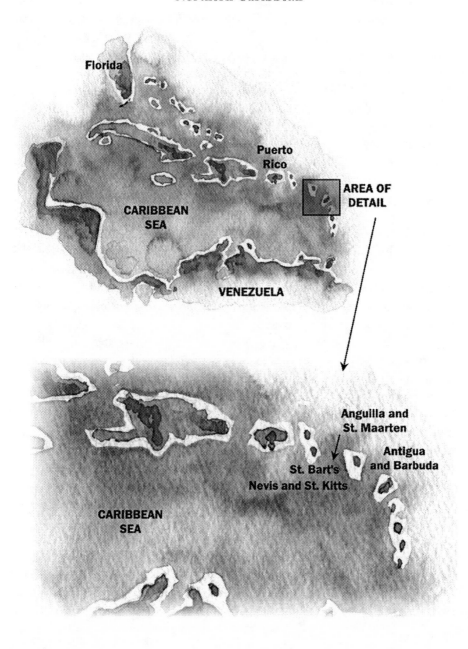

Southern Caribbean

To yachties, the southern Caribbean is known as the Windward Islands. The range is about 300 miles long, stretching from Dominica in the north all the way to Trinidad in the south, close to the northern coastline of Venezuela.

Because the Windwards are so far from the northern yachting hubs of St. Maarten and Antigua, fewer power-driven megayachts cruise in this area. Plenty of sailing yachts head down, though, and many captains aboard the partially and fully crewed sailboats consider the Grenadines section of the Windwards to be "the next Virgin Islands." The landmasses are relatively close together, the waters are sparkling, and the yachting infrastructure is improving every season. Bareboating options, too, are sure to increase in the Grenadines for all of these reasons.

However, while some of the Windward Island peoples have built nicely manicured facilities and are fairly well-off in their personal lives, the poverty ashore some of these farther-flung southern Caribbean islands—especially in the wake of devastating hurricanes—can make it emotionally challenging to visit onboard a sparkling, top-dollar, private yacht. My personal experience in the Windwards is limited to a charter I did nearly a half-dozen years ago as a guest of Fraser Yachts Worldwide onboard the 137-foot motoryacht *Lady Jenn,* but even during that one trip, I experienced this disconnect.

My schedule allowed only three days during an itinerary that other charter brokers were enjoying for an entire week onboard *Lady Jenn,* so my impressions are admittedly limited. I got to see just St. Vincent and St. Lucia, and my most lasting memory outside of St. Lucia's awe-inspiring Pitons (twin peaks more than 2,000 feet high) was of young, shoddily clad boys waiting at the dock to beg for money the minute I stepped off the yacht's dinghy. Having said that, the charter brokers who stayed onboard *Lady Jenn* after I flew home visited Bequia, Mustique, and the northern part of the Grenadines, and each broker reported stepping onshore to find far more tourism-friendly people with higher standards of personal living, not to mention sweeping sandy beaches and glimmering turquoise waters.

The upshot is this: Work with a charter broker who knows the area and the boats there if you want to charter in the Southern Caribbean. Things change from season to season, and some charters will be more successful than others depending on hurricane destruction, local conditions, and the kind of boat you cruise onboard.

The Windward Islands

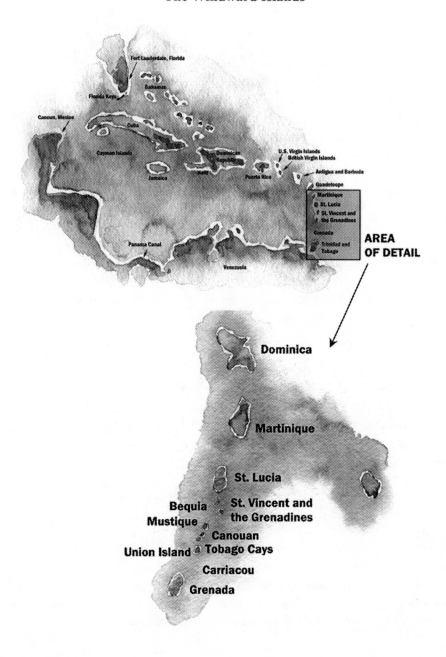

Because getting to the Windward Islands requires longer airline flights and in some cases greater travel expenses, many people opt to do two back-to-back weeks aboard a private yacht there. The thinking is that if you're going all the way down, you might as well make the most of the trip and see a good deal of the region.

With that in mind, the following itinerary for a two-week Windward Islands charter is recommended by Yachting Partners International.

Day One: Martinique. Board your yacht at Fort de France, where restaurants and shops are aplenty.

Day Two: Martinique to St. Lucia. Anchor in Rodney Bay, where you can play in the water all day and enjoy drinks ashore come nightfall.

Day Three: The Pitons. These are the majestic mountains on St. Lucia that I mentioned earlier in this section. Just a fabulous sight. They'll blow your mind.

Day Four: St. Lucia to St. Vincent. This is the longest leg of your charter, at 40 nautical miles (a half day or more spent cruising, depending on the yacht). You can arrive at Cumberland Bay, where nature still rules the scenery.

Day Five: St. Vincent to Bequia. Explore centuries of maritime history after arriving in Admiralty Bay. You'll also find shops and restaurants in Port Elizabeth.

Day Six: Bequia to Mustique. This island is mostly private, with nature trails that wind to and from the unspoiled beaches.

Day Seven: Mustique to Canouan. Little-known to most cruise ship passengers, Canouan is a quiet, secluded spot that's perfect for walking onshore or swimming in private coves.

Day Eight: Canouan to Tobago Cays. The coral reefs and vodka-clear waters are spectacular for water sports in and around these small, deserted islands.

Day Nine: Tobago Cays to Union Island. Clifton is the harbor you'll likely make way for on Union Island, with bustling shops and cosmopolitan restaurants galore.

Day Ten: Union Island to Petit St. Vincent. Lots of charter guests enjoy snorkeling and swimming here, as the island is small and does not cater to large groups of tourists.

Day Eleven: Petit St. Vincent to Carriacou. Fresh-water oysters are the real find on Carriacou, which also offers terrific snorkeling and scuba diving, if you're certified.

Day Twelve: Carriacou to Grenada. Known as Spice Island, Grenada offers open-air bus tours that will not only show you the sights, but also introduce you to the smells of nutmeg and cinnamon growing in the wild.

Day Thirteen: Grenada. You can explore some more on shore or simply retire to your private yacht for a final day of relaxation on the water.

Day Fourteen: Grenada. It's off to the airport for your flight back home.

The Bahamas

As I've mentioned several times now, I love the Bahamas. If I were a fisherman, the Abacos part of the region would probably be my favorite, but I much prefer swimming with the fishes to catching them, and that's what the Exumas are about. The water is remarkably clear, the marine life is terrifically abundant, and the reefs are in very good condition because no commercial vessels or cruise ships ever go near them.

Both the Abacos and Exumas regions are great for first-time charterers. Marsh Harbour in the Abacos is a major hub for Bahamas bareboat operations, including the one run by The Moorings, while Paradise Island just north of the Exumas is a favorite hub for many fully crewed yachts—including many of the world's largest, most luxurious power-driven megayachts.

One of the best memories I have from charters in the Bahamas is being caught on Harbour Island, just east of the Exumas in the shadow of Eleuthera, during a windstorm right before Christmas 2004. I was a guest of Koch, Newton & Partners (a company that is now part of Merrill-Stevens Yachts) onboard the 85-foot motoryacht *Princess Marcie.* Capt. Dave Laird and I had to make our own fun ashore after Mother Nature canceled our plans to go cruising.

I found myself sitting beneath a white canvas umbrella atop the pink porch of The Harbour House restaurant, watching golf carts whir down the main street and listening to locals greet one another with a friendly "Hey, mon." The azure bay was just a few steps away, but I was mesmerized by the scene: slow-going, sun-drenched, and downright nap-inducing. I enjoyed a cool drink on that restaurant's porch for well longer than it should've taken me to sip it, completely content in knowing Harbour Island simply doesn't know how to rush. Later that night, Laird and I sampled the dinner specials at The Rock House, where rooms run from $275 to $655 a night (talk about civilization). It was the classic yin to the rest of the day's yang, and I recommend either the grilled yellowfin tuna with sesame cucumber salad *or* the cider pork tenderloin with goat cheese mashed potatoes.

If you're more of a culture vulture, you might enjoy an experience I had in the Exumas aboard the 120-foot motoryacht *Joanne.* Capt. Dan Webster introduced me to Thunderball Cave—yep, the same one from which Sean Connery escapes in the eponymous movie. We swam and snorkeled in the cave, and even though no helicopters full of Bond girls in skimpy thongs came to our rescue, we did enjoy a late-afternoon rum punch at nearby Thunderball Bar onshore. Then, we cruised back to the marina and docked next to private motoryachts named *Octopussy* and *Moonraker*. Perfection!

One week makes for a terrific Bahamian charter starting and ending at the Atlantis Resort and Casino marina on Paradise Island or at the Marsh Harbour hub. However, if you have two weeks to spare, you might consider a one-way charter that starts at the top of the Bahamas, on Grand Bahama Island, and ends at the last archipelago in the region, the Turks and Caicos Islands. There are international airports on both Grand Bahama and Providenciales, in the Turks and Caicos chain, and the trips I've made to Provo, as it's locally known, were filled with some of the most spectacular scuba diving I've ever done.

Following is a weeklong itinerary, round-trip to Nassau, suggested by Camper & Nicholsons International.

Day One: Paradise Island. After flying into Nassau, it's a quick ride to the Atlantis Resort and Casino to meet your yacht. You can try the steep, intimidating water slide, which includes a see-through tube running through a shark aquarium, or you can try to win a few bucks at the blackjack tables.

Day Two: Paradise Island to Warderick Wells Cay. This 176-square-mile natural marine preserve boasts fabulous coral reefs and great snorkeling, along with plenty of hiking trails for exploring on land.

Day Three: Warderick Wells Cay to Staniel Cay. This is where you'll find the aforementioned Thunderball Cave, which is a short dinghy ride from Big Major's Beach. Its best-known resident is Emily, a wild pig that will swim out to your dinghy to look for snacks.

Day Four: Staniel Cay to Compass Cay. There's a huge, nature-made hot tub on Compass Cay known as Rachel's Bubblebath. What better way to relax after a day of pretending to be James Bond?

Day Five: Compass Cay to Shroud Cay. This island is pretty much made of mangroves and makes for spectacular snorkeling adventures.

Day Six: Shroud Cay to Allan's Cay and Highbourne Cay. Allan's Cay is infested with iguanas, all of which you can feed in the wild. (I've done it, and it's not as creepy-crawly as it sounds.) From there, it's a quick hop to Highbourne Cay, where spotted rays are among the marine life you may encounter with your snorkel.

Day Seven: Highbourne Cay to Harbour Island and Eleuthera. You can have dinner in my favorite top-dollar restaurant, The Rock House, or simply watch the excitement at your yacht's helm as your captain or a local pilot take your boat through the treacherous maze known as Devil's Backbone Reef.

The Bahamas

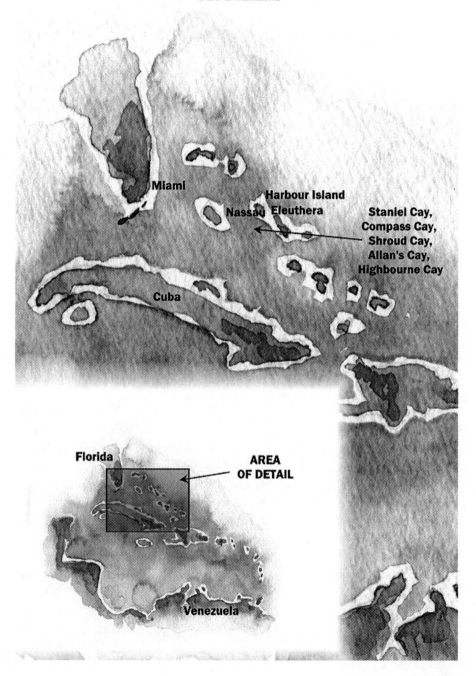

Day Eight: Eleuthera to Nassau. You'll usually have time for one last swim in the warm, blue waters before it's time to fly back home.

Western Mediterranean

Bareboating is more mom-and-pop-shop in the Mediterranean than it is in the Caribbean, but there are plenty of boats to be found. If you want to enjoy a fully crewed yacht charter, there is no more sought-after destination. Yachts that cruise the Caribbean during the winter and the Mediterranean during the summer usually raise their base rates by 20 percent in the Med. The demand for bookings on Europe's southern shore is simply that high.

For the purposes of yacht charter, the Western Mediterranean is broken down into several major regions. I've visited most of them on separate charter trips, and I believe I could return to each a dozen more times before I'll have truly experienced everything that each destination has to offer.

To the west is Spain's Balearic Islands, due south of Barcelona. Its main island is Mallorca, with Menorca and Ibiza to the east and west, respectively. My most recent trip to the Balearics was as a guest of Camper & Nicholsons International aboard the 141-foot motoryacht *CD Two.* Because of high winds, we could not cruise to the world-renowned discotheques on Ibiza, but I thoroughly enjoyed discovering the village of Valdemossa on Mallorca. It looks like a postcard, with old stone streets lined with boutique shops and outdoor cafes. Palma de Mallorca, where we—and most yachts—were based, is a fully modern city functioning within centuries-old architecture. Simply fabulous.

Northeast of the Balearics is the Côte d'Azur, or French Riviera. It's known for its world-class restaurants and resorts, and it includes both Antibes and St. Tropez—two of the most fashionable, big-money charter destinations in the world. I cruised here aboard the 171-foot motoryacht *Solemates*, and the region did not disappoint. The place is a perfect backdrop for Hollywood stars and billionaire moguls alike.

If you continue east along the Mediterranean coast from France, you'll cross the border into Italy and the marinas of San Remo and Genoa. These are favorite pickup and drop-off points for fully crewed yacht charters, which can include itineraries that either head due south to the islands of Corsica and Sardinia or stay along the Italian Riviera and head south along the Cinque Terre coastline. I found the Cinque Terre stunning during a cruise I did there aboard the 136-foot sailing yacht *Infatuation*—row after row of buildings painted in almost iridescent reds, oranges and yellows. Our route also took us to a small island called Elba, an old hideout of Napoleon Bonaparte's.

You can also find charter yachts in southern Italy, between Naples on the mainland and the island of Sicily to the south. The area nearest Naples is known as the Amalfi Coast, and it includes Mount Vesuvius as well as the ruins of Pompeii. I have yet to visit there myself, but I hear nothing but great reviews from the charter brokers who have made the journey.

Following is just one of many possible itineraries recommended by Nigel Burgess in the Western Mediterranean. As with the Southern Caribbean, many vacationers like to charter one way and stay longer than a week, to make the most of the long trip overseas.

Day One: Antibes to St. Tropez. Don't forget your most fashionable outfits when you visit the restaurants and clubs of St. Tropez. You'll be in the French Riviera's most scorching hot spot, and you'll want to look the part.

Day Two: St. Tropez to Isles de Lerins. After enjoying the fabulous nightlife on shore in St. Tropez, you can cruise to an anchorage between the two Isles de Lerins—where chirping cicadas will lull you to sleep.

Day Three: Isles de Lerins to Calvi, Corsica. The French refer to Corsica as "The Beautiful Island," for good reason. Its mountains tower high above the bays where your yacht will dock, sometimes more than 6,000 feet overhead. Calvi itself is a charming little town with adorable shops and restaurants.

Day Four: Calvi to La Girolata. The bay known as La Girolata is in the middle of a Corsican national park. You can get there only by donkey or by boat—and the donkeys are certainly less comfortable than even the smallest, oldest of yachts.

Day Five: La Girolata to Campomoro. Water skiing and swimming are musts in this delightful Corsican spot, and the small town of Propriano is nearby if you want to spend a little cash in the local boutiques.

Day Six: Campomoro to Bonifacio. At the southern tip of Corsica, Bonifacio is a natural fjord that delves into sandstone cliffs. Your yacht will enter through a narrow cut, after which the waters open up to a wide, secluded harbor. The view is unparalleled.

Day Seven: Bonifacio to Cavallo/Lavezzi. The Lavezzi islands are rocky, but the town of Cavallo is smooth. That is to say it's highly fashionable, with expensive villas and a private airstrip.

Day Eight: Lavezzi to the Budelli Islands. The Budellis are across the French-Italian border, your gateway to the Italian island of Sardinia. Swimming and snorkeling are musts in the warm, clear waters.

Western Mediterranean

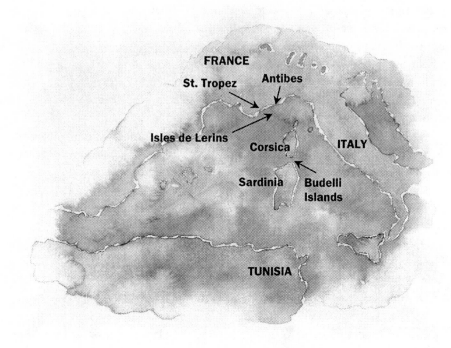

Day Nine: Budelli to Porto Cervo, Sardinia. The seas along this route are almost always flat calm, so much so that you sometimes feel you are cruising on a lake instead of the Mediterranean Sea. Porto Cervo itself boasts world-class shopping.

Day Ten: Porto Cervo to Cala di Volpe. This large bay is popular for charters, so you can spend a good deal of time "yacht spotting" and trying to guess who's onboard which boat. Sandy beaches ring the bay, and golfers can enjoy a round onshore.

Day Eleven: Cala di Volpe to Porto Rotondo. This port is smaller than Porto Cervo but is fashionable nonetheless. Top-notch restaurants are tucked in between virtually every kind of shop and boutique you can imagine.

Day Twelve: Porto Rotondo to Olbia. There is an international airport in Olbia, a town on Sardinia. You can pick up last-minute trinkets here before heading back home.

Eastern Mediterranean

The Eastern Mediterranean, as I briefly mentioned in Chapter Five, is sort of a land of its own when it comes to private yacht charter. There are lots of mom-and-pop bareboats in this cruising ground, and the powerboat division of The Moorings, called NauticBlue, opened a base a few years ago off the coast of Athens. There are also fully crewed yachts available in Greece, Turkey, and, more and more often, Croatia.

This is a classic cruising ground in the sense that people have been visiting here during boating vacations for generations, but in some cases, the destination may feel more like an emerging cruising ground because its infrastructure is not on par with that of other places, like the Western Med. You can enjoy a terrific charter here, but the standards of luxury and service can be lower than onboard top-dollar yachts that cruise back and forth from the Western Mediterranean to the Caribbean, competing for charters as part of the worldwide marketplace. And even on a top-notch, top-dollar charter yacht here, your cruising itinerary may have to be organized not entirely around your easiest starting and stopping points, but around conflicting national regulations among the countries.

It bears repeating that working with a knowledgeable broker or trusted bareboat company in the Eastern Mediterranean is a must.

The charter I did onboard the 85-foot motoryacht *Oh Que Luna* centered on Greece's Aegean Islands, a classic Eastern Mediterranean itinerary. On the advice of two knowledgeable brokers, independent American Ann-Wallis White and

British ex-pat Rosemary Pavlatou of A1 Yacht Trade Consortium in Greece, I started and ended the charter in Athens and along the way visited the islands Aegina, Poros, and Hydra. To be honest, I found the city of Athens itself somewhat dirty, crowded, and uncomfortable to walk around as a woman traveling alone, but in the nearby islands I felt completely entranced.

On Aegina, there is an acropolis that is smaller than the world-famous one in Athens, but that you can get so close to without any crowds, you can see every crack in the ancient stone. Poros has a bustling promenade of shops and outdoor cafes that I loved meandering in and out of, while Hydra—my favorite—has a single, spectacular harbor where getting one of the few slips large enough to hold our yacht made me feel almost like royalty. The island has no cars, nor any roads; only mules carrying people and goods up and down the steep, stone, mountainside steps. I explored dozens of narrow stone alleyways, getting more than a light workout for my legs and finding everything from tucked-away craftsmen's shops to spectacular sunset views.

Following is an 11-day, one-way charter itinerary in Turkey suggested by Yachting Partners International.

Day One: Bodrum to Kargicik Limani. Fly into the international airport at Bodrum and head off to the coastal city of Kargicik, where swimming awaits.

Day Two: Kargicik Limani to Dirsek. Scenery is the order of this day's cruise, with your yacht cruising down a narrow inlet surrounded by high hills.

Day Three: Dirsek to Orhaniye. At Orhaniye, you'll find a water sport unlike those virtually anywhere else: walking. A more than 900-foot-long sandbar is submerged in water that's about knee-deep. You can keep your feet cool while working on your tan.

Day Four: Orhaniye to Bozburun. The small village of Yesilova is here, along with protected waters that are crystal clear and inviting for swimmers.

Day Five: Bozburun to Ekincik. You can leave your yacht for a day trip up a river at Ekincik, which is close to the ruined city of Caunos.

Day Six: Ekincik to Gocek Sound. Pine forests surround the bays in Gocek Sound, with lots of trails to explore onshore.

Day Seven: Gocek. With a guide, you can walk through gorges and forest trails to an abandoned monastery and village that are far from any remaining civilization.

Day Eight: Gocek to Kekova Roads. There's a castle at Kekova Roads that you can climb up to from the old village, which is near a quaint anchorage for your yacht.

Turkey

Day Nine: Kekova Roads to Gemiler Sound. Ruins and artifacts line the ocean floor, and you can see them during a glass-bottom boat tour. The nearby sea caves are also worth exploring.

Day Ten: Gemiler Sound. Hiking and dinghy rides will keep you more than busy in this spot, where the scenery is as inviting as the water.

Day Eleven: Gemiler Sound to Gocek. Depart your yacht near a different airport and prepare to head home.

New England

Every time I step onboard a charter yacht in New England, I find myself in the midst of a unique experience. That's saying a lot, because I've lived in New York, New Jersey, and Connecticut nearly my entire life, with plenty of opportunities to explore by car as far north as Maine.

A charter that starts in New York City—while not technically part of New England—is many people's summertime favorite, especially during the Fourth of July, when you can watch the Big Apple's fireworks display from your private yacht's deck. Cruising along New York's Long Island to the tony Hamptons and the fishing mecca of Montauk are also good charter choices, as well as easternmost launching-off points for entering the waters of New England proper. Nantucket, Martha's Vineyard, and even Boston are well within cruising distance, on your way to the massive coastline in Maine, which has hundreds of islands and rocky spits to explore just offshore.

Yet, as with other charter destinations, you wouldn't want to try to see all of New England in one cruise. In fact, my favorite New England charter never left the waters around Boston, Massachusetts. I was aboard the 120-foot motoryacht *Sovereign*, invited by longtime charter broker Missy Johnston of Northrop & Johnson in Newport.

The United States was still reeling at the time, fresh from the terrorist attacks of September 11, 2001. *Sovereign's* captain, a local expert named Tom Hartman, worked with Johnston to create a memorable itinerary that celebrated American history. We started by cruising into Plymouth and docking just across the harbor from the re-created *Mayflower*. We visited nearby Plimoth Plantation, a living history museum where we walked among costumed Pilgrims and Native Americans in extraordinarily lifelike villages. Our charter later took us to Salem, notorious for the witch trials so aptly described in Arthur Miller's *The Crucible*. The themes in all of these places—of hope, of freedom, of terror, of justice—were a startling reminder that all of us living in the shadow of Al Qaeda had others who came before us, with their own burdens to bear.

If you are interested in American history, I highly recommend a New England charter like the one I enjoyed aboard *Sovereign*. Yet if simply relaxing and exploring are more in your nature, you'll have plenty of options as well. A charter I did one fall onboard the 118-foot motoryacht *Time for Us* didn't involve much sightseeing at all beyond watching the bright orange, yellow, and red leaves wave from the treetops along the shore in Maine. It was a pure and gorgeous experience.

Following is a weeklong itinerary from Boston, Massachusetts, to Newport, Rhode Island, as recommended by Camper & Nicholsons International.

Day One: Boston. You can't possibly just fly into Boston and then head straight to your yacht. The city is rich with history—and is immensely walkable for tourists. Simply watching the activity in Boston Harbor, site of all that famously dumped tea, is thrilling in and of itself.

Day Two: Boston to Plymouth. You can climb aboard the *Mayflower II*, a re-created version of the famous sailing ship that is afloat in the harbor just off Plymouth Rock. Actors in period dress will talk to you and explain their "journey" aboard the ship, which feels startlingly dark and small compared with the one you arrived onboard.

Day Three: Plymouth to Provincetown. This town is at the tip of Cape Cod, across the bay from Plymouth. You can go exploring on land or collect shells along the beaches. The sunset over the open bay is spectacular.

Day Four: Provincetown to Nantucket Island. Fishing is still a big deal on Nantucket Island, and you can cast a few lines with novices and professionals alike. Or you can swim in the harbor while working up an appetite for dinner at one of the fresh seafood restaurants onshore.

Day Five: Nantucket Island to Martha's Vineyard. Charming villages full of quintessential New England shops and restaurants continue to make Martha's Vineyard a favorite destination for locals and tourists alike. Gingerbread cottages line the streets along with the mansions that ship captains called home during the 1800s.

Day Six: Martha's Vineyard to Hyannis and Falmouth. If you've heard of the Kennedys, you've heard of Hyannis. The seaside town is home to the John F. Kennedy Memorial Museum, along with terrific waterfront seafood restaurants. It's just down the coast from Falmouth Harbor, where your yacht can anchor at night.

Day Seven: Falmouth to Newport, Rhode Island. Your charter will end in Newport, the premier yachting hub in all of New England. Classic sailing yachts race in the harbors while boats of every other shape and size pack the waterways. It's a memorable charter ending point, one filled with nautical history.

New England

7

Sample Itineraries: Emerging Charter Grounds

I know that the word "emerging" is used often in politics to describe third- and second-world countries. Rest assured, that's not the meaning it has in the context of private yacht charter vacations. On the contrary, emerging charter markets are stunning destinations—many of them inside the borders of the United States—that simply have yet to build up the marina infrastructure and worldwide reputation of classic charter regions.

In emerging charter markets, you should expect to find the same level of onboard quality and service that you would receive in classic charter grounds, but you also must realize that your choices of yacht are likely to be far more limited than in, say, the Caribbean. Fewer bareboat and fully crewed yachts spend time in these emerging markets. Sometimes, it's because there are not enough marinas to hold more yachts. Other times, it's because a nation's laws make the legalities of charter too challenging or costly for yacht owners and bareboat companies to bear. In still other cases, it's because the emerging cruising grounds are geographically too far away from classic cruising areas, and there's just not yet a constant demand for charters.

Hawaii is a good example of these phenomena. In terms of general tourism, the Hawaiian Islands are very high on the list of places vacationers want to visit. Yet despite the place being surrounded by water, yacht charter is almost non-existent there.

There are several reasons why this is true. For starters, Hawaii is far from any major continental hub where yachts might receive repairs and take on crew. Whereas yachts cruising in the Bahamas and northern Caribbean can get back to Fort Lauderdale fairly easily for such things, a yacht in Hawaii would have to cruise farther, to the Seattle or San Diego areas, to reach a major boatbuilding or repair yard. Second, once the yacht makes it to Hawaii, it's going to have a problem finding a slip at a marina. Whereas the waterfront resorts in southeast Florida, the Bahamas, and the Caribbean are usually built with boating in mind, the waterfront resorts in Hawaii are not. Especially for the larger, fully crewed yachts, there just aren't many places to dock in the Hawaiian Islands.

Yet another reason why charter is almost impossible to find in Hawaii is that the vacation season there is during the winter months, when most fully crewed yachts are in the Caribbean. When the summertime season arrives, most of those Caribbean-based yachts move across the Atlantic Ocean to the Mediterranean. Think about how much farther, and at how much more expense, a yacht would have to cruise to go from Hawaii back to the Mediterranean in time for the summer season. It's just not worth it to most yacht owners.

That's not to say that yacht charters never happen in Hawaii. I had the pleasure of cruising there for a week onboard the 96-foot motoryacht *Kakela* in early 2002, as a guest of Bob Saxon & Associates, a charter company that now is part of Camper & Nicholsons International. *Kakela*—which means "castle" in Hawaiian—was owned by a millionaire who lived in the islands and wanted his yacht near his home all year-round. He kept her docked on the western shore of Oahu, at the only regional marina that could accommodate a yacht of her length.

Bear in mind that 96-footers are about half the size of many of today's fully crewed charter yachts, and you start to understand the industry's infrastructure problems in Hawaii. Patti Medenwald, first mate aboard *Kakela*, told me that there were more boats registered in Utah at the time than there were in the whole of the Hawaiian Islands. It's hard to believe, I know, especially because Hawaii is so lovely to explore by boat. The scuba diving, fishing, and whale watching are spectacular. Yet Hawaii's far-flung distance from the rest of civilization, along with the other problems for yacht captains who need provisions and supplies, have kept it from developing in terms of charter.

Other destinations that fit this bill include Jamaica, the Cayman Islands, the California coastline, and Bermuda. As with Hawaii, there's absolutely nothing "emerging" about their tourism infrastructure in general. You can even visit them aboard cruise ships. Yet they have not developed as steady markets for private yacht charter, which is why you will rarely find available bareboats or fully crewed yachts there.

The rest of the destinations discussed in this chapter fall somewhere on the spectrum between Hawaii and the Caribbean: There are yachts to be found, but, for whatever reason, the destinations have not yet blossomed into full-blown charter hubs.

My advice, should you want to charter in one of these destinations, is to go for it—by working with a reputable bareboat company or a charter broker. I've done just that in most of the emerging markets described in the following pages, and I have yet to be disappointed.

Alaska

When I ask industry experts why there aren't more fully crewed yachts available for summertime charters in Alaska, they almost always reply by saying the season is just too short. Unless a yacht's owner wants to visit Alaska himself, the expense and time required to move a yacht all the way up the Inside Passage to Juneau simply doesn't make it worthwhile to offer charters there.

Luckily for those of us who want to visit Alaska, there are more than a few yacht owners who want to see the place by boat, too—and who are happy to allow a few charters onboard to help offset their costs of getting there. I hardly ever hear of bareboat opportunities in Alaska, but I do hear of a decent number of partially and fully crewed yachts heading up there each summer.

One such yacht is the 120-foot motoryacht *Kayana*, which I cruised aboard from Juneau to Sitka as a guest of CEO Expeditions. I happened to board the yacht right around the same time a cruise ship was taking on passengers in Juneau, and the contrast could not have been more startling. I was one among ten guests welcomed aboard *Kayana* the way you might be welcomed into a private home, whereas the dozen or so landing craft carrying passengers out to the cruise ship held at least 20 people apiece. It looked like an invasion.

Keeping that many people on schedule requires sticking to your itinerary no matter what, and the cruise ship did just that. In fact, right about the time they blew past us in Tracy Arm, our amiable and experienced captain, Russ White, noticed something sticking up from the water in the distance. He carefully nosed *Kayana* closer, keeping a watchful eye on the underwater radar so as not to hit anything, and we soon found ourselves circling the tip of an iceberg.

Now, a cruise ship would never divert from its path to spend a few hours checking out something like this, but we could—because yacht charter guests can set their own schedules. *Kayana*'s crew unloaded a large, rubber dinghy, and the ten of us literally got close enough to the iceberg to touch it. We stayed until we'd had our fill of photographs, and then returned to the yacht, where chief stewardess Lisa Reedy was waiting on deck with a broad smile and ten large, steaming mugs full of hot chocolate.

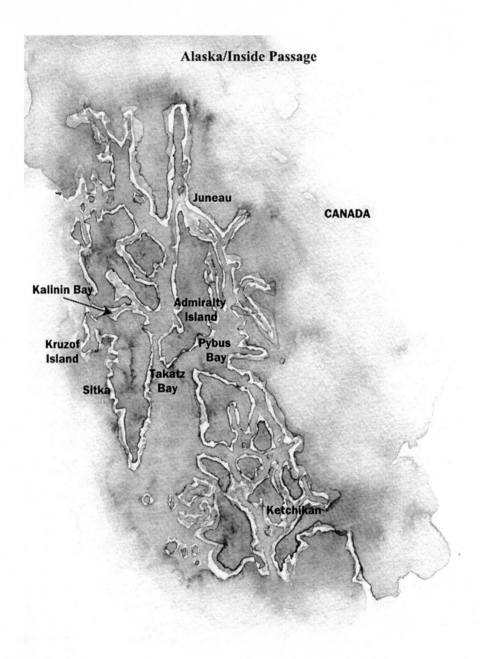

We repeated experiences like that throughout the week, including standing in a stream full of spawning salmon that writhed and wriggled right over the tops of our waterproof boots. Again, not the kind of thing you can do with hundreds of people at a time, but when there are only ten guests onboard, you can get awfully close to nature.

Following is a weeklong itinerary for cruising in Alaska, suggested by CEO Expeditions.

Day One: Juneau to Tracy Arm. This is literally the tip of the iceberg, based on my personal experience.

Day Two: Tracy Arm to Admiralty Island. The Tlingit natives of this region refer to Admiralty Island as the "Fortress of Bears." You'll see a few, to be sure, since the island has the greatest known concentration of grizzlies in the world.

Day Three: Brothers Island to Pybus Bay. Orca whales and dolphins are known to hang out around Brothers Island, so have your camera ready. Pybus Bay is on the southeast coast of Admiralty Island, and more bears may put on a show for you later that night.

Day Four: Pybus Bay to Deep Cove, Baranof Island. The walls that line Deep Cove are more than 4,000 feet high—a spectacular sight to behold. There are waterfalls, too, which make for a stunning backdrop to the day's fishing and hiking.

Day Five: Deep Cove to Takatz Bay. Kayaking is excellent in Takatz Bay, where tidal creeks will take you inland. Just remember to watch out for bear tracks!

Day Six: Takatz Bay to Kalinin Bay, Kruzof Island. Fishing, hiking, sightseeing—whatever your favorite part of the charter has been thus far, you can choose to do more of it along this passage. Your captain will adjust the yacht's direction accordingly.

Day Seven: Kruzof Island to Sitka. The town of Sitka has an interesting history, much of it based on fishing. It's worth exploring around town a bit before heading off to your hotel or back toward the airport.

Florida

Fort Lauderdale is the yachting capital of America. Most major yacht management companies have offices in this coastal city, and more charter brokers call Fort Lauderdale home than any other place in the United States. Pretty much every fully crewed yacht that heads to the Caribbean stops first in Fort Lauderdale to provision supplies, make repairs, and the like, and a host of bareboat companies do major business each October at the Fort Lauderdale International Boat Show—the biggest in the country.

Plenty of fully crewed charter yachts are based in Florida year-round, since many yacht owners have waterfront homes there with docks. There are bareboats to be had in Florida, too, some based on the Gulf Coast and others on the Atlantic side. Hopping along the Florida Keys is a terrific cruising adventure, as is heading offshore to lesser-known islands like the Dry Tortugas. You can even combine Florida and the Bahamas as a single destination during a charter, depending on how much time you have and whether you care to cruise for a day offshore.

In most cases, yachts based in southern Florida are marketed as having "Florida/Bahamas" availability, but more often than not, vacationers are more interested in the Bahamas than in Florida. It's for this reason, as opposed to a lack of infrastructure, that Florida is listed in this chapter on emerging charter grounds. It's easily well more developed for charter than any other place in this chapter, and it could arguably be featured in the chapter about classic cruising grounds instead, but it often just isn't in people's minds when choosing a locale for a charter vacation. Especially for Americans, who no doubt have made plenty of trips to Walt Disney World in Orlando, the state of Florida can seem like a "been there, done that" vacation option.

A lot of yacht owners, though, really enjoy cruising in Florida, and the boating I've done in the region has been pretty darn good. One charter in particular comes to mind: a cruise I made in 2004 aboard the 100-foot motoryacht *Melimar*, round-trip from Key West to the Dry Tortugas as a guest of International Yacht Collection.

The Duval Street bars in Key West are a lot of fun (especially after the cruise ships pull out and take their crowds with them), but what I enjoyed most about my Florida cruise was discovering the Dry Tortugas. These seven islands lying about 70 miles west of Key West have a rich history of shipwrecks and shady characters. Now a national park, the Tortugas are home to Fort Jefferson, one of the largest coastal forts ever built. I was one of a half-dozen or so boaters exploring the fort during my visit, and I stood in the battered stone cell that once held Dr. Samuel Mudd. He's the physician who set the broken left leg of gunman John Wilkes Booth following Abraham Lincoln's shooting at Ford's Theater. The good doctor earned $25 for tending to Booth before being tried and convicted as a conspirator in Lincoln's assassination. The phrase "your name is mud" is said to derive from these events, and I felt shivers as I toured the former jail cell, thinking about how guards might have spit the phrase through iron bars and into the doctor's face.

The Florida Keys

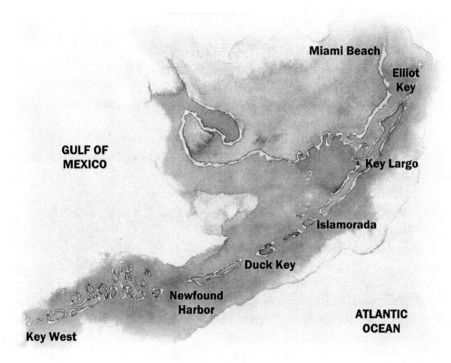

Cruising aboard *Melimar* back to Key West, I was certainly ready for a stiff, relaxing drink. Luckily, the bars that make up the "Duval Crawl" do not disappoint.

Following is a weeklong charter itinerary in Florida recommended by Camper & Nicholsons International.

Day One: Miami Beach to Elliott Key. You can enjoy the Art Deco lifestyle in this fast-moving city as long as you like, then head off to a quiet anchorage for snorkeling amid fish, lobster, and colorful coral.

Day Two: Elliott Key to Key Largo. Bars and restaurants are as plentiful as excellent scuba diving sites in Key Largo. Be like Bogey and Bacall, and have it all as you sail away.

Day Three: Key Largo to Islamorada. Fishermen of all stripes love Islamorada, which is a series of six islands ringed by offshore sailfishing, shallow-water bonefishing, and bay fishing for redfish and tarpon.

Day Four: Islamorada to Duck Key. Most visitors to Duck Key enjoy the facilities at Hawk's Cay Resort and Marina, where a half-dozen restaurants complement the stunning scenery.

Day Five: Duck Key to Newfound Harbour. On the edge of Newfound Harbour is Little Palm Island, where a world-class spa will rub and buff away any remaining calluses you have from your pre-charter days.

Day Six: Newfound Harbour to Key West. If you don't want to do the Duval Crawl from bar to bar, you can relax with a fresh conch dinner at one of several excellent seafood restaurants on the water.

Day Seven: Key West. Stay until sunset and enjoy the carnival atmosphere that envelops Mallory Square. Wave to the party boats coming in for the night while you dodge fire-baton-twirling jugglers balancing on unicycles.

Spanish Virgin Islands

The Spanish Virgin Islands are west of the "regular" Virgin Islands and, despite their name, are American-owned. Puerto Rico, Vieques, and Culebra make up the whole of the area, along with the tiny, nameless islets that surround them.

Why are these picturesque islands so undeveloped in terms of charter? Mostly because the U.S. military has traditionally used them for target practice. Culebra hasn't been hit regularly since the 1970s, but Vieques still took a socking as recently as a few years ago from fighter pilots honing their skills.

I've never heard of a boater being injured by these well-publicized ordnance drops, but they were enough to keep marina and other yachting infrastructure development to a minimum. Resorts are starting to rise now, overlooking the crystal waters full of excellent fishing and snorkeling, but in general there are fewer restaurants, shops, and the like than in other tourist-friendly destinations.

That's a good thing to some people, who prefer to cruise far away from civilization and the crowds that go with it. If you're an experienced bareboater with more than a week's worth of time to cruise, you can get to the Spanish Virgins aboard a chartered boat from St. Thomas or Tortola. If you're looking for a fully crewed yacht, you often can find one moving through the area on its way someplace else or perhaps one that's willing to cruise over from the "regular" Virgins for an extra delivery fee or as part of a longer charter in the region.

My first charter in the Spanish Virgins is scheduled to occur right around the time this book goes to print, aboard the 115-foot motoryacht *Ragazza*, as a guest of Merrill-Stevens Yachts. Here's a look at a weeklong itinerary suggested by *Ragazza*'s captain, with a note that any of these places can be intermixed into an itinerary that includes the traditional Virgin Islands.

Day One: Puerto Del Rey to Puerto Ferro. Your first destination is Green Beach on the west end of Vieques, where you can have lunch onshore. The overnight anchorage at Puerto Ferro is a blazing phosphorescent bay that lights up the night.

Day Two: Puerto Ferro to Bahia Icacos. This unspoiled anchorage is within the U.S. Navy Weapons Range, which has kept it from blossoming as a tourist hotspot for the past 50 years. The snorkeling is excellent, and you are in no danger.

Day Three: Bahia Icacos to Bahia Almodovar. You'll cross Vieques and head for the island of Culebra. The lights of St. Thomas come up on the horizon as the sun sets, a beautiful sight after a day of snorkeling.

Day Four: Bahia Almodovar to Ensanada Honda. On the way to a nighttime anchorage full of restaurants, bars, and boutiques, you'll stop for a custom-prepared luncheon on a private beach.

Day Five: Ensanada Honda to Cavo Luis Pena. This evening's anchorage is an uninhabited wildlife refuge, a real get-away-from-it-all destination.

Day Six: Cavo Luis Pena to Isla Palominos. Spend the day exploring the refuge's trails, then anchor along a beach where you can watch the sun set over El Yunque Mountain, which is home to Puerto Rico's rainforest.

Day Seven: Isla Palominos to Puerto Del Rey. If time permits before your return flight, check out the casino at the famous Conquistador Hotel in Fajardo.

Spanish Virgin Islands

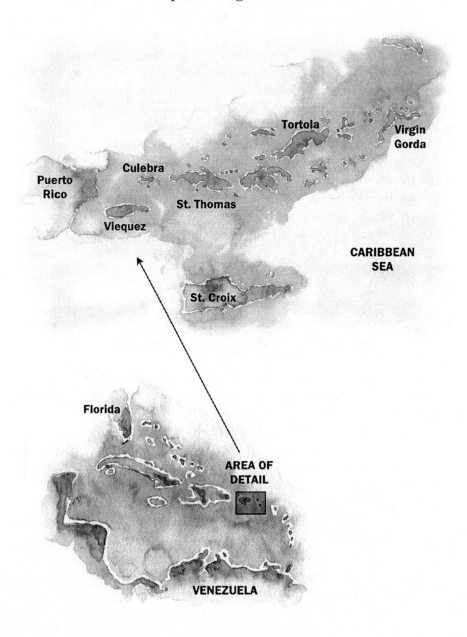

Chesapeake Bay

You'll find bareboats, instructional, and fully crewed yachts alike on the Chesapeake Bay, though the biggest, fanciest motoryachts don't tend to be in this region too often. Still, you sometimes can catch those biggest yachts in the Chesapeake on their way from the Caribbean toward New England for the summer.

Bareboats in the Chesapeake range from sailing catamarans to trawlers to everything in between. Don't be fooled by the word "bay," though. The Chesapeake is a very real boating environment—it can churn up swells as nasty as anything you'll find along the Atlantic coast, give or take a hurricane tidal surge. Still, it's a lovely place to bareboat not just because of its well-found marinas and dock-and-dine seafood restaurants, but also because it's not so big that you feel like you might get lost and sail off by accident toward Europe.

"It's a very forgiving environment," explains Bill Shermer, co-owner of Blue Goose Charters, which offers bareboat and instructional trawler yachts. "The Chesapeake is relatively shallow. It's not like going out into the Northwest, where there are heavy tides, heavy currents and big rocks. The Chesapeake is generally a sandy clay or mud bottom. There are some rocks, but not enough to worry about. Especially the north end of the bay, it's well marked in terms of charts. You can pilot with a basic understanding of charts and just keeping your eyes open. If you do have the misfortune of running aground—which usually we only hear about with sailboaters—it's usually not such a big deal. You can get towed off without much fanfare unless you hit a rock or an oyster bed."

Crewed charters in the Chesapeake can be quite lovely as well. In Chapter Two, I mentioned the charter I did aboard the 60-foot motoryacht *Irony* with my immediate family, in honor of my father's 58th birthday. Our charter was limited to one part of the bay, where the biggest tourist-friendly town is St. Michaels, yet I still felt that I got to know the place in a way I don't know others where I have spent far more time exploring. (And did I mention the crab cakes? There's a reason Maryland is famous for them!)

Irony's captain and mate, husband-and-wife team Dan and Libby Cole, own a bed and breakfast in the town of Oxford, where the yacht is based. They like to take guests from Oxford to St. Michaels, then to other destinations along the bay that fit with the guests' personalities. In the case of our family, that place was up the Wye River offshoot, to a sportsman's club called Pintail Point.

My father, you see, is a lifelong skeet and trap shooter, and Pintail Point has a sporting clays course with a Wobble trap that we just knew Dad would love. The place also has a small dock where *Irony* fits just fine, so we had our own bed and breakfast with personal chef docked just off the property's grounds during our two-day stay. In the mornings, a member of the Pintail Point staff would collect us in a golf cart and drive us along the winding, shaded paths to the sporting clays action. We'd take the golf cart back to the yacht come lunchtime, then return to the course for the afternoon's shooting games.

As cool as Pintail Point itself was, the best part about being there was that we were with the Coles aboard *Irony*. They truly understood what it meant to take care of their guests, going so far as to deliver freshly baked snacks and sodas to us during our afternoon round of shooting. They also had plenty of cruising lined up for us when we finished our few days at the sporting clays course, and we all enjoyed watching their home waters go by while sipping drinks on deck and listening to the sea gulls swoop overhead.

I'd go back every summer if I could, not just to the small part of the Chesapeake that I already know, but to other parts as well, including the historic boating hubs of Annapolis, Maryland, and Norfolk, Virginia. I'd also love to scoot a ways up the Potomac River toward Washington, D.C., just to take a look around.

Following is a possible weeklong itinerary on the Chesapeake Bay, suggested by the Coles from their experiences with guests aboard *Irony*.

Day One: Annapolis to Rock Hall. After a day of exploring the rich maritime history in this great American city, cruise to the Eastern Shore and Rock Hall, which has three museums and a trolley that offers tours around town.

Day Two: Rock Hall to Chestertown. The cute main street and shops here offer interesting history and delicious eats alike.

Day Three: Chestertown to Kent Narrows. This popular boating hub is a great place to pick up provisions or partake in a pub crawl. Just be careful if you're bareboating: Keep the red day markers to starboard (the boat's right side) whether you're entering or exiting. Otherwise, you'll run aground.

Day Four: Kent Narrows to Pintail Point. This cruise, up the Wye River offshoot, is stunning in terms of scenery. Many a Washington, D.C., diplomat has his summer estate along this waterway, and you can enjoy the architecture as you make your way to the dock at Pintail Point for an afternoon of sporting clay shooting or golf.

Day Five: Pintail Point to St. Michaels. Stay as long as you like for the games at Pintail Point, then cruise onward to "The Town That Fooled the British Navy" in Colonial times. It is by far the bay's most popular cruising destination, thanks to charming shops, museums, galleries, and restaurants.

Chesapeake Bay

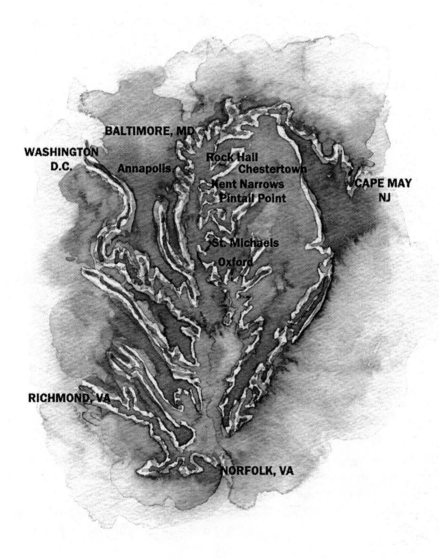

Day Six: St. Michaels to Oxford. This destination is home of the Ruffled Duck Bed and Breakfast, which the Coles own (and help to run when they're not onboard *Irony*). You'll be welcomed like locals anywhere you wander, even if it's down to the oldest home in town, now occupied by boatbuilder Eddie Cutts, Jr.

Day Seven: Oxford to Annapolis. Enjoy a scenic cruise back up the bay to Annapolis, returning in plenty of time for your afternoon flight back home.

Great Lakes

The Great Lakes are beautiful for boating, as anyone who cruises there regularly will tell you, but they haven't developed as a main charter hub because of their location so far inland in the United States.

Most charter yachts that want to cruise there during the summer have to go all the way up the New England Coast, into Canadian waters, and around Nova Scotia to the Gulf of St. Lawrence, where they can meet the St. Lawrence River and finally head westward toward the Great Lakes. There are other routes, of course, including up the inland Mississippi or Hudson rivers, but they, too, take a lot of time and come with the additional challenges of commercial boating traffic, shallow areas, and locks that are too small for some larger yachts to fit inside. As with so many other beautiful boating areas, the Great Lakes simply have yet to overcome their geographic location to develop a chartering reputation.

There are hints, though, that this may soon change. "The infrastructure has always been there, but for commercial shipping," explains Grant Eccles, a partner with Barrie, Ontario-based Lakeshore Excursions, which helps charter captains get what they need in the region. "It's being utilized in a great way now by yachters who are seeing that we do have the first-class facilities they need, for stocking supplies, servicing, and repairing the yachts up to about 130 feet, even in small cities. There are a lot of people coming here quietly, on their own boats, but really the area is undiscovered in terms of charter. It's for people who want to do something off the beaten path, who don't necessarily want to follow where hoards of other people are going.

"In one week, you could pick one region of one lake," Eccles says. "Or, where they come together, you could visit Lake Michigan, Huron, and Superior in one week. Or, you could stay along the St. Lawrence River. There's Montreal, Quebec City, and a most unique area full of fjords. It has the world's largest concentration of whales in the summertime, humpbacks, beluga, and blue whales. If you prefer a different style, we have the Montreal Grand Prix every summer. It all depends on what you want to do."

The Great Lakes

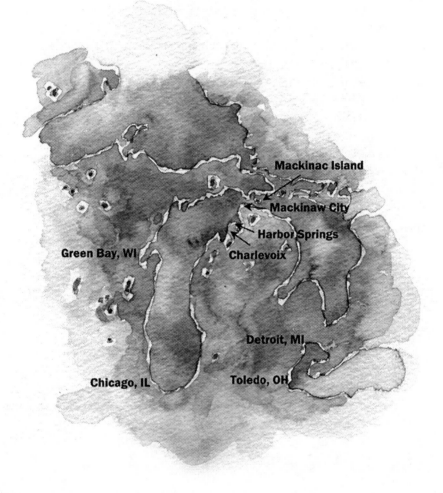

My first charter in the Great Lakes is being planned as this book is being written. I'm hoping to visit during the summer of 2006, as a guest of International Yacht Collection onboard the 85-foot motoryacht *New Moon II*. Stay tuned at *www.CharterWave.com* for my post-charter review.

In the meantime, here's a Great Lakes itinerary suggested by International Yacht Collection.

Day One: Charlevoix, Michigan. Spend the afternoon exploring the unique shops in this resort town. Enjoy dinner at the famed Grey Gables, a 19th-century Victorian house that now serves as a restaurant.

Day Two: Charlevoix to Bay Harbor. After breakfast onboard, take a short cruise to Bay Harbor. Enjoy this outstanding resort, with manicured beaches, upscale shopping, and great restaurants. There are several Jack Nicklaus-designed golf courses to be played as well.

Day Three: Bay Harbor to Mackinac Island. This 40-mile cruise is to a quaint island that does not allow motorized vehicles. Horse-drawn buggies will get you to the Grand Hotel, where high tea is served on the porch every day at 3 PM sharp.

Day Four: Mackinac Island to Les Cheneaux Islands. Enjoy nature by day, then a dinner cruise on your way to the anchorage at Les Cheneaux Islands. Look for moose drinking at the water's edge, and watch the northern lights.

Day Five: Les Cheneaux Islands to Mackinaw City. After a day's cruising in the scenic islands, stop in at the nearby wooden boat museum and then cruise for the night to Mackinaw City, a historic Native American town.

Day Six: Mackinaw City to Harbor Springs. You'll usually find several mega-yachts cruising in this watery playground of the Fords, Chryslers, and other well-known local families. The town is upscale, and the restaurants are exquisite.

Day Seven: Harbor Springs to Charlevoix. Enjoy a leisurely morning onboard before your afternoon flight back home.

Pacific Northwest

I'm just going to come right out and say it: I *love* the Pacific Northwest. Of the dozens of countries and countless cruising regions I've visited, the one that I chose to return to during my honeymoon in 2005 was the Pacific Northwest. In particular, I returned to Eagle Nook Resort, a wilderness lodge I first visited in 2003 during a "surf and turf"—a trip that combined a charter onboard the 85-foot motoryacht *Endurance* with a few days on land at the lodge, which the yacht's owner also happened to own.

There are many reasons I so enjoy cruising and exploring in this region, which stretches from Seattle up to Vancouver Island, Canada. For starters, there are the San Juans, a group of close-together islands full of hiking trails and tree-lined vistas. Then there are the bigger cities like Victoria, at the southern tip of Vancouver Island, where I never fail to find handmade local jade jewelry in the shops. And, if you can find yourself a knowledgeable charter captain, you can make your way up the west coast of Vancouver Island, known as "The Graveyard of the Pacific" for all the old-time sailing ships it's swallowed. That's where the Eagle Nook Resort is, tucked inside Barkley Sound, where you'll find nothing but humpback whales, sea lions, bald eagles, king salmon, pristine forests, clean waters, clear blue skies—and a few lucky vacationers like me who prefer thick-soled Timberlands to skimpy bikini bottoms. There are no roads to the place. You have to either land in a seaplane or cruise in aboard a chartered yacht, which is just my style.

There are plenty of bareboating opportunities in the San Juans, along with instructional charters aboard everything from sailing monohulls to catamarans to twin-engine powerboats. Some of the advanced instructional courses will take you beyond the San Juans to the Canadian Gulf Islands and even British Columbia's Desolation Sound—where the scenery amazes pretty much every boater who ever makes it there. You can, of course, get to these destinations during a regular bareboat charter or fully crewed yacht charter, too, depending on how much time you have in your vacation schedule.

Some fully crewed yachts call the Pacific Northwest home, but for the most part, you'll end up booking charters aboard bigger boats that are headed from the western coast of Mexico up to Alaska for the summer (or are returning on the opposite course). This means the opportunities for fully crewed charter in this region tend to be best during the spring and fall, on either side of the summer cruising season in Alaska. Have no qualms about this. My honeymoon on Vancouver Island was at the end of September, just before the start of the annual rainy season, and we had a full week of bright sunshine, temperatures in the mid-60s and more wildlife around than I could count. I also did a springtime charter from Seattle to the San Juans a half-dozen years ago aboard the 100-foot motoryacht *Katania,* as a guest of CEO Expeditions. I remember the weather being cool but perfectly comfortable—and outstanding for hiking, a favorite pastime in the region.

Following is a weeklong itinerary that includes the San Juan Islands, plus Seattle and Vancouver Island, as suggested by CEO Expeditions.

San Juan Islands

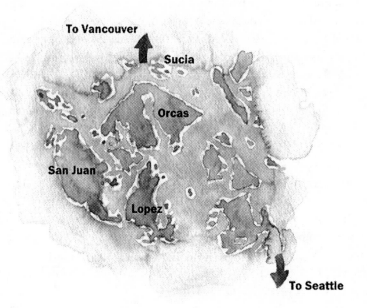

Day One: Seattle to Sucia Island. Depart through the busy Chittenden Locks on Seattle's Lake Washington and end up in a quiet cove on Sucia Island, where hiking trails and wildlife rule.

Day Two: Sucia Island to Roche Harbor, San Juan Island. Roche Harbor is lined with picturesque white buildings that house a few shops, a small hotel, and a restaurant. I recall the food being only decent, but the view was spectacular as sunset fell across the yachts in the marina.

Day Three: Roche Harbor to Victoria. This city on the southern tip of Vancouver Island offers plenty of shopping and restaurants. If you have time, hop in a taxi for a visit to the nearby Butchart Gardens, some of the most beautifully manicured grounds I've ever seen.

Day Four: Victoria to Nanaimo. The city of Nanaimo is on the eastern coast of Vancouver Island, along the wide though weather-protected Strait of Georgia. You can wander the shops and restaurants or enjoy bicycling, hiking, kayaking, and other active pursuits.

Day Five: Nanaimo to Desolation Sound. Don't let the name of this body of water dissuade you: Desolation Sound is anything but. It's filled with stunning scenery, and the waters are warm enough during the summertime months for swimming and diving.

Day Six: Desolation Sound to Prideaux Haven. This anchorage is one of many inside Desolation Sound, and it has lots of small coves that are perfect for discovering by kayak.

Day Seven: Prideaux Haven to Seattle. You'll catch a seaplane not too far from your Prideaux Haven anchorage for the two-and-a-half-hour scenic flight back to Seattle.

South Pacific

For the purposes of yacht charter, the South Pacific comprises Australia, New Zealand, and the islands to their north including tourist favorites like Fiji, Bora Bora, and Tahiti. Think of Auckland, New Zealand, as Fort Lauderdale, Florida—a hub of boatbuilding, provisioning, and repair activity—with the tropical islands to Auckland's north being similar to Fort Lauderdale's nearby Caribbean, a playground where yachts can cruise.

One difference between this South Pacific and the Caribbean, though, is that the islands are scattered in groups instead of in a long, arcing row that boats can follow like a trail. The island groups themselves in the South Pacific are pretty far apart, too, meaning that once a charter yacht gets to a group of islands, it's likely to stay there. The Fijian islands are one example; you wouldn't want to cruise from there all the way up to the Marshall Islands and back during a weeklong charter.

"You'd do Tahiti—maybe seven, ten, or 14 days there," explains Allan Jouning, a longtime yacht captain who now helps to arrange charters with Fraser Yachts Worldwide in Auckland, New Zealand. "Or you could do seven, ten, or 14 days in Fiji. Or in Tonga. Or in the Great Barrier Reef in Australia." Just not all together in one charter. "From Fiji to Australia is 2,000 miles. You've got to pick an area to charter."

Another way the South Pacific differs from the Caribbean is that there are far fewer charter yachts available there—though the number is growing. "There are bareboats in New Zealand, the Whitsundays [off Australia], Tonga, Tahiti," Jouning says. "In Fiji they have bareboats, but you have to take a Fijian person with you. I've had bareboaters who've done it, and they weren't too sure at first, but after having done it, they said it's fantastic. He cooks, cleans up, knows all the villages—it makes it easier for people chartering in those areas.

"The crewed boats, we're not getting the 150-footers because no [yacht owner] is really prepared yet to base a boat out here like that," Jouning says. "We've got a few that are 100 to 125 feet, and we get plenty of inquiries for the bigger boats, but the only way you'll get one of those is to catch it coming through on a world cruise."

No matter what kind of charter you choose, you're bound to have an adventure. The whole of the South Pacific is far more than just a tropical playground. "The South Island of New Zealand, there are fjords like in Norway and Alaska," Jouning says. "On the North Island, you've got warm waters and beaches. Australia, most of the chartering is on the Great Barrier Reef, which is around the same latitude as Fiji, so that's tropical. You can also charter out of Sydney, which is like a big city, like chartering in New York for a week. Places like Fiji, they're sort of like the Virgin Islands were 25 years ago. It's very nice cruising, but without the [boating] traffic that you have right now. The Virgins, though, they're no more than about forty miles long. Fiji is two hundred miles of islands. We're getting some interesting surf charters now, too. The guests love to find the breaks and just live there in comfort for a week."

I've cruised onboard three different charter yachts in the South Pacific, all about two years ago as a guest of Fraser Yachts Worldwide. Jouning was along for part of my trip, as were several charter brokers from the company.

First was the 102-foot sailing yacht *Pacific Eagle*, with her owner, Peter Stewart, at the helm. We were in the Marlborough region of New Zealand's South

Island—well known for producing tasty wines, but not well known for much else. Stewart has a venison farm there and has lived on the South Island all his life, and he was one of the first to offer charters there, hoping to introduce tourists to the rolling hills and quiet countryside where he grew up. We enjoyed some fabulous hiking, along with delicious mussels caught fresh off the boat, not to mention more than our share of tasty wines from vineyards, including the popular Cloudy Bay.

My second charter in the South Pacific was onboard the 108-foot motoryacht *Askari* with an extremely knowledgeable captain named Lon Munsey. He introduced me to the Bay of Islands, a rich cruising ground on New Zealand's North Island where we found everything from fine dining to spectacular golf resorts to traditional Maori dances and songs. At the risk of sounding like too much of a pop culture junkie, I can tell you that the people were just as interesting as the young girl in the Oscar darling *The Whale Rider*, and the scenery was just as spectacular as it looks in *The Lord of the Rings* trilogy. The scuba diving was good here too, despite the waters being far cooler than anywhere in the tropics. I especially enjoyed a wreck dive here, with the site's history keeping my mind off the ocean's temperature.

Last on my South Pacific itinerary was a weeklong charter aboard the 115-foot motoryacht *Surprise*, which I mentioned in Chapter Five. It's one of my most memorable yacht charters of all time, not just because the yacht is gorgeous, the captain is skilled, and the crew are quite good, but also because it was so different from every other yacht charter I've experienced. Captain Carol Dunlop, you see, is running the first fully crewed megayacht ever to be permanently based in Fiji, and she draws on the three decades' worth of personal connections she has made both in the major cities and in the outlying islands to introduce charter guests to the *real* island nation. We didn't visit anything remotely like the hula shows that are put on for tourists in other tropical locales. Instead, our crew performed the proper introductory ceremonies with tribal leaders onshore and then led us into actual villages where we could talk to the church leaders, pay a few dollars for the handmade crafts laid out on blankets, or even kick around soccer balls with the children. There were no marinas at all, and we anchored off shores where there were literally no lights after sundown. The moon and stars were brighter than I've ever seen them, the earth itself as quiet as a private thought.

My point in telling you about these three different South Pacific experiences is, of course, that the region is vast, as are the charter experiences you can find within it.

Following is a sample itinerary for a weeklong charter that includes Tahiti and Bora Bora, as suggested by Fraser Yachts Worldwide.

The South Pacific

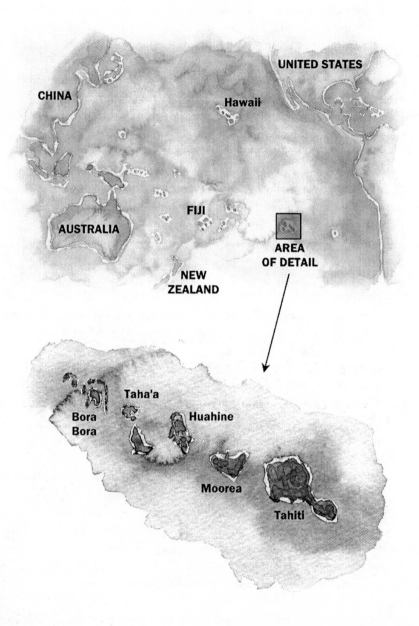

Day One: Tahiti to Moorea. Take a short, hour-and-a-half cruise to the island Moorea, where you can tour the landscape with a four-wheel-drive vehicle. Cool off with a swim in the warm waters before dinner onboard your yacht.

Day Two: Moorea to Huahine. Your yacht will move to a second anchorage on Moorea during the day, when you can enjoy snorkeling, swimming, fishing, and simply relaxing on the beach. After dinner, cruise to Huahine to anchor for the night.

Day Three: Huahine. Your first anchorage at Huahine may offer an opportunity for horseback riding or deep-sea fishing. Or, you can lounge onboard your yacht and simply take in the tropical scenery.

Day Four: Huahine. Your second anchorage at Huahine may offer chances for scuba diving, hiking, or cycling. If you had your fill of any one of those activities during Day Three, you can try whichever one you skipped.

Day Five: Huahine to Taha'a. You'll stop at the island of Raiatea along the way, cruising inside a stunning reef to visit pearl farms onshore. Your anchorage for the night will be at Taha'a, as you make your way toward Bora Bora.

Day Six: Taha'a to Bora Bora. The two-hour cruise to Bora Bora is well worth the trip, with everything from onshore hiking to in-water shark feedings. And the scenery, which you can view from your yacht, is stunning.

Day Seven: Spend the morning relaxing onboard or taking in more of the sights on Bora Bora. An evening flight from the island's airport will return you to Tahiti, so that you can begin your trip back home.

Seychelles, Maldives, and South Africa

The Seychelles, due east of Kenya and northeast of Madagascar in the Indian Ocean, were among the islands affected by the massive tsunami that struck in December 2004. They were not hit as hard as some spots in Sri Lanka and Thailand, though, and they've worked hard to get their tourism infrastructure back up and running. The Maldives, farther east than the Seychelles and off the southern point of India, were also affected by the tsunami. Repairs continue there.

There are bareboat charters in the Seychelles and Maldives, and you can sometimes find fully crewed yachts as they make their way to or from South Africa or Europe. While the Seychelles, Maldives, and South African coast are considered safe for charter, most brokers do not recommend itineraries that go up the eastern coast of Africa toward the Suez Canal, as the area tends to be frequented by pirates (who stalk even the largest cruise ships).

The Seychelles

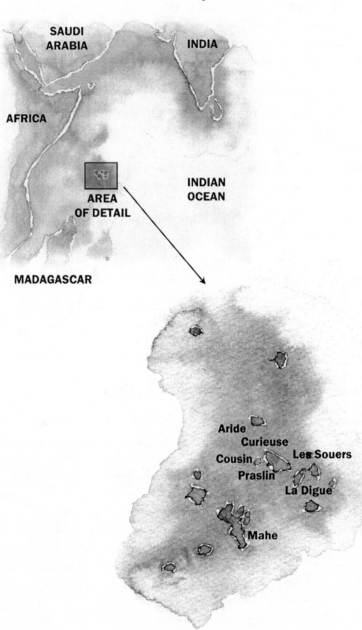

I was on my way to my first charter in the region as this book went to print, and I was quite excited because my fellow writers and editors who have gone there for boating-magazine articles all loved it. They describe the Seychelles, in particular, as being more beautiful than the Caribbean, with fewer boats and less commercialization. Look for details from my charter—onboard the spectacular, $195,000-per-week, 161-foot-long motoryacht *Teleost* as a guest of Fraser Yachts Worldwide—to become available soon at *www.CharterWave.com*.

Following is a seven-day itinerary for chartering in the Seychelles, as suggested by Fraser Yachts Worldwide. It is different than the one *Teleost* had planned for me when this book hit newsstands, so keep in mind that this itinerary is one option among many in the Seychelles.

Day One: Praslin to Curieuse. You will board your charter yacht in St. Anne, on Praslin, before setting sail for the nearby island of Curieuse. There, you can see the giant tortoises that are bred in a conservation station.

Day Two: Curieuse to the Les Souers. The Les Souers Islands are privately owned, but they welcome charter yacht guests for swimming in the warm waters or hunting shells on the beaches. Cocos Island is also nearby, and its snorkeling is fantastic.

Day Three: Les Souers Islands to La Digue. Oxcarts and bicycles are the main modes of transportation on La Digue, which has about 2,000 residents. You can tour restored plantation houses on shore or go scuba diving off of granite boulders. Snorkeling is quite good as well.

Day Four: La Digue to Praslin. The plant and animal life on Praslin is so remarkable, its Vallee de Mai forest has been named one of the world's smallest World Heritage Sites. Some say it is the actual Garden of Eden.

Day Five: Praslin to Cousin Island. Snorkeling, diving, and beachcombing are the order of the day for sun worshipers here, but if you prefer to explore onshore, this nature reserve boasts everything from birds to geckos.

Day Six: Cousin Island to Aride Island. Bird watching and fishing are the main pursuits on Aride Island, or you can simply relax on your yacht and lounge away your last full day of vacation.

Day Seven: Your yacht will return you to Praslin, where you can dine onshore before catching your flight back home.

Western Mexico, Central America, and the Galapagos Islands

The Sea of Cortez has long been a favorite cruising destination for California yachtsmen who visit onboard their own boats, but private charter vacations have yet to really take off from those turquoise waters all the way down to the Panama Canal. While cruise ships regularly visit commercial ports along this stretch, known as the Mexican Riviera, marinas dedicated to servicing charter yachts are still few and far between. That means that only the most self-sustaining, largest, fully crewed charter yachts typically cruise here, since there are relatively few places to provision and get repairs onshore.

A good example is the 125-foot motoryacht *Centurion*, which I cruised onboard along the western shore of Costa Rica in early 2000 as a guest of Venture Pacific Marine. *Centurion* is a yacht built for long-range, expedition-style cruising. She has extra-large fuel tanks, extra-large food storage freezers, and other features that make her virtually self-sufficient for far longer than other yachts her size might be. The owners of Venture Pacific Marine decided that a yacht like *Centurion* could open up new markets for charter, and they chose to work with Costa Rica Expeditions, a nature/adventure tour company, to create cruising itineraries where no marinas exist at all. My week onboard was filled with scuba diving, whitewater rafting, and hiking through tropical dry forests where the roars of the howler monkeys were as loud as high-speed trains.

It was a terrific experience, similar to the one I enjoyed onboard another Venture Pacific Marine yacht, the 180-foot motoryacht *Revelation* in the Galapagos Islands. The islands are about 600 miles west of Ecuador, due south of Guatemala, and are teeming with the same iguanas and giant tortoises that you may have seen in the Russell Crowe film *Master and Commander*. The islands are tightly monitored in terms of yacht traffic—to protect the wildlife—which means that few charter yachts can ever go there unless they are locally owned and operated. The ones that get through the paperwork and regulations, like *Revelation*, do so at great expense and investments of time.

Still, these areas all along the western coast of the Americas are picturesque and enchanting, and as the yachting infrastructure continues to improve, more charters should become available there.

Following is an itinerary for a weeklong cruise in the Galapagos Islands, suggested by Ricardo Arenas and Yvonne Mortola, the husband-and-wife team who own Sail'n Galapagos. It's an Ecuadorian company that helps charter yacht captains plan itineraries for guests like you in the islands. I know both Arenas and Mortola personally—and they really know their stuff. Not just the boats; Mortola is also an excellent, licensed nature guide on the islands.

The Galapagos Islands

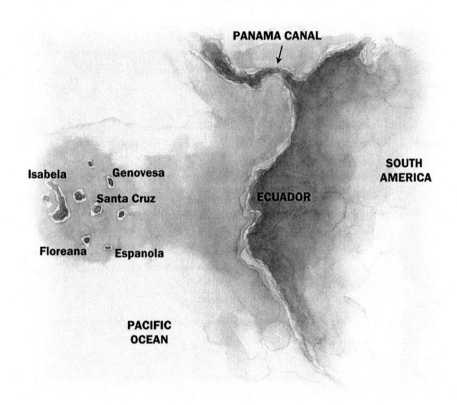

Day One: Baltra to Santa Cruz. Hike along the lava rocks, where you will see extremely tall prickly pear cacti as well as yellow land iguanas.

Day Two: Santa Cruz to Genovesa. You can climb Prince Phillip's Steps in the morning, taking you to a trail full of Nazca boobies, red-footed boobies, frigate birds, small marine iguanas, finches, mockingbirds, and doves. In the afternoon, at Darwin Bay, you can add swallowtail gulls and sea lions to your day's encounters.

Day Three: Genovesa to Bartolome. Stop first at Santiago, where tide pools and large grottos await, full of playful sea lions and scampering marine iguanas. Sally Lightfoot crabs will glow bright red, and fur sea lions will enhance your understanding of the species. On Bartolome, you can hike up a volcano and photograph penguins during a dinghy ride.

Day Four: Bartolome to South Plaza. First, a stop at North Seymour Island to see blue-footed boobies and snorkel with the sea lions along the shore. Then, it's on to South Plaza, where land iguanas await with yet more sea lions.

Day Five: South Plaza to Santa Cruz. Visit the Charles Darwin Research Center, where tortoises are raised year-round. Later, it's a walk through the lava tube in the Highlands area, home to giant tortoises in the wild.

Day Six: Santa Cruz to Floreana. Visit Post Office Bay, where an old whalers' mail drop is stuffed with postcards that you can help deliver back home (or leave one of your own, and see if it ever returns to you by way of another boater). Later, it's a walk to the flamingo-filled lagoon for photographs of the tall birds in the wild.

Day Seven: Floreana to Espanola. Snorkel at the aptly named Turtle Rock before taking your longest hike of the week. It includes a famous blowhole on land as well as lava lizards and wide-winged albatrosses.

Day Eight: Espanola to Santa Cruz. A short tender ride along the mangroves in the morning will offer you a glimpse at various swimming rays, sharks, pelicans, and herons. From here, it's a quick dinghy ride back to the airport on Baltra.

Thailand and East Asia

I have yet to experience a yacht charter in this part of the world, but the yacht captains I know who have been there rave about it. Thailand, in particular, is getting a lot of buzz on the marina docks these days, which means that more and more yachts are going to want to visit there—and that more and more infrastructure will be built. I don't hear much about bareboating opportunities in this part of the world, but among the fully crewed yachts, Thailand is becoming a hot spot.

The Far East, including China, doesn't typically generate as much excitement in terms of charter, bareboat or crewed, but the director of charter for Fraser Yachts Worldwide believes that situation will change rapidly during the next five years.

"As soon as China is ready in a few years with infrastructure—hear me now—in a few years you will see us there," says David LeGrand, who oversees the charter division of Fraser Yachts Worldwide from his office in Monaco. "As more and more boats are built, the harbors [in the Mediterranean] are full. It's spreading out. Another main area needs to be developed for August. China has some very interesting possibilities."

Until that happens, your best bet for finding a fully crewed charter in this part of the world is in Thailand, where there's more than enough to keep you busy for two weeks if you want to make the most of the long flight over.

Following is an itinerary suggested by Nigel Burgess, starting and ending near the international airport in Phuket.

Day One: Patong Beach, Phuket. Board your yacht for a relaxing dinner onboard after a long day (or more) of airline travel. Freshly caught fish will be a nice change of pace from the food, even if you've flown first class.

Day Two: Phuket to Similan Islands. It's a three-hour cruise to the Similan Islands, where snorkeling is beautiful amid the coral reefs and tropical fish. Whale sharks and manta rays are often spotted in these waters, which also are a favorite among scuba divers.

Day Three: Similan Islands. There are nine islands in this chain, well more than you can enjoy in just a single day. This second day of exploration can include walking through lush forests and visiting villages onshore.

Day Four: Similan Islands to Koh Surin. Sea gypsies live on Koh Surin, existing on nothing but an economy of fishing and shell collecting. You can learn about their way of life in between snorkeling trips to the pristine reefs.

Day Five: Koh Surin to Richelieu Rock. Whale sharks like this area, which again makes it a favorite among scuba divers. Most charter guests choose to spend the whole day, and many say it is a highlight of a charter in this part of the world.

Day Six: Richelieu Rock to Ao Bang Thao. This was Asia's first fully integrated resort complex, with beautiful beaches lined by clubs and hotels. You can enjoy lunch onshore, then swim and nap before a night on the town.

Thailand

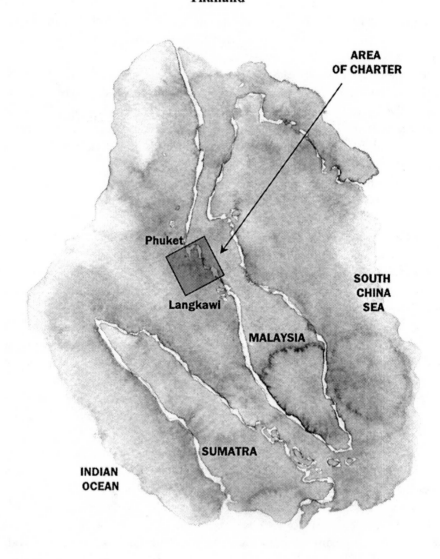

Day Seven: Ao Bang Thao to Koh Phing Kan. It's a four-hour cruise to Koh Phing Kan, which was the setting for the James Bond film *The Man With the Golden Gun.* The rock formations are fascinating, and you can explore the lagoon by dinghy.

Day Eight: Koh Phing Kan to Koh Dam Hok. By day, you can swim, snorkel, dive, or fish in the beautiful waters. By night, a quick tender ride will take you to Krabi for dinner at a resort nestled into a dramatic sea mountain backdrop.

Day Nine: Koh Dam Hok to Koh Dhang Nah. It's just an hour's cruise to Koh Dhang Nah, where the lagoon is a lovely place to relax and read a book onboard your yacht. This is a terrific mid-point in your charter for simply lounging and napping amid stunning scenery.

Day Ten: Koh Dhang Nah to Langkawi, Malaysia. This Malaysian island is a tourist favorite with plenty of shops and souvenirs. There is also a picturesque freshwater lake nearby that makes for memorable photographs.

Day Eleven: Lagkawi to Koh Muu. Your second day in Langkawi can be spent fishing with your yacht's crew or visiting the traditional fishing villages onshore. A beach picnic is usually in the cards as well, before setting sail to anchor for the night in Koh Muu.

Day Twelve: Koh Muu to Phi Phi Island. The extinct volcano on Koh Muu is unforgettable—you can enter its crater by swimming for ten minutes through a cave. Talk about your day's adventure while dining off the shore of Phi Phi Island, where vertical cliffs climb straight out of the sea.

Day Thirteen: Phi Phi Island to Patong. This city, near Phuket, is a quick ride from the international airport.

Scandinavia and Northern Europe

The Baltic and Norwegian seas are home to many boats, but few of them are ingrained in the worldwide charter market. During my six years of covering international charter yacht shows for various magazines, I've met only one charter broker from Scandinavia, a Norwegian man. He explained that there are a fair number of six-guest sailing yachts available for partially crewed or fully crewed charter in this region, but outside of that, the infrastructure is still in its infancy. I thanked him for his local knowledge and told him I looked forward to seeing him at next year's boat show, but he never returned. When I e-mailed him during the editing phase of this book, I received no response.

Such is the state of yacht charter in Scandinavia and Northern Europe. You do stand a decent chance of finding a high-end, fully crewed luxury yacht in and around the Netherlands, since the Dutch build some of the finest motoryachts on the world's waters today. Owners of those yachts usually want to be onboard themselves when the launches are brand-new from the shipbuilding yards, but in some cases, you can find a yacht willing to take charters in the Baltic or North Sea—at a top rate, since the yacht will literally be untouched by other guests.

Other fully crewed yachts may be cruising the area because their owners want to see Oslo, Copenhagen, Stockholm, Helsinki, St. Petersburg, and other major worldwide cities near the coastline. A good charter broker can tell you when these opportunities arise, and you may be able to squeeze in a charter between the owner's personal use of his yacht.

No major yacht companies promote a sample itinerary for charters in Scandinavia and Northern Europe, so ask your charter broker for details if this is an area you hope to visit.

North African Coast and the Red Sea

This historic region is one I have yet to visit, but it does have bareboating and fully crewed charters available. The scuba diving in the Red Sea is said to be quite spectacular, as are the resorts along the Egyptian coastline that lure European vacationers. I've even heard of fully crewed, high-end charter yachts taking guests through the Suez Canal and then on to visit such storied cities as Cairo and Tripoli before cruising northward to Western European ports.

The charter guests I've spoken with who have done this route are all Americans, and each told me they found the trip fascinating, though slightly uncomfortable. The War on Terrorism creates challenges for U.S. residents traveling in this part of the world—sometimes, real challenges such as unfriendly locals, and other times, perceived challenges such as paranoia about safety. I have never heard of anyone aboard a fully crewed yacht or a bareboat suffering any kind of injury, physical or psychological, anywhere in this region. In fact, many yacht captains say the local businesspeople happily welcome charter guests of all nationalities—just as resort and restaurant owners do in all other tourism areas worldwide.

Still, the charters I do hear about from this region are limited in number, so working with a knowledgeable charter broker or bareboat company will be important if the Red Sea or Northern Africa are your dream vacation destinations.

Following is a weeklong itinerary in Tunisia suggested by the captain onboard the 172-foot motoryacht *Taipan III*, which has cruised in these waters.

North African Coast

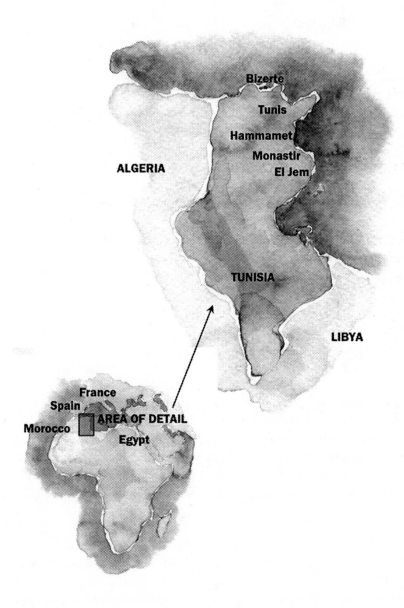

Day One: Bizerte. Arrive at your yacht, tour the city, and enjoy a freshly prepared seafood dinner before climbing into bed early with jet lag.

Day Two: Bizerte to Bon Anchorage. After four hours underway, you'll find yourself in a calm anchorage where snorkeling and other water sports are the order of the day.

Day Three: Bon Anchorage to Hammamet. The shopping is quite good here, but so are the water sports if you'd like to enjoy another day at the beach.

Day Four: Hammamet to Tunis. This city of contrasts, new and old, offers opportunities to dine onshore at night, or return to the boat for a meal prepared by your chef after a day of touring around on foot.

Day Five: Tunis to Monastir. The walled city here is a sight to see, as is the Bourguiba Mausoleum, named in honor of the father of modern Tunisia. A castle dominates the waterfront museum, and there is excellent nightlife nearby for some late-evening adventure onshore.

Day Six: Monastir to El Jem. This inland city is a short drive from your marina, with a roman amphitheater that is considered the most important in North Africa. It's reportedly second in size to the amphitheater in Rome, Italy.

Day Seven: El Jem to Monastir. There should be time for more water sports and sunbathing before you need to head off to the international airport for your flight back home.

Getting There

There is no doubt: It's a big world out there, and the more you learn about all it offers, the more you will want to think about different yacht charter vacation itineraries.

You've learned in this chapter, as well as in Chapters Five and Six, that different charter grounds offer different levels of boat availability. That fact, along with your preferences for a certain style of yacht and a given onboard experience, will have a lot to do with helping you choose the right charter for your vacation.

Another factor will, of course, be the cost of whichever yachts are available in the destinations you most want to see. That's what we'll explore in Chapter Eight—what you can expect to pay for various types of charters in different cruising locations.

8

Comparing Prices

If all you have ever booked in the past is a cruise ship vacation, then you're used to receiving thick, glossy booklets that list each ship, each itinerary, and the price for each type of cabin during a given set of dates. With the simple flip of a few pages, you can compare how much you will pay for a seven-day itinerary in a balcony cabin onboard one ship versus a seven-day itinerary in a balcony cabin onboard another. You will know exactly which ports of call each itinerary offers, and even exactly how much you will spend on excursions above the price of the cruise ship cabin itself. If you look to the back of those glossy booklets, you can even see the price for airfare packages and airport transfers, along with predetermined gratuities.

These kinds of booklets make it easy to comparison shop for a cruise ship vacation, and you may be disappointed to learn that similar booklets do not exist for private yacht charters. You can find literature about suggested cruising itineraries as well as literature about yachts and their base rates, but nowhere will you find specific yachts with specific itineraries and total package prices listed side-by-side like cruise ship trips.

You also will not find printed brochures that itemize the variable costs of yacht charter. These additional costs can be substantial, typically adding 25 percent and sometimes as much as 30 or even 50 percent to the charter yacht's advertised weekly rate. Among these variable expenses are food provisions, wine and beer, fuel fill-ups, marina fees, ship-to-shore transfers, taxes, national park fees, crew gratuities, and even cruising guides and toys like water skis in some cases.

These add-ons are not listed as standard fees because every charter is different. Two different groups can charter the same exact yacht in the same exact place and run up a completely different set of bills.

For instance, one week's guests onboard a powerboat may want to zip back and forth to a dozen different top-dollar island marinas a day, burning up fuel and spending lavishly on restaurant lunches before snacking on caviar and Dom

Perignon champagne back on the boat each night. That same powerboat, the next week, may host charter guests who want to use far less fuel and cruise to just three islands during an entire week, always anchoring in the harbor instead of paying marina fees, and dining on freshly caught seafood after days spent snorkeling with the yacht's free equipment.

Yachts—bareboat and fully crewed alike—have to account for these differences by making more costs variable than cruise ships do. You have the opportunity to do whatever you want onboard any charter yacht you choose, but unless you book one of the rare yachts that offer an all-inclusive rate, you need to understand that your choices will be reflected in higher or lower variable costs.

A good charter broker will be able to help you estimate your variable costs in advance, based on what you tell her about how you want to use the boat during your vacation. She will know how much fuel a given yacht tends to use, how far apart the islands are in your chosen destination, what a particular yacht's chef is capable of producing on certain budgets, what dockage rates the local marinas tend to charge, how pricey the region's restaurants are (if you plan to dine ashore), and other details that should give you a reasonable idea about your overall expenses.

Good bareboat company operators, too, can talk you through many of these costs beforehand, though with you literally at the helm of your own ship, you will ultimately be the person who determines how much money gets spent. You could end up paying an extra 50 percent on top of the yacht's base rate, or you could keep the purse strings tight, even taking your own snacks from home to stock a bareboat's galley instead of buying midday munchies ashore.

No matter what total amount you expect to spend in your charter budget, a key factor to remember is that when comparing cruise ships to private yachts, it is the per-person rate that matters in terms of what you're getting for your money. A $20,000 yacht may look at first blush like a ridiculous expense next to a $2,000 cruise-ship cabin, but after you add in typical expenses such as daily excursions and onboard alcohol purchases, the better per-person deal—and the better vacation—is often the yacht.

Here's an example to help you understand that point. Crystal Cruise Lines, a high-end cruise-ship company, offers Alaskan cruises that run round-trip from San Francisco. You're on the ship for 12 days, but only five of those are actually in Alaska, plus two spent cruising the Inside Passage. So let's call it seven days in the actual destination, which is comparable to a week's stay onboard a yacht that you board in Juneau and disembark in Sitka. If your goal is to see Alaska—and not to be entertained by dancing girls on the ship—you're getting just as much time in your cruising ground during a seven-day yacht charter as you are during a 12-day cruise ship journey.

Cost Comparisons

This chart shows the per-person cost for a weeklong cruise—after typical expenses* are added to published base rates. For cruise ships, the rates shown apply to a couple who book a cabin. For yachts, the rates shown are for the entire boat, meaning couples who are friends would book the boat, each take a cabin, and split the total cost equally.

The base rates that cruise ships publish may appear to be cheaper than the base rates private yachts offer, but when you add in typical expenses, yachts often end up being comparable to or even less expensive than cruise ships on a per-person basis.

	Base rate	Total Cost Per-Person *
Royal Caribbean Cruise Line Ocean-view cabin for two people, 3,114 guests onboard ship	$929	$1,865
Crystal Cruise Line Mid-range ocean-view cabin for two people, 1,080 guests onboard ship	$2,775	$2,788
Seabourn Cruise Line Mid-range ocean-view cabin for two people, 208 guests onboard ship	$3,849	$3,325
36-foot bareboat sailboat Entire yacht for eight guests total in four cabins, high-season top rate	$4,410	$689
48-foot bareboat powercat Entire yacht for six guests total in three cabins, high-season top rate	$7,950	$1,656
Partially crewed 60-foot motoryacht Entire yacht for six guests total in three cabins, high-season top rate with captain and chef	$13,000	$2,709
Fully crewed 80-foot sailing catamaran Entire yacht for ten guests total in six cabins, high-season top rate with three crew	$22,000	$2,658
Fully crewed 80-foot motoryacht Entire yacht for eight guests total in four cabins, high-season top rate with three crew	$25,000	$3,906

* For cruise ships, includes $200 per person, per day for excursions, wine, liquor, sodas, snacks, and gratuity. For yachts, includes extra 25% of base rate for fuel, provisions, dockage, gratuity, and other typical expenses.

Of course there are bargain deals aboard Crystal Cruise Lines, as with all cruise ships, but if you want a more exclusive experience that even comes close to comparing with a private yacht charter, it's top dollar. The penthouse aboard *Crystal Harmony* in August runs a whopping $19,000 per person (give or take a thousand), but a similar level of luxury can be had in cabins on the same deck, according to an online company that specializes in cruise ship advice. Those cabins run about $9,500 per person—not at all outrageous for the quality level of vacation we're discussing.

Now, consider the charter motoryacht *Kayana* and her sistership *Katania*, both part of the CEO Expeditions fleet. *Kayana*, at 120 feet long, carries ten guests comfortably, while *Katania*, at 100 feet long, holds six. Again, you have a crew and chef catering exclusively to you and your friends, and you can change your itinerary along the way to do whatever you want.

Each yacht's base rate is far more than the advertised cruise-ship cabin prices, but if you fill one of the private yachts with your friends, the per-person price will be about $7,000. That is a good $5,000 less per couple than the cruise ship trip would cost—including typical charter expenses like fuel, alcohol, and food.

This is just one example of charter pricing, and a good charter broker can help you figure out the math for other yachts that interest you. In general, the important thing to remember is that even when a yacht's base rate looks far more expensive than a cruise-ship cabin's price, the yacht's per-person cost may well be better after typical expenses are added for each trip.

Many things will contribute to your charter yacht's base rate, and the rest of this chapter is devoted to explaining those factors.

Size and Style

The size and style of your yacht are among the biggest factors in its weekly rate. As a general rule, the following three axioms apply:

- Bareboats are less expensive than crewed yachts;
- Smaller yachts are less expensive than bigger yachts;
- Sailing yachts are less expensive than power-driven yachts.

A small bareboat sailboat is typically going to be your best bet for an inexpensive charter vacation, while a large fully crewed megayacht is likely to cost you the most. The spectrum is wide, to be sure—from less than $2,500 a week for a yacht at one end to well more than $250,000 a week for a yacht at the other—but for the most part, you can count on price ranges for yachts of similar size and style staying about the same at any given price point in between.

For instance, fully crewed 60-foot sailing yachts that carry six guests apiece will typically all fall into a similar price range. There will be a different price range for 40-foot bareboat powerboats that carry four guests apiece, but all of those bareboat powerboats should have similar rates amongst themselves.

When you get into the fully crewed, big-money sailing yachts and megayachts, the prices can vary within size categories depending on other things (like the fact that one yacht used to belong to Aristotle Onassis while another has an anonymous owner), but for the most part, you should be able to compare even top-dollar charter yachts within the pricing categories of size and style.

Classic vs. Emerging Charter Grounds

You learned in Chapters Six and Seven that different levels of yachting infrastructure make for different numbers of boats cruising in different regions of the world. This fact translates not just into itineraries, but also into charter rates. It's a simple rule of commerce: Where there is less competition, you're almost always going to pay more.

The greatest concentration of bareboats, for instance, tends to be in the Virgin Islands—a classic cruising ground where various owners of bareboat fleets need to compete for your vacation dollars. By contrast, if you want to go bareboating over in the emerging charter ground of Tahiti, you will have fewer reputable companies to work with and, therefore, will likely pay more for the same exact size and style of bareboat.

When it comes to fully crewed yachts, the same holds true. A megayacht cruising in the classic Caribbean charter grounds during the winter may head off for the emerging charter grounds of the Indian Ocean the next year—and may charge a higher weekly rate for the same exact number of guests. It's simply a function of supply and demand. If there are 12 competing megayachts in the Caribbean but only two in the Indian Ocean, the yacht owners can raise their prices and still expect to get charter bookings.

Age and Pedigree

Think about buying cars for a moment. An older Mercedes will cost you less than a recent model, while even a brand-new Toyota will cost you less than some older

Mercedes. It's a matter of age and pedigree. Older cars tend to be less expensive, while fancy name brands cost more.

So it is with charter yachts—to an extent.

If only the biggest, newest, fanciest, brand-name, fully crewed yacht will suit your tastes, you're going to pay for the privilege of chartering it, no matter what part of the world it's in.

"At the top of the market, there is a massive pricing effect with quality," explains Rupert Connor, president of Luxury Yacht Group in Fort Lauderdale. "People want the best at that extreme end of the market. The yacht owners who have tried to enter that market at a budget level, they're failing. The clients are willing to spend $400,000 a week [for a charter vacation], and they want top quality. For instance, the owner of a pedigree boat understands quality and is generally going to be willing to pay more to retain a better crew."

However, at more affordable price points—from bareboat sailboats all the way up to fully crewed 80- to 120-foot motoryachts—there are so many boats becoming available for charter these days that brand-name pedigree doesn't necessarily translate into higher weekly rates.

Part of that is because of increased competition: A four-cabin yacht is going to have to compete with other four-cabin yachts, no matter how nicely it's constructed. In addition, production boatbuilders have begun to turn out yachts up to about 120 feet long that, in many ways, are comparable to custom-built yachts in terms of quality.

"The difference in quality between a [custom-built] Swan 65 sailboat with a captain onboard and a bareboat Beneteau, which is a production sailboat, you may not see as much of a difference," Connor says. "On the other hand, if I had a 130-foot Westport [motoryacht] compared to a 130-foot Delta [motoryacht], I know I would encourage the client to go toward the Delta pedigree. The price difference may not be all that much, but the experience onboard a larger pedigree yacht will be different."

In my opinion, most people who are new to charter have a hard time discerning the factors that separate a pedigree yacht from a lesser brand of boat, whether you're talking about a 30-footer or a 300-footer. I remember thinking the first 120-foot motoryacht I stepped onboard was spectacular, until I went back a few years later after having toured countless other yachts of similar size. Today, I know that same 120-footer is a perfectly decent yacht, but certainly not a head-turner among people who really know the ins and outs of yacht charter.

Yet for the purposes of a first-time charter client, that same 120-footer will offer a fantastic vacation. I'd have no qualms about recommending it to my own family and friends for their first charters—particularly because they could probably book it at a slightly lower weekly rate than the newer, brand-name boats in the same size range.

"Somebody new to charter, as with any new experience, do it for the [price] figure that's comfortable for you," Connor advises. "Once you are experienced, you will appreciate the comforts that a pedigree yacht will give."

It would take countless pages to categorize every brand of yacht and the prices its pedigree may or may not command, but there are a few names you should know in the arena of big-money, fully crewed charter. Megayachts built by Lürssen, Feadship, and Amels tend to come with the highest price tags, while among top-dollar sailing yachts, you'll usually find the brand names Royal Huisman and Perini Navi.

As a general rule, most reputable bareboat companies don't buy poorly built yachts from lesser shipyards, simply because bareboats get a lot of use and therefore require a lot of maintenance—a cost that would only increase for the bareboat company if the boat were shoddily constructed from the start. You'll usually be able to find bareboats built by reputable companies, including Grand Banks when it comes to trawler yachts and Beneteau in the world of monohull sailboats.

Number of Crew

Yacht crew are an entirely different breed than cruise ship crew. When you're on a cruise ship, you probably don't know the names of the people who make your beds or clean your toilets. The service in the dining areas is probably good, but not first-rate proper. For many cruise ship crew, a main goal is herding large numbers of people into certain areas to satisfy them as quickly as possible.

Onboard yachts, crew function entirely differently. There are typically two to 12 crewmembers aboard the majority of charter yachts (except for bareboats, of course), and you are likely to get to know at least half of them by name during your charter. They don't think of their jobs as simply making your bed or cleaning your toilet. They think of themselves as service-industry professionals who strive to meet your needs before you even know that you need anything. They often have college degrees, work with smiles through 24-hour days, and understand how to be both fun-loving and discreet, whichever suits your personality. They are the yacht owner's personally chosen staff, not hired hands culled from blind advertisements in college campus newspapers.

They are—no matter the size of your yacht—simply offering a far better class of service than cruise ship crew, anywhere.

To tell you the truth, getting to know the crew is often one of the highlights of my charters. Yacht crew aren't as diverse as cruise ship crew—most yachties are young, white adults from New Zealand, South Africa, Australia, Europe, and the United States—but they are definitely smart people, albeit with a wanderlust that keeps them from settling down. They have amazing stories to tell about all the destinations they have visited. There's usually at least one shutterbug working onboard each yacht, too, which is also a highlight for me. I'm just getting into digital photography, and many of these yachties have been testing out the best equipment for years.

As important as training and personality are, though, they're not the main factors that affect charter pricing when it comes to crew. Instead, it's the ratio of crew to guests that you need to look at when comparing yachts. Onboard some yachts, you will have more crew than guests—better than one-to-one service. That, of course, usually comes at a price premium, but how can you argue with paying a little extra to literally have more than one person focused completely on your needs, and your needs alone?

Expertise of Crew

In some cases, demand for a specific yacht increases based on the crew's expertise. Repeat customers may enjoy a longtime captain's way of handling things, for instance, or a seasoned stewardess's penchant for throwing the best parties afloat.

A lot of times, though, it is the chefs who make some yachts more sought after than others, thus increasing the yacht owner's ability to ask for—and sometimes get—higher charter rates. The chefs who work onboard fully crewed yachts compete for awards at virtually every industry-only boat show held around the world each year, preparing everything from their best clam chowders to their finest legs of lamb.

The chef onboard the 115-foot motoryacht *Harmony*, for instance, won a major annual chef's competition about five months before this book went to press, and that yacht's management company, The Sacks Group, was reporting having to take bookings a year in advance because of demand for his cooking.

Sometimes, your crew will have unadvertised talents as well. They can include everything from having a stewardess who does manicures or massages to a deckhand who was raised in a local village and can get you into the *real* excitement onshore come nightfall.

Those kinds of abilities may not transfer into a higher charter rate, but they can affect your pocketbook in other ways.

"One point that's very important," says Ann Landry of Ann Landry Yachting in Fort Lauderdale, is that "your crew will know where to buy the best jewelry, the real artistic pieces. And they won't be getting a cut from the junk jewelry store like a cruise ship taxi driver might. The yacht crew know where their yacht's owners shop. That's where they'll send you."

Unusual Amenities vs. Standard Features

When you categorize yachts in terms of price groups, you're likely to find boats with similar features onboard. Bareboats, for instance, will usually come with sheets for each bed, a basic set of dishes and silverware in the galley, and a VHF radio at the helm. A more expensive bareboat may have all of those standard amenities, plus a nice television in the main saloon and a newer dinghy that you can take along on your charter.

The same principle holds true for fully crewed yachts, though in the higher-end price categories, the unusual amenities can be extraordinarily cool. Top-deck hot tubs, once considered a luxury, are an expected feature onboard megayachts, as are satellite Internet communications and plasma-screen televisions. Features that can help a megayacht to stand out in the crowd nowadays include onboard gyms, full-size fishing and diving dinghies (in addition to the smaller ones), and at-rest stabilizers (which keep the boat motion-free even in rolling seas).

Of course, the more of those newfangled features you want, the fewer yachts will have them—and the higher their prices are likely to be.

"When you're talking about cruise ships and how they offer different things, there are also different levels of cruise ships," explains Carolyn Cox Titus, a terrific charter broker with Nautor USA in Newport, Rhode Island. "This is kind of like that, except you always get your own private yacht at the end of the day. There are a lot of differences, and it's kind of like the difference between an inn, a Motel 6, and a five-star hotel. Boats really do vary, and pricing depends on the condition of the boat as much as on the crew or the toys onboard. You can have a really nice Feadship [megayacht], but if it's poorly maintained, there's a problem. The charter industry polices this, along with the professionalism of the crew."

You will have to decide whether extra features on the best-outfitted yachts are worth paying for, should your choice come down to two otherwise similar yachts in the same destination. Sometimes the answer will be yes, but don't be afraid to opt for the yacht with fewer features if you think it will suit your needs just fine.

I personally find extras like the full-size fishing and diving dinghies to be extremely worthwhile—because I'm a scuba diver who likes to fish. I also like having a hot tub onboard, because I usually get sunburned during the day and the hot water soothes my skin at night.

But the onboard gyms, for me, are not worth the extra cash. I prefer to get my exercise hiking along inland trails and then swimming back to the yacht from the nearest shore—especially when I'm onboard a crewed yacht with a deckhand who will collect my camera and clothes from me on the beach and then have them waiting, dry and secure in my cabin, after I sidestroke my way to the yacht's swim platform.

In the same vein, while I think truly unique features like the arcade onboard the 173-foot motoryacht *Passion* are tremendously cool, I'm not a gamer. The ability to play *Golden Tee* is not going to entice me to pay more for a charter onboard that particular yacht because I would be just as happy with a less-expensive yacht carrying a few stacks of Texas Hold 'Em chips.

My PGA golf professional husband, though, would disagree. And you might, too.

Seasons and Events

Just as hotel rooms near Walt Disney World are most expensive during the weeks when children are on school vacations, yachts are most expensive during the weeks when demand for charters peak. The terms "high season" and "low season" describe the busiest and slowest booking times onboard yachts, but the terms are a bit misleading, because they tend to be periods of a few weeks instead of actual seasons, like the entirety of the winter.

"High season is the most in-demand dates," explains Jan Henry, a longtime crewed yacht charter broker in the Fort Lauderdale office of Fraser Yachts Worldwide. "For instance, if you're chartering in the Caribbean, it's Christmas/New Year's. In the Mediterranean, it's July and August, the Cannes Film Festival, and the Monaco Grand Prix. Low season would be anytime that it's not high season. The prices vary from owner to owner, but high season could be anywhere from 15 percent to as much as 30 percent more. It all depends on the yacht's owner and what he believes he can charge."

If you're used to booking cruise ship vacations, you might think it worthwhile to wait for a last-minute deal to try to avoid high-season prices. Sometimes that works, but most reputable brokers advise against it.

"If you wait until the last minute, you may get a good deal, but not on the best boats," Henry says. "In high season, people sometimes wait until the bitter end, but I don't recommend it. Then you're left with the boats that nobody else wanted."

My advice regarding high seasons and special events is this: Unless you really want to be at a certain place at a certain time, skip the "best weeks of the year" and book your charter right before or after them. Your odds of having good weather are almost identical, the local shops and restaurants will usually still be open, and you're likely to miss out on all of the crowds that drove you to consider a private yacht charter in the first place.

Multi-Week Charters

You can sometimes lower your weekly charter rate by booking more than one week in a row. This holds true for bareboats and crewed yachts alike—depending on the company or yacht owner involved.

A lot of first-time charter guests are nervous about booking more than one week on a yacht, but it's not necessarily a bad idea, especially if you're flying to a far-off location and can take two weeks instead of one to relax. Many top-dollar charter guests who have cruised onboard yachts before book them for a month or two at a time during their vacations.

"Typically, you get some kind of a break on a multi-week charter," says Louise Dailey of Jubilee Yacht Charters in Osprey, Florida. "A lot of it depends on the season and how busy the yacht is. If it's off-season, you can negotiate a better rate. If you're in the Virgin Islands and the boat has a charter coming up in St. Maarten, you could get a break on a second week that would help to reposition the yacht [by cruising to that destination instead of back to where you started]. The boat's got to go that way anyway."

Similarly, if you were the charter client who had the booking coming up in St. Maarten and were willing to book an extra week's stay onboard, you might get the yacht's owner to lower or even eliminate the repositioning fee. If you're booking more than just a single week of charter, you have a negotiating tool. The yacht owner will now gain two, three, four, or more weeks of charter business by moving his boat to your port of choice—and he may be willing to shoulder the repositioning costs himself if he stands to earn enough weekly charter income after the yacht is moved.

Again, this is where a good charter broker can be invaluable. She will know which owners are typically willing to negotiate these kinds of deals, as well as what fees they have compromised on with other clients in the past.

Owners' Whims

At the base of all these tidbits and tips lies the fact that the yacht's owner controls its weekly charter rate. Yes, in the case of fully crewed charters, he may take advice from a management company about pricing his yacht competitively, but the bottom line is that the boat's owner can do whatever he wants, whenever he wants in terms of the weekly charter rate.

This is a gray area of the fully crewed charter business that many brokers don't like to discuss, simply because negotiating with an owner is not always possible. In fact, it's probably closer to being a rare occurrence than a common one, but I know that it happens because I have had yacht owners and their captains tell me directly that their fully crewed yacht's weekly rate was negotiable—especially when the yacht's owner was an American.

American owners, you see, tend to think of yacht charter as more of a business when compared with European yacht owners. The latter are not typically as consumed with making a buck as the Americans tend to be, and thus could care less about negotiating with a charter client. A European owner's rate for a fully crewed charter is typically the rate you will pay, no matter who you are or what deal you offer.

Sometimes, though, you can find wiggle room with the American owners. One, a California entrepreneur who owns a 94-foot motoryacht, explained his thinking to me this way: "I don't want to be the guy with the highest charter price. I'm in the industrial real estate industry. I'd rather have my buildings rented at a low rent than go have to find a special tenant who'll pay the highest rent, but have the building vacant for two months. I look at the boat the same way. I've priced it very reasonably for what it has, and people will know they're getting a deal. It's a business. You've got expenses, depreciation, repairs—but not a lot of income. Still, you have to run it like a business."

Good charter brokers will know which fully crewed yacht owners think in these terms, yet another reason to consult with a knowledgeable expert before booking your vacation.

Whatever You Desire

The point of all of this is that when you compare the price of one 65-foot yacht with the price of another 65-foot yacht, you need to consider exactly what is included in that price. Crew-to-guest ratios, special amenities and features, location, time of year—all of it will affect the vacation that you end up getting for your money.

Yes, yachts of similar size and style are likely to be priced in the same range. But don't make the mistake of simply choosing the least-expensive boat you are offered in a given destination.

Whether you're considering a bareboat or a fully crewed yacht, you must take every detail of the charter agreement into account. Even something as seemingly minute as different pickup and drop-off times might sway you from one yacht toward another. Sometimes, factors you never even imagined will become primary in your thinking.

"When I'm helping clients narrow their choices down, I focus on amenities and crew personalities," explains crewed yacht charter broker Barbara Stork, who works with The Sacks Group in Fort Lauderdale. "What the charter client likes to do, whether they have children, what their expectations are, if there are four or five boats that are similar and in the same price range, you go with the amenities and the crew that go with their personalities and what they like to do. For instance, I get to know the yacht owners, too, because if they have children, their yacht is going to have a kid-friendly crew.

"When it comes down to two or three really similar boats," she adds, "it usually comes down to price or personal taste on décor. You might want a more modern-looking interior or a more classic interior."

The point is that price does matter—but it's not the only thing that matters. Keep that in mind as you consider the following price ranges for different styles of charter yachts.

General Pricing Guidelines

Even given all of the variables outlined in this chapter, you can put a general dollar figure on prices for different sizes and styles of boats. For the most part, yachts are marketed with *base rates*—which include only the yacht and crew, if one exists. Extra fees will apply, including food, alcohol, fuel, marina dockage, and crew tip, all of which can add one quarter or even one half again to the total cost of a charter.

A handful of yachts are beginning to offer inclusive rates, which factor in some or all of the variable fees that you're likely to encounter. There is no consensus among bareboat fleet owners and fully crewed charter brokers about whether inclusive or base rates are the most cost-effective for you as the guest, so you'll have to do your own math and try to determine what makes the most sense on your particular itinerary.

In my opinion, inclusive rates certainly make comparing prices easier, especially when you're looking at a private yacht charter versus a cruise ship trip. However, inclusive rates also eliminate one of the key benefits that draw people to yacht charter in the first place: personal choice. If you want to be able to do whatever you choose on the water, it's sometimes worth it to forgo an inclusive fee and simply pay your way as you go onboard the perfect charter yacht for your needs.

Also, when considering the following prices, remember that charter yachts offer weekly rates. These rates are for the entire yacht—there are no by-the-cabin bookings. In some cases, a yacht's fee may be lower if you use only two or three of the five guest cabins onboard, but in many cases, you will be booking an entire yacht at its regular weekly rate no matter how many people you plan to bring onboard.

Bareboat companies will sometimes list per-person prices, to help you figure out how much you're spending on each member of your family or group. However, with most bareboats and crewed yachts, you will need to divide the weekly rate by the number of people in your charter party to determine how much each yacht will cost, per person.

Last, if you're considering booking a yacht of any kind through a charter broker, remember that the yacht's owner pays the broker's commission, not you. It's a cost you do not need to factor in, for a service you should not go without.

Following are general base rates that you can expect to find for different categories of charter yachts. Remember, there are a lot of variables and, usually, additional costs. Use the prices listed in the following pages only as guidelines for your planning purposes. I've chosen these particular companies and boats because they are typical of what you will find across the board and because I know these companies to be reputable based on my personal experiences.

Bareboat Sailboat Rates

For the sake of easy comparisons, the following prices are for bareboat sailboats offered by Sunsail, one of the world's largest companies with bases from the Americas to the South Pacific and Thailand.

An Oceanis 373 (which is 36 feet long and carries up to eight guests) charters for $4,410 per week during high season and $2,100 per week during low season from the Southern Caribbean base of St. Vincent.

The slightly larger Oceanis 393 sailboat (which also carries up to eight guests) charters for $3,360 per week during high season and $2,170 per week during low season from the Australian base in the Whitsunday Islands.

That same Oceanis 393 charters for $3,290 per week during high season and $2,170 per week during low season when chartered from one of Sunsail's two bases in Greece.

The larger Beneteau 50 (which carries as many as 12 guests) charters for $9,310 per week during high season and $4,760 per week during low season from the St. Vincent base.

That same Beneteau 50, carrying 12 guests, charters for $5,600 per week during high season and $4,760 per week during low season from the Whitsunday Islands base off Australia.

A slightly larger Beneteau 523 that carries the same 12 guests charters for $8,190 per week during high season and $5,250 per week during low season from one of Sunsail's bases in Greece.

Bareboat Powerboat Rates

Again, for the sake of easy comparisons, the following bareboat powerboat prices are all from Virgin Traders, which offers bareboat and crewed powerboats in the Virgin Islands. The company's base is in Tortola, so that is where your charter will start and end.

A Virgin Trader 44 trawler yacht that sleeps seven people and cruises at 10 knots charters for $6,600 per week during high season and $4,950 during low season.

The Horizon 48 is four feet longer than the Virgin Trader 44, but the Horizon sleeps only six people—each in a cabin with a double or queen bed and its own bathroom, which is ideal for three couples splitting the charter rate equally. The Horizon cruises a bit faster, too, at 15 knots. Its rate is $7,950 during high season and $6,215 during low season.

Among the largest in the Virgin Traders fleet of bareboat powerboats is the Horizon 56, which sleeps eight people in four cabins (three of which have their own bathrooms). All the cabins have double or queen-size beds, again a good feature for three or four couples splitting the charter bill. The yacht's speed is 15 knots. High season weekly rate is $9,240, while low season weekly rate is $8,085.

Bareboat Catamaran Rates

As you learned in Chapter Three, catamarans can be either sailboats or powerboats. The basic layout is the same onboard both styles of catamaran: One style has a sail on top of it and an auxiliary engine, while the other has bigger, more powerful engines and no sails at all. Still, prices tend to follow the general rule of power being more expensive than sail.

Sailing catamarans and powercats look a lot alike and often have identical interior layouts, but powercats usually charge higher rates.

For the sake of easy comparisons, the following prices are all taken from CharterWorld, a company that does not own the boats it markets, but that does have an excellent searchable database, *www.CharterWorld.com*, of boats drawn from many fleets.

A Lagoon 380 sailing catamaran (about 38 feet long) that carries eight guests and is based in the British Virgin Islands charters for an average weekly rate of $3,635.

A larger Leopard 4500 sailing catamaran that carries those same eight guests in more spacious accommodations is based in Antigua with an average weekly rate of $4,495 per week.

Back in the Virgin Islands, a Powercat 52 that carries as many as ten guests charters for an average weekly rate of $8,350.

Instructional Sailboat Rates

Offshore Sailing School offers its Fast Track to Cruising program in six locations: St. Petersburg, Fort Myers, and Captiva Island in Florida; The Florida Keys; Jersey City, New Jersey; and Tortola in the British Virgin Islands.

You need no prior sailing experience to enroll. After you complete the seven- to ten-day program (depending on how you choose to set up your lessons), you will be certified to operate a bareboat sailboat—and you will be entitled to a 15-percent discount on any sailboats you book through the school's partner company, The Moorings.

The cost for the Fast Track to Cruising program depends on where you take the class and what season you choose to cruise.

Least expensive is the course in New Jersey, which is $1,790 for seven days total. That cost is tuition-only, so you either sleep at home at night or book a hotel separately. You also pay for all your own meals at restaurants or in brown bags that you take from home.

The most expensive, high-season course through Offshore Sailing School is in Tortola, which costs $4,550 for ten days total. That price includes all your meals and a liveaboard cabin based on double occupancy. If you want a cabin to yourself, single supplements will raise your rate to $5,195.

Instructional Powerboat Rates

Florida Sailing and Cruising School offers powerboat instruction in partnership with Southwest Florida Yachts, a bareboat company based in Fort Myers. You take back-to-back "Basic Handling" and "Inland Cruising" courses during a seven-day period, after which you are certified to charter a bareboat powerboat—and entitled to receive a one-time, ten-percent discount on a weeklong charter with Southwest Florida Yachts.

The cost of the weeklong, combination course package is $1,795 per person onboard a 32-foot yacht; $1,895 per person onboard a 36-foot yacht; and $2,095 per person onboard yachts up to 42 feet long.

Prices include your accommodations onboard the yacht, your instructor and course materials fee, and fuel for the boat. Meals are extra. If you want to take along a spouse or child who does not want to learn, but who wants to stay onboard the yacht, the cost is half the regular price.

Crewed Sailboats to 80 Feet

Typically, sailing yachts available for crewed charter start around 40 to 45 feet long. At that small end of the range, from about 45 feet to about 55 feet, you're likely to find yachts that carry two to four guests at prices ranging from $4,500 per week to as much as $15,000 per week (with the latter being all inclusive).

Slightly larger yachts in the 60- to 80-foot range that carry as many as six guests typically start around $7,500 per week and run as high as $35,000 per week (with the latter being all inclusive).

Eighty-foot sailing catamarans can carry as many as 12 guests (versus the six or eight onboard same-size monohull sailing yachts). Those yachts tend to start around $20,000 per week and can hit the $35,000 all-inclusive mark as well.

Crewed Sailing Yachts 80 Feet and Larger

Monohull sailing yachts in the 80- to 95-foot range typically carry six or eight guests, though you can find similar-length sailing catamarans that hold ten or 12 guests at a time. In general, the price for yachts in this size range is from $20,000 to $45,000 per week.

You'll be able to get eight or ten guests onboard monohull sailing yachts that are 100 to 125 feet long, at base rates ranging from $40,000 to $70,000 per week.

Above 125 feet long, you get into the big-money sailing yacht charters. These boats are typically in the $125,000 to $150,000 range and carry ten or 12 guests, with the world's largest sailing sloop, the 245-foot-long *Mirabella V*, taking 12 guests a week at a whopping low-season weekly rate of $275,000.

Crewed Powerboats to 80 Feet

Crewed powerboats typically start around 50 or 60 feet long. At that lower end of the range, say from 50 to 70 feet, you can usually fit six guests comfortably onboard. The base rates range from about $14,000 to about $25,000.

Onboard crewed powerboats from 70 to 80 feet long, you will be able to bring six or sometimes eight guests—though one couple's cabin may have twin beds and a bathroom shared with another cabin. Base rates for this size yacht range from about $20,000 a week to about $30,000 a week.

Crewed Megayachts 80 Feet and Larger

This is the most expensive category of charter yacht in the world. For yachts in the 80- to 100-foot range, you're likely to get eight guests, maximum, onboard. The base rates can be anywhere from $25,000 to $50,000 per week.

Megayachts from 100 to 150 feet long are the heart of this segment of the market, carrying anywhere from eight to 12 guests at a time. Each cabin has its own bathroom—and many of those bathrooms are as big as some cabins onboard smaller powerboats. Prices trend from about $25,000 a week all the way up to about $165,000 per week.

At the top of the charter scale are megayachts 150 feet and larger. These are your highest-dollar, highest-glamour boats, and you will pay for the privilege of climbing onboard them. Base rates typically start around $120,000 per week, with one of the world's most expensive 12-guest motoryachts—the 228-foot *Floridian* (owned by Wayne Huizenga, who started Blockbuster Video and now owns the Miami Dolphins)—chartering for a base rate of $400,000 per week. For those of you doing the math at home, that's more than $33,000 per person for the week, even before expenses like food and fuel are added.

The super-size megayachts that you read about in Chapter Three are a breed unto themselves, usually chartered only by corporations or royal families that have 25 to 35 guests in their vacationing party. The prices for those yachts start around $350,000 per week and can rise to well more than $1 million per seven-day journey when expenses are included in the bill.

Adding It All Up

Once you have chosen a size and style of yacht that you like, selected a destination where you want to cruise, and gotten an idea of the price range that fits your budget, your next step is to consider exactly who will be traveling with you—and how different people in your group may be more comfortable onboard some yachts more so than others.

Charter brokers refer to this as determining the *complexion* of your charter party. One couple traveling alone may think they will be happy onboard the same yacht that a large family with several small children finds attractive, but in most cases, two different kinds of yachts will do a far better job of serving the two different kinds of traveling groups.

In Chapter Nine, you'll learn how certain yachts are ideal for certain groups of vacationers—and how you can match the right yacht to your own charter party's complexion.

9

Your Charter Party

Your charter party's *complexion*, as brokers call it, will have a lot to do with the charter yacht vacation you ultimately choose. Who is traveling with you is one factor over which you have complete control—and you should think through your guest list *thoroughly* before sending out those invitations.

Unlike onboard cruise ships, you will never be 12 decks away from the guests you invite along with you for a private yacht charter. The total space onboard yachts—even the world's largest—is by sheer physics far smaller than the total space onboard cruise ships. You'll typically dine as a group at every meal, for instance: three times a day for seven days or longer. You'll be riding in the dinghy together more often than not, and you'll rarely be sunbathing alone.

Yes, you will be able to find quiet nooks for getting away, reading a book, and stealing solitary moments—especially onboard the larger, crewed yachts—but if you want to make sure everyone in your group stays happy in tighter-than-usual quarters, it pays to compare different yachts' arrangement plans with specific guests in mind.

For instance, if you are traveling with three other couples who all want to split the week's cost equally, you can save yourself from squabbling by looking for a yacht that has four equally, or almost equally, sized cabins—each with an en suite bathroom. On the other hand, if you are grandparents treating your children and grandchildren to a charter, nobody is likely to argue about you selecting a yacht with a super-deluxe master stateroom for yourselves. What they may complain about, though, is having children placed in cabins with double or queen-size beds. For kids, you should look for cabins that have twin-size mattresses and even Pullmans.

When you travel with a small group of family or friends onboard a private yacht, nobody should be thinking about who has the better stateroom or who has to share a bathroom—but we all know what goes through certain people's minds (especially chronically complaining in-laws). It's best to head those kinds of problems off before they have a chance to fester, out at sea, where there are very few witnesses…

Seriously, professional charter brokers have good ideas about what features and amenities you should look for when planning for charter parties with different complexions. Most of these suggestions apply to sailing and power-driven yachts, bareboat and crewed alike.

One Couple Traveling Alone

When your only travel companion is your significant other, you have a real advantage. You know each other's habits, you know each other's preferences, and you can choose a yacht with all of them in mind.

For instance, if you're taking your honeymoon, you can focus on finding a yacht that has romantic little design features—like tables for two on deck, where you can enjoy champagne at sunset in a quiet harbor. On the other hand, if you're a couple seeking adventure along the lines of fishing and scuba diving, you can look for a yacht that carries a fighting chair and a dive compressor.

"A lot of it depends on how much open sea you're going to be crossing," explains Gina Robertson, a charter broker with YachtStore in Fort Lauderdale, Florida. "I'd recommend a larger boat for crossing longer passages, but if you're just gunkholing around a couple of islands, a smaller boat would do. The minimum size sailboat would be about 40 feet, for a powerboat, about 50 feet. That way, there's still room for a crew and toys onboard. And you'll want a really good master cabin. The other cabins don't matter now. You can use them to store luggage."

If you're a single couple traveling alone but are willing to pay extra for the feeling of having a bit more space onboard, consider chartering a yacht that typically carries six or eight guests, tops. Any yacht larger than that is likely to be overkill, unless you're a mogul trying to impress a Hollywood starlet.

"You can even negotiate a lower rate sometimes," Robertson says of couples booking larger yachts for charter. "Most people want to max out a boat. That's the tendency. If the boat takes eight guests, they bring eight. But if it really only will be two people, and we put that in the contract and you're bound to that, a lot of times the owner will knock off ten or 20 percent.

"The smaller the boat, too, the more likely it is that you're going to get an all-inclusive rate," she continues. "Those are tiered anyway, for two, four, or six people. So if they don't have a tiered rate [on the yacht you prefer], we can make one up based on what other, similar boats are doing. I hardly ever get a no. They want the business."

Group of Single Friends

The most important design element for groups of single friends to look for is a yacht with multiple cabins that have twin beds and Pullman berths. Most adults do not like to sleep together unless they are a couple.

"Twin beds aren't en vogue except in pricier boats," explains longtime broker Ann-Wallis White, who owns Ann-Wallis White Charter Yacht Consultants in Annapolis, Maryland. "The average 65- to 90-foot European-owned boat is much more suitable for a bunch of singles because it has a big cabin for daddy bear and then a bunch of baby bear cabins. The boats that have a lot of single beds tend to have been built for European owners, and there are some great cabins with singles. Or, if you only have four people, you can book a 50-foot catamaran, and everybody will have a cabin all to themselves."

White also recommends taking the crew's personalities into account for singles charters, say, if you're a group of female friends cruising together.

"You have to choose a crew that isn't gender biased," she says. "I would have to choose a captain that liked and respected his wife. There are different kinds of guys. Who wants to be on vacation with a guy who's rude to his wife if she's the chef, or looking at you funny?"

Couples Splitting the Bill

As I mentioned earlier in this chapter, couples splitting a yacht vacation's bill equally will want to feel like they are getting similar accommodations for their money. It's virtually impossible to find a yacht outfitted with cabins that are 100 percent identical; in fact, there is a need for more crewed yachts with more equally sized accommodations.

Still, there are some yachts out there where the differences are small enough to be overlooked. "Sometimes, one couple will have a bathtub when another has a shower, but I try to find boats where nobody feels like they're getting the short end of the stick," explains Liz Howard, who became a crewed yacht charter broker in the San Diego office of Fraser Yachts Worldwide after spending a decade working as a chief stewardess onboard boats. "I also try to meet with as many of the couples as I can, so that I can get to know them a little bit. First-time charterers, especially, they have no idea what to expect, and quite honestly, I need to *earn* my commission. With a good broker, it's a lot more than just signing a contract and walking away. I find that meeting with all the couples helps me to understand their personalities better, and then I can put them onto the right kind of boat with the right kind of crew."

Interestingly, I've found that classic yachts tend to have more equally sized staterooms than newer ones, perhaps because the standards of luxury have risen in recent decades and today's yacht owners want super-deluxe grand master suites for themselves. Still, there are new charter yachts with similarly sized cabins out there, especially onboard bareboat and crewed catamarans where all the guest staterooms are inside the yacht's pontoons.

One last detail to consider for couples splitting the bill: Count the number of chairs at the dining tables drawn on the yacht's accommodations plan. Some yachts sleep eight people comfortably, but fit only six people comfortably in the main eating area. If you're all paying the same amount, you don't want to feel like you're squishing in at the kiddie end of the dinner spread.

Families With Children

The aforementioned twin beds are one thing to look for when chartering a yacht with small children in mind, but even more so than that, you need to look for a yacht that is receptive to allowing children onboard in the first place. With bareboats, you can take whomever you like, as long as your contract does not prohibit children younger than certain ages. With fully crewed yachts, though, the option of taking small children may be nonexistent.

"If the owner and the captain say no children under 13 years of age—and most of them say that—sometimes, that's the way it is," explains Sandy Taylor, a Fort Lauderdale-based broker with Northrop and Johnson who specializes in fully crewed yachts. "The crew aren't baby-sitters. They have jobs to do. Important jobs. But sometimes, if you bring a nanny, there are some boats you can work with, and there are some crew that absolutely love children. That's what a charter broker has to know, the right boat that's kid-friendly.

"Some cabins have nanny beds," Taylor continues. "It could be a twin bed in the same room as the kid, or a smaller bed next to a larger bed. There are boats that are set up for that, and if they are, the owner probably has kids, which means it's going to be a safe and friendly boat for children, with a crew that likes children."

In terms of safety, yachts that are better for children tend to have higher side and bow rails, easy-to-navigate staircases, and swim platforms that can be closed off from the main deck when the yacht is underway (so that nobody wanders down to them and falls overboard).

In terms of fun, crew who are good with kids are a must. A good broker can tell you which crew really go out of their way to set up games and put together theme nights for the children to enjoy.

Pirate night is one example of a favorite theme onboard many crewed charter yachts, and kids tend to love it. Capt. Russ White and chief stewardess Lisa Reedy onboard the 120-foot *Kayana*, for instance, went so far as to "find" a treasure map floating in a bottle near the yacht's swim platform when their youngest guests were preparing for a dip in the water. They used the yacht's dinghy to help the kids follow the map to an onshore cave, where they had stashed a treasure chest filled with candy, toys and keepsake *Kayana* T-shirts.

Giving pirate night a different spin, Capt. Dave Laird and chief stewardess Soni Ricci planned a pirate night that actually began in the morning for their young guests onboard the 85-foot motoryacht *Princess Marcie*. First mate Raul Valdivia cruised by the yacht's aft deck, where the children were trying to decide what water sports to enjoy that afternoon, and shouted to them from the dinghy: "That other boat, up there, the crew told me they just saw some pirates!" The crew continued to build the kids' anticipation until that evening, when Ricci decorated the entire main deck with treasure chests, skulls and crossbones, and the like. Each crewmember arrived to serve dinner dressed in tattered T-shirts, black eye patches, and pirate bandanas; music straight out of Disney's *Pirates of the Caribbean* played over the sound system; and Ricci had painted "tattoos" on every crewmember's biceps and faces (she later offered to paint tattoos on the kids as well).

The scene was so realistic that it even got the attention of children aboard another yacht. "We were stem-to-stern at the marina with another boat, and it had four or five kids on it, and they were all on their aft deck, gripping the rail and looking over here," Valdivia recalls. "You could see the want in their eyes. They were running to their parents screaming, 'There are *pirates* on that boat! *Real pirates!*'"

In addition to crew who are good with kids, you can also look for yacht design factors that will enhance the entire family's experience. Larger yachts, particularly power-driven megayachts, may have separate play areas for kids, but even onboard smaller motoryachts, you can often find a sky lounge—an upstairs saloon of sorts where the kids can play Nintendo while the adults are down one deck in the main saloon enjoying cocktails and jazz.

Some crew are better than others when it comes to creating theme nights. Here, the chef, mate, and stewardess onboard the 85-foot motoryacht *Princess Marcie* show their decked-out costumes for a typical "Pirate Night" extravaganza.

Another good feature to look for when chartering with children is smaller, separate dining areas. A sitting area originally designed for cocktails and hors d'oeuvres on deck, for instance, can be turned into a kids' table—or a teenagers' getaway from the adults, if you prefer to call it that—while adults eat in the main dining room.

Sugar Daddies

When you're paying for the yacht and taking family and friends along for the ride, the odds are that nobody will pipe up with an argument about you having better digs than they do. This is the time to go for the utmost style and comfort in a master stateroom—especially onboard the world's more expensive fully crewed yachts, where those cabins can be as extravagant as floating palaces. In many cases, they are full beam, meaning they take up the entire width, from one side of the yacht to the other.

"*Aurora*, a 163-foot Perini Navi, has an excellent master cabin for a sailing yacht," explains Barbara Dawson, a longtime crewed yacht charter broker who works in the Palm Beach, Florida, offices of Camper & Nicholsons International. "It is full width with a walkaround queen bed and a seating area, too. The sofa has a pullout and can be made into a double berth. The cabin can be subdivided into two private cabins with their own baths. This type of layout is perfect for a family with a small child or with extra staff."

In the power-driven megayacht world, Dawson is a fan of the master stateroom onboard *Excellence III*, a 187-footer that takes 12 guests at a base rate of $365,000 per week. I, too, found *Excellence III*'s master stateroom to be downright gorgeous when I was onboard a few years ago. It's on the yacht's main level, all the way forward for privacy, and includes a massive bed, sitting areas, and a his-and-her bathroom that was so big and beautiful, I'd have been happy sleeping inside of *it*.

These kinds of master staterooms typically dwarf the other cabins onboard most yachts, but that's not to say that your guests will be riding in steerage down below. The guest cabins of this caliber are far nicer than most cabins you'll find onboard cruise ships at any price—and even onboard the smallest bareboats, the cabins are generally as comfortable as inside cabins aboard cruise ships, albeit sometimes with shared bathrooms.

Onboard some partially and fully crewed motoryachts in the 70- to 80-foot range, if I were the sugar mommy footing the bill, I might even choose the VIP cabin instead of the master cabin, depending on how the yacht is laid out. In some cases on yachts this size, the master cabin is all the way forward in the boat's bow—with a spectacular view of whatever lies ahead outside the cabin windows—while the VIP is toward the middle of the yacht, known as *amidships*. In these cases, I always offer to take the VIP, because amidships is where you're likely to feel the least motion underway. The folks in the master all the way forward may have a bigger bed and a prettier view, but I tend to sleep better.

Business Groups

As with groups of single travelers, business groups and corporate charterers will want to look for yachts that have an abundance of twin beds. Unless you're inviting your business partners to take along their spouses, they're probably going to want a cabin—or at least a bed—to themselves.

There are other considerations for business travelers, too, including spaces where work can be done and meetings can be held. While only a handful of very large yachts have conference rooms onboard, you certainly can look for boats that have larger dining tables and outdoor seating areas, places where groups of people can spread out comfortably with printed materials and laptop computers.

Business groups don't always want to work underway; in fact, most corporate charters are simply about building relationships, says the affable Nick Trotter of Meridian Yacht Charters in Irvington, Virginia. He once spent more than a year organizing a corporate charter that a business owner gave to his favorite suppliers as a thank-you gift. The businessman chartered five yachts at once for an entire week in the Caribbean, and then invited the suppliers to take their spouses for a vacation they'd never forget—and that the suppliers would want to be invited on again by staying in the businessman's good graces.

"You would never see his company name on anything at all—no bags, no hats, nothing like that, which they thought was cool because it's very high class," Trotter recalls. "It was more about building relationships than promoting his product. This is invitation-only, and there is a business aspect to it. You have to be good enough to go."

A good broker in this situation will help you find yachts that are suitable for the charter's purpose as much as for the complexion of the group. "We've got another corporate group, for instance, and they're going out in the Med this summer," Trotter explains. "It's a bunch of people who don't know each other, bringing in customers. In that situation, we look for yachts that have layout versatility. We don't know what the makeup of the charter party will be, so we look for things like twin beds that can slide together to form doubles."

Onboard larger yachts, satellite communications should not be a problem. However, if you're considering a medium- or smaller-sized yacht for a business group, be sure to ask your charter broker about the Internet, satellite television and telephone capabilities.

Groups of More Than 12 People

Because of international regulations, most charter yachts can carry only 12 guests at a time. Yes, there are the super-size charter yachts that take upward of 30 guests, but they fall into a different category of construction codes than "regular" charter yachts. For the most part, if you're talking about a private yacht charter vacation, you're going to have no more than a dozen people onboard at any time.

So what do you do if your charter party contains more than 12 guests? You have two options: Book one of those super-size yachts, or work with your bareboat company or charter broker to organize more than one yacht at a time, in what is known as a *tandem charter*.

Tandem charters have their pros and cons. By definition, when you have two or three yachts cruising together, you are going to have two or three different onboard atmospheres—some that will be more appealing than others, and which can leave some guests feeling like they're onboard "the lesser yacht" in the group. Also, different yachts have different performance capabilities, meaning one might cruise faster or slower than another. The same goes for the kinds of toys onboard, the skill level of the chef, and the quality of service the crew can provide.

Many of these things are challenges that can be surmounted by a good charter broker, but the demand for better large-group options has led to a recent trend in building super-size yachts that can carry more guests onboard a single boat. One of the newest such launches is the 228-foot motoryacht *Sherakhan*, a project initiated by the owner of a "regular" yacht who saw the market for super-size charters growing faster than any other type of charter business.

Of course, there is a cost factor to booking a super-size charter yacht. *Sherakhan*, for instance, can accommodate 26 guests, but her base rate is just shy of $440,000 per week—which may be well more than even a few tandem yachts put together. Hence the continued appeal of tandem charters despite the challenges of finding several similarly outfitted yachts available at the same time.

If you find yourself weighing the costs of a super-size yacht versus a tandem charter, remember that with tandem charters, the owners of each yacht will be different people. Your broker will have to work overtime to even try to get a "group discount" for booking more than one yacht at a time—meaning that your overall costs may be nearly as high as if you'd simply booked the super-size yacht in the first place.

If you have a group larger than 12 guests, you can book a tandem charter, which means several yachts at a time. These two fully crewed yachts, *Katania* (left) and *Kayana* (right), are part of the CEO Expeditions fleet and together can take 16 guests.

Tips for Choosing Your Group

In many cases, you'll know who is going to be part of your charter party before you even start looking for a yacht to match your needs. If it's your immediate family, for instance, you can't very well take Dad and leave Mom home without hearing complaints during holiday dinners for years to come. Yet if you find yourself in the opposite situation—trying to decide which of your friends make the guest list and who stays home—there are some ways to make smart decisions.

I'll tell you straight up: I wouldn't take anybody with me on a charter yacht that I wouldn't have as an overnight guest in my home. Remember, you are going to be living with these people on this yacht for a week—and the yacht is going to be smaller than your house, in most cases. Friends who are especially needy, who demand to have things done their way and their way only, are going to grate on your nerves after about a half day on the water (and you can't just walk away across the ocean's surface to escape their presence). On that same note, a girlfriend who cannot fathom traveling without six full-size, hard-sided pieces of luggage is going to require an awful lot of space and accommodating onboard, at everyone else's expense.

Difficult relatives are a different sort of challenge, since you may have no choice but to invite them along. My advice in this situation is to be gracious about finding out what they want to do during the charter, and then make sure those activities are available on a nearly constant basis. If the relative in question is a shopaholic, for instance, you can ask the captain to forgo anchoring in secluded harbors and instead dock every afternoon at a marina in a town full of boutiques. Your shopaholic relative will then get off the boat and go do what she wants while you can enjoy the yacht in solitude for at least a few hours a day.

If you're splitting the price of the charter among couples, I'd also advise you to stick with couples who want to spend generally the same amount of money for the week. If you have four couples in total, and three out of the four have bigger vacation budgets, that fourth couple is going to feel an awful lot of stress about paying for the kind of yacht and provisions you might choose. This will come out on the boat, at some point, perhaps in the form of an argument. That's no way to spend your vacation.

More often than not, money will be a concern only when you're splitting the cost of the charter evenly among several couples. Typical problems come in other varieties and are more common than you may imagine.

Common Problems

The single problem that I hear about most often on yachts is drugs. In particular, teenagers with marijuana. While onboard cruise ships, the crew may overlook a group of 16-year-olds passing around a joint, on a charter yacht the consequences can be far more severe.

"Right in the contract that you sign, it says illegal drugs are just not tolerated," explains Sandy Carney, a terrific crewed yacht charter broker in Newport, Rhode Island, who works for Churchill Yacht Partners. "The charter will end, wherever you are, and you will not get your money back. You are off the boat and on your own. It's illegal for the crew and the guests to partake in any illegal drugs. If the captain catches you using something, he has the right to end the charter then and there and put you ashore, wherever you are. You have no recourse against the owner.

"I've only known of one instance in all my years where it happened," she recalls. "In that instance, the captain gave them a warning. He explained that he could lose his license, the boat could be seized by the Coast Guard—there are huge consequences. For the most part, if the crew find drugs while cleaning up the cabins, they'll throw it out. They won't say a word; it just won't be there when you get back to your cabin."

That level of intolerance for drugs exists onboard even the most luxurious megayachts in the world. Early in 2006, Microsoft cofounder Paul Allen—who owns the 303-foot power-driven *Tatoosh*—reportedly fired six crewmembers after they tested positive for drug use. This is a million-dollar-a-week charter yacht that has entertained the likes of Steven Spielberg, Bono, and Cameron Diaz. I've never heard of any of those celebrities using drugs onboard chartered yachts, but I have heard about others whose names you would know just as well—and not only were they booted off their very expensive charters mid-cruise without a refund, but were also blacklisted across the industry from ever chartering again.

Weapons are a less-common problem onboard charter yachts, simply because most families and friends don't carry them on vacation, but it's worth noting that guns and other threatening implements can bring your charter to an abrupt end, again without a refund. If you're arranging a charter to a sporting clays range or hunting facility, you can talk to the captain in advance about taking your unloaded shotguns or other sporting equipment onboard. Just be honest up front, and be sure you have all the correct permits for wherever you will be cruising.

Last, you will need to respect the rules that a handful of yachts have regarding red wine. When onboard carpets are brand-new and lightly colored, some yacht owners do not allow charter guests to drink red wine inside. Popping a merlot cork outside, where the decks are teak, is perfectly acceptable, but guests who've knocked back one too many glasses commonly try to wander inside, spilling and ruining the carpets.

Even if you offer to replace the stained flooring, you'll do the yacht little good—because the owner's cost is not just the new carpeting, but also the down time the yacht will have for the repair work and the charters it may have to cancel because of it. That can be tens or even hundreds of thousands of dollars.

Thus, if you find yourself onboard one of the few yachts with these red wine rules, follow them. It will save you much arguing and money in the long run.

Special Needs

As you think more and more about who will be a good fit for your charter party, you no doubt will come up with one or two people who have special needs. They may be diabetic, or cancer survivors who don't like the sun, or even family members who don't always get along. In some cases, you'll simply have too many people to fit onboard one single yacht, in which case you'll have to charter two or three at a time in a tandem situation.

All of these special considerations can be accommodated if you work with a good bareboat company or charter broker. The types of things you should bring to their attention during your vacation planning stages are discussed in further detail in Chapter Ten.

10

Special Considerations

Now that you've narrowed down your charter party and made sure you're selecting a yacht that will keep everyone generally comfortable, you need to consider which, if any, of your guests have special needs.

Special needs are not problems. Rather, they are any considerations that require particular attention from your bareboat company, charter broker, or yacht crew. A person who uses a wheelchair fits into this category, as does a couple celebrating their 50th wedding anniversary. In both cases—and in a host of others—you need to make your bareboat company, charter broker, or yacht crew aware that something about your charter is not standard. That way, they can make the necessary preparations, be it having an extra-wide *passarelle* (boarding ramp) or ordering an extra-special bottle of celebratory champagne.

Every industry expert I have talked with about special needs over the years says the same thing: They wish more people would speak up in advance.

Remember, the people running these yachts are not like the crew onboard cruise ships. Yachties consider themselves several steps above in terms of attitude and professionalism, and they want to provide you with a vacation experience to match. If you tell them beforehand that a member of your party is, for instance, diabetic, they'll go out of their way to make sure the galley is stocked with as many sugar-free treats as they can find. Yet if you wait until after you step onboard to bring up this medical condition—notifying the chef somewhere between far-flung islands in the middle of nowhere—the result will be a charter guest who may have to go without his sugar-free chocolate fix, not to mention a yacht chef who feels like a cad because he has no way to make his guest as happy as possible.

In addition to discussing any special needs in advance with your bareboat company or charter broker, you should make your wishes known in writing by filling out your *provisioning sheet* (in the case of bareboats) or your *preference sheet* (in the case of crewed yachts). These sheets are sent to you at least a few weeks in advance of your charter, and your job is to complete them in a timely manner—listing everything from what kind of food and wine you want stocked on the yacht to what kind of activities you are most eager to enjoy onboard.

Again, do not be shy when filling out these sheets. The worst things you can write are, "We'll do anything!" and "We love all kinds of food!" Of course you won't, and of course you don't. Think about the television show *Fear Factor*, and consider your written answers again.

In fact, what I typically do is fill out my preference sheet with explicit instructions regarding whatever fad diet I'm trying at the time—"Atkins-friendly meals only" and that sort of thing—and then call the charter broker to let her know I'm sending the completed sheet back to her, so the crew can start their provisioning. "By the way," I add toward the end of our conversation, "please note the special instructions that I wrote regarding my low-carb diet. I need the chef to keep that in mind during provisioning."

It never fails, and I'm never disappointed. You can enjoy the same 100-percent success rate by considering the suggestions in the rest of this chapter for handling different types of special needs.

Special Diets

Special diets are actually one of the easiest considerations to handle. If you're bareboating, you're in charge of your own food—and you know exactly what you can and cannot eat. If you're booking a crewed yacht, you'll probably be in even better shape, since you'll have a personal chef who will cook both your personal favorites and new recipes that suit your needs and tastes.

"When I started in this business 30 years ago, a cook was hired just walking down the dock in the Virgin Islands," recalls charter broker Beverly Parsons of San Diego-based Interpac Yachts. "The captains picked whoever was cute and hoped that they could put something decent on the table. Now, even on smaller yachts, most chefs can actually be called chefs. They're professionally trained at places like the Culinary Institute and Le Cordon Bleu, and clients are continually amazed at what comes out of these tiny little galleys.

"It would be misleading to say that every boat can serve several meals at each sitting, but more and more people are demanding it and getting it," she continues. "It's not always easy for the chef. On a small sailing yacht, for instance, we have to guide the charter client toward the right yacht. Yes, special diets are definitely doable. The broker just has to help you carefully pick the boat."

I've experienced this onboard several fully crewed charters, most memorably one in which a traveling companion was a vegetarian. In that case, onboard the 100-foot motoryacht *Melimar*, chef Felipe Cuellar prepared meals for the vegetarian woman that not only were different from the others served simultaneously at the table, but that looked the same, with similar-colored ingredients and presentation on the plate. Had I not known this woman was getting vegetarian meals prepared separately, I probably never would have noticed that they were different.

Even better, the woman had worried that Cuellar, like other chefs she had spoken with in the past, would try to serve her fish instead of beef—not realizing that fish, too, was a problem for her. Not so in this case. Cuellar created everything from tofu salads to pasta specialties that left her more than content while the rest of us enjoyed perfectly cooked chateaubriand in a morel-white truffle infusion sauce, oven-roasted quail with black bean, mango, and ginger salsa, and rack of lamb with sweet potato and asparagus in a red wine reduction.

Remember: Ask for what you want, and your broker will work to find it. Whether you have a sensitive palate or serious allergies to some foods, your provisioning and preference sheets are the place to make your needs clear.

Medical Concerns

One of the only things you will not have onboard a private yacht that you would have onboard a cruise ship is a dedicated medical facility. Notice I didn't say doctor—most cruise ships don't have those nowadays, either, relying instead on physician assistants and registered nurses who are not cruise line employees. But cruise ships do have infirmaries where you can receive care for your nicks, scrapes, and other minor medical problems, and that may even stock commonly requested prescription medicines. Private yachts, unless they are quite large, do not have such dedicated treatment facilities.

That's not to say there is a lack of medical care onboard yachts (unless you're bareboating). Crewed charter yacht captains and additional crewmembers are required to have training in basic first aid as well as a substantial first-aid kit stowed onboard. Longer-serving captains and crew, simply by the nature of their jobs, also have a general understanding of common medical concerns onboard yachts—painful sunburns, severe seasickness, scrapes from certain kinds of coral, skin allergies to tropical fruits like mangos, and the like.

"They do a special course for professional yachts-people, and if they don't do it, they don't get their [certification] papers renewed," explains Anne Sterringa, a charming crewed yacht charter broker with Camper & Nicholsons International in Palma de Mallorca, Spain. "It's part of international law, and they have to renew it every few years, always have it up to date. It's the same as what they have to do on passenger ships and cruise ships. The regulations are the same for the officers [onboard larger yachts].

"It's actually not just your normal first aid," she adds. "It goes a lot further. The captains must have it, and it comes with a complete medical kit that has to comply with international law, depending on how big the boat is. They're not doing surgery, but if there's a bad cut, they could probably stitch that together."

Medically trained crew also can keep an eye on any specific problems you make them aware of in advance, and even tailor your yacht's itinerary around special medical needs. If someone in your group has a heart condition, for instance, the captain can talk with you about setting an itinerary that focuses on leisurely beachfront strolls instead of serious inland hiking. That way, your guest with the heart condition won't feel like he's missing out on anything along the way.

Onboard the larger crewed yachts, there are sometimes additional medical options, as well. "Some boats have an online link with a medical service," Sterringa explains. "There are two or three of these services [worldwide], and they stay in touch with the boat if the yacht's owner pays for it. You're in contact with doctors 24/7 in case somebody's worried about it, and they will explain what to do in real time in an emergency. All the specialties are available, depending on what the problem is, be it having a baby or being sick.

"It's available to every boat," she says, "but you need a reliable communication system, so that type of service ends up being [only] on the larger motoryachts and bigger sailing yachts."

No matter what combination of medical services are available onboard your chosen yacht, your best bet is to tell your charter broker in advance about any medical conditions you have—and then mention them on your preference sheet, as well. Also make sure you take your daily medications with you, along with inhalers, disposable contact lenses, and anything else you cannot replace without a doctor's prescription. Even less-significant items, such as a favorite pain reliever, will be difficult to find in some charter destinations.

After all, there are no pharmacies on windswept beaches or in bays full of icebergs.

Handicapped Accessibility

Most charter yachts—power or sail—are, unfortunately, difficult to get around for people who use crutches, canes, and wheelchairs. Since yachts are private vessels owned by private people, they do not have to adhere to the same standards of access that hotels and cruise ships acknowledge with specially outfitted bathrooms, elevators, and handrails. There is no Americans with Disabilities Act when it comes to people's private vacation boats.

Charter yachts are privately owned boats that do not have to offer handicapped accessibility. Here, guests board a dinghy for a shore excursion from the 120-foot motoryacht *Joanne*. Obviously, the walk down the stairs would be impossible for guests who use wheelchairs.

Additional challenges are created by any given yacht's motion underway. I have fully functioning legs and arms, and I use them all the time to help steady myself when I'm onboard a yacht that is moving through the water. Even long-serving crew do the same, almost unconsciously leaning up against walls and other fixed objects all day long to keep from swaying back and forth with the yacht's rolling, no matter how subtle that rolling may be.

Even at the top end of the price scale, with motoryachts that have elevators, it can be challenging to find handicapped-accessible yachts. A yacht sales broker once told me the story of a multimillionaire who lost the use of his legs to old age. He desperately wanted to continue yachting, but could not find a boat that had hallways, seating, and an elevator that were sized to suit his wheelchair. Then one day the sales broker took the man onboard the 153-foot motoryacht *Argyll*, which was built by North American Yachts and Shipbuilding as the first handicapped-accessible luxury yacht in the world. After a quick tour, the multimillionaire broke down in tears, pulled out his checkbook, and bought the yacht on the spot, still sitting in his wheelchair amid the freshly decorated Ralph Lauren décor.

If it's that hard to *buy* a yacht with handicapped accessibility, you can imagine how much harder it is to find one available for charter. *Argyll* is one of the half-dozen or so that I know of in the marketplace, with a charter rate of $125,000 per week, plus expenses, for ten guests (not exactly the bottom of the barrel in terms of pricing).

If you don't have that kind of financial reserve at your disposal, you'll have to take what little you are likely to find in terms of charter yachts with handicapped accessibility. My advice is to work with a good broker, who will know about any other yachts like *Argyll*, even on a smaller scale, that happen to find their way into charter.

Pets

I'm one of those weirdos who treats pets like kids. My hounds, Floyd and Stella, have the run of our home. I attended puppy kindergarten classes. I buy my dogs Christmas presents. I even call my neighbor regularly to ask if her golden retriever can come over for play dates in our back yard.

Like I said, I'm a pet fanatic—one of those people who has trouble leaving the dogs behind when it comes time to take a vacation. If a hotel says pets are welcome, I take 'em along. And if a yacht ever told me my pooches were welcome, I'd take them along with me there as well. Heck, Stella will hang her head out of anything that moves to get her ears flapping in the breeze. What better place for her than on the bow of a boat?

In my years of charter travel, though, I have yet to hear that offer from a charter yacht captain, bareboat or crewed. I do know of some partially crewed yachts that will allow small dogs onboard—and where the captains themselves have a small dog of their own living down below, in the crew's quarters—but for the most part, if you're used to traveling with pets, you're going to have to adjust to the idea of leaving them in a kennel before you book your private yacht charter.

There are a few exceptions out there, and a good charter broker can help you find those handful of pet-friendly yachts if you can't vacation without your favorite Fido. Just don't get your hopes up.

Sun vs. Shade

One of the things some people fear when first looking into private yacht charter is that they will be trapped outside in the sun all day—in places like the Caribbean, where that sun can be scorching to the skin. It's a valid concern, especially if you're fair-skinned, like me. I've succumbed to sun torchings so blazing hot that I feared they were first-degree burns.

Luckily, when it comes to yacht charter, you can put aside the fear of being fried. Bareboats and crewed yachts alike come in different shapes and sizes, but they all have some sort of interior gathering area where you can sit comfortably out of the sun, often in air conditioning. Most charter yachts also have shaded outdoor areas where you can enjoy the fresh breeze without barbecuing your skin.

You can look for shade-making features on the accommodations plans of charter yachts you are considering. Some have permanent *biminis*, which are overhead sun shades, while others have retractable biminis that the crew will arrange however you wish from day to day. Onboard larger yachts, you may also find small tables with umbrellas (that typically go up only at anchor, so they don't blow away). Any motoryacht larger than about 80 feet long is also likely to have at least a partially covered aft deck, meaning that the top deck of the yacht hangs over the back end of the main deck, creating a shady area for sitting and sometimes dining.

If you're bareboating, be sure to take along plenty of SPF 30 or higher just in case your shady areas get too crowded by other guests in your party. Onboard crewed charter yachts, a variety of suntan lotions will usually be available for you to use, along with aloe creams should your skin protection fall short. Larger crewed yachts that boast a lot of watersports equipment sometimes also have lightweight wetsuits called rash guards or skins that you can wear without feeling hot or uncomfortable in the water. If you're bareboating, you can pick up one of these lightweight skins for less than $50 at many sporting-goods stores. I wear them even when I'm just swimming in tropical charter climates, where severe sunburn can start after less than ten minutes of exposure.

Scuba Diving

Plenty of yacht owners use their boats for scuba diving, but few allow charter guests, even certified ones, to dive directly from the yacht. The issue is liability and insurance rates, and most yacht owners choose to save themselves money and aggravation by instead offering less-expensive, less-dangerous activities like kayaking and water skiing.

If you're a diver and you're bareboating, you can always rent your own tanks and weights from a local dive company and then do whatever you want during your charter—unless expressly prohibited in your bareboat contract. But onboard crewed charter yachts, you almost always will be forced to go *rendezvous diving*, as it's known, with a local company that your yacht captain knows.

I'm a certified diver and have done plenty of rendezvous diving from charter yachts, never with even the hint of a problem. In most cases, the dive company came right out to the yacht to pick me up, and later dropped me off on the yacht's swim platform after our dives were done. Once or twice, my yacht's captain has taken me in the boat's dinghy to meet the dive operator, and then returned to pick me up at the operator's base even before the day's diving was over. When my group wanted to be the only ones with the dive operator for the day, the captain arranged it, no questions asked. The bill can simply be added to the overall yacht charter tab.

Only two or three times have I ever been allowed to dive right off the back of the yacht—and I'll admit, it's pretty cool. No gear to lug, no wait to take a hot shower, and, usually, snacks out and waiting upon my post-dive arrival. One yacht I was onboard even had an owner who was very into diving, and he installed underwater flood lights that lit up the sea for diving day or night. Tremendously cool stuff.

The upshot is that if you're bareboating, you may be able to dive right from your yacht, but onboard crewed charter yachts, you should not expect that privilege.

However, if your broker can find a yacht that takes divers, by all means go for it. It's like being onboard a liveaboard dive cruise, only with the diving being just one of many activities available upon your command.

Golf

One of the reasons my husband doesn't enjoy yacht charters as much as I do is that he's a golfing fanatic (an actual PGA professional). If he has to go for more than a week without seeing a green or a tee, he practically breaks down into convulsions.

Unfortunately, most of the places I visit onboard charter yachts—the tips of icebergs, uninhabited islands, quaint fishing villages—simply don't have 18 holes anywhere nearby. And I never ask to go anywhere that does, since I don't know a bogey from a Bacall.

That's not to say that you can't combine golf with a yacht charter, though, if smacking a ball around in the grass with a metal stick is one of your favorite vacation activities. In fact, if you plan for golfing in advance, you can enjoy an entire itinerary wrapped around long drives and short putts. Bareboat companies and crewed yacht captains know their local cruising grounds well and can point you toward the best courses on your route. Crewed yacht captains will schedule tee times in advance for you, along with any lessons or equipment rentals you would like. Onboard mid-size and larger yachts, there is even stowage space for you to bring your own clubs.

Some yachts even promote golfing charters. The fully crewed 130-foot motor-yacht *Sacajawea*, for instance, issued a marketing flyer in spring 2006 through International Yacht Collection for a "Great Golf Getaway." The yacht was preparing to move from Hilton Head, North Carolina, up to Newport, Rhode Island, for the spring, and Capt. Mitch Mitchell had organized stops along the way at many of the East Coast's finest golf courses.

There's no reason you couldn't create a similar itinerary for yourself onboard a bareboat, depending on your charter location.

Birthdays and Anniversaries

Booking a private yacht charter vacation is an excellent way to celebrate a milestone. Whether you select a bareboat or a fully crewed yacht, you can have your closest friends and family around you in a fabulous destination that will make the event even more memorable for your scrapbooks and keepsake videos.

If you choose a bareboat, you'll need to do the party planning yourself. This includes everything from carrying hats and streamers in your suitcase to working with your bareboat company to find a good bakery near its marina base. Remember to take along candles for the cake, along with cards, gifts, and special brands of champagne if they're important to you. Especially if you plan to cruise the out-islands far from civilization, you'll have trouble finding any of the above after you arrive to meet your yacht.

Should you choose a crewed yacht for your milestone celebration, you need do nothing more than inform your charter broker about the special occasion. She will talk with the yacht's captain and crew about arranging a party to remember, allowing you to be involved as much or as little as you like.

I happened to turn 30 onboard the 171-foot motoryacht *Solemates*, somewhere off the Côte d'Azur. I was the only guest onboard for a short week's charter (I was working on a feature article for *Yachting* magazine), and the yacht's 13 crewmembers realized something was up when I started receiving a flood of e-mails from friends and family back home in the States. I admitted that it was my big 3-0 and told them not to worry about making a fuss. After all, it was only me onboard.

Like many charter yacht crews, though, they just couldn't help themselves. I returned to the yacht after a day of reporting and taking photographs onshore to find the dining area decorated floor-to-ceiling with Happy Birthday signs and balloons, as well as colorful beads, masks, and feather boas the crew had brought back from the annual carnival held in Venice. I'd actually thought something was wrong at first, since the crew put up signs directing me away from the dining area because they were "polishing the floors"—an unusual occurrence during a charter. But it was all a ruse, meant to hide the festivities until chef Thierry Molimard had finished baking me a lovely, personal cake of chocolate (my favorite!). The crew, at my insistence, even joined me in celebrating that night.

I can honestly say it was one of the most memorable milestones in my life, and I highly recommend asking your charter broker to help you arrange a party just like it to celebrate your own special occasion.

Weddings and Honeymoons

I hear about honeymoon charters fairly regularly, but not nearly as many wedding charters. The legalities of tying the knot in a foreign destination can be complex, but I still think chartering a yacht for a wedding ceremony and reception—perhaps followed by a private honeymoon cruise through the islands—is a fabulous idea.

You could easily hold the ceremony on the yacht's aft deck, with any spillover guests watching the vows being exchanged from a cocktail area set up on the dock. Then the crew could unveil a full-blown reception in the main gathering areas onboard, with guests able to move from room to room and from deck to deck as they please. At midnight, the party could end—with the newlyweds literally sailing off to begin their life together while friends and family waved from onshore.

Like I said, a fabulous idea, especially onboard the right kind of yacht. If it were my wedding budget, I'd spend it on a power-driven megayacht in the 150-foot range. It would have a large master stateroom where the bride could feel pampered as she dresses; a large aft deck that would simply drip with flowers during the ceremony itself; enough space inside the main saloon and on the upper decks for a terrific night of dancing and buffet dining; and a crew area that would allow enough room for additional caterers, florists, and wedding planners to do their work out of sight of the guests.

You would have to keep in mind that the yacht's charter fee would be in addition to the budget for your ceremony and reception, and you would have to limit your guest list to somewhere in the range of 100 people, since you would want friends and family to be able to move comfortably around the yacht during your reception. You also might have to take your legal vows back home at town hall before the big day, especially if you plan the yacht event in a nation where the marriage laws aren't what you want them to be.

Still, with land-based weddings running well into the six-figure range these days—and with the cost of the yacht charter including your honeymoon—it's truly a fabulous way to say "I do."

Family Bonding

Most of us take vacations in the first place because we need a bit of down time. In the case of families, we often equate that down time with a rekindling of relationships, a chance to spend "quality time" together away from the day-to-day hassles and headaches that drag on our nerves.

A yacht charter amplifies this quality time well more than a cruise ship vacation might, for the simple reason that all kinds of charter yachts are smaller than cruise ships. Your charter party, by the sheer fact of physics, will be spending more time together.

"My family chartered a sailboat when I was 12," recalls Katie Macpherson, an up-and-coming crewed yacht charter broker with International Yacht Collection in Fort Lauderdale, Florida. "It was a 78-footer, me and my parents, plus two younger brothers. We went cruising in the British Virgin Islands, and we met up with one of my friends who was with her family at the Bitter End Yacht Club. Instead of going onshore and eating meals, we ended up being on the boat the whole time. We used the water toys, we invited them for dinner, it was a controlled environment where we could goof off and have fun—all the kinds of stuff you couldn't do in a restaurant or even on a cruise ship. We made a swing off of the boom and would swing as high as we could and then jump into the water. It was just so much more than any vacation we ever went on. It was the one that really brought us together. It's an enclosed environment. It's so much more intimate.

"One of my clients, he and his family chartered last summer in the Mediterranean," she adds. "His son was about 19 or 20 and had done an exchange program in Italy, and the two younger ones were still in high school. It was a way to bring everyone together as a family before they each had to go their separate ways in life. When they come onto the boat, they can catch up and ride the Jet Skis and have meals together. That's what's missing from so many families today. They don't even make time to have dinner together anymore."

Ann-Wallis White, who owns her own agency in Annapolis, Maryland, has arranged similar family charters that left the parents delighted. "Once upon a time there were these two beautiful sisters, and Leslie the lump," she recalls. "They went on a charter on a 60-foot boat. The two sisters were luminary, good students, skinny—all those things people want other people to be. The crew kind of took pity on Leslie, who was dumpy and dopey. The chef never let anyone near her galley, but she let Leslie help her. The captain never let anybody drive the boat, but he took a shine to her, too. They let her do things they didn't even let the dad do. The father came up to me a year later and said, 'I just really wanted to thank you for the choice you made in terms of the crew. Those people really took a shine to our youngest, Leslie. The way that they related to her made us see her in a different light. She just blossomed. She turned into a near-Olympic class dinghy racer.'"

One fully crewed yacht captain once told me a story about a very wealthy man who arranged in advance to bring his family closer together. The man told the captain before the charter that his teenage sons had become difficult to control, and that no amount of money sent to boarding schools or boot camps was making a difference. He asked the captain to think about ways to help him use the charter time as a bonding experience.

The captain gave the matter a great deal of thought, and when the family arrived, he explained to the teenage boys that there was going to be a strength contest onshore. He drove them in the yacht's dinghy to a deserted beach, where the crew had left a large anchor in the sand with several lines (of rope) tied to it. The captain told the sons that the contest was to see who could drag that anchor farther down the beach, and that he wasn't taking them back to the yacht until somebody was declared the winner.

Well, the teenage sons pulled and pulled on that anchor until their palms swelled with pain, and by the time they got back to the yacht, their arms and legs were so exhausted that it was all they could do to lift their forks at dinner. The yacht's chef was in on the scheme to bring the father and boys closer together, too, and made sure to serve a seven-course meal that night with small bits of food on each plate that kept the boys hungry for more—and sitting at the table with their father. He, in turn, used the opportunity to have a serious conversation with them about their futures, and the boys were so physically beaten down that they actually listened. For hours.

Even if you have no yacht captain and crew to help you, yacht charter can be a great way to bring your family closer together. Bareboating is an especially good bonding experience for parents with teenagers—who typically like to do their own thing, but who will become so involved in helping to steer and navigate the yacht that they'll forget they're even doing so with their parents by their sides.

They will even feel a sense of empowerment if you let them act as captain for a leg of the journey, with you acting as their crew and taking orders the way they feel they have to every day of their lives. I'm not talking about orders like, "Scrub the deck, fish bait!" Instead, I'm talking about orders like "Trim the jib, I'm tacking to port"—orders that, when followed, show how family members can work together to accomplish anything.

Nude and Gay Charters

Some people book charter yachts for the express purpose of having a private environment in which they can be themselves. Nudists and gay groups can fall into these categories, and some yacht crews will cater to their needs better than others.

In at least one worldwide database that charter brokers use to keep track of bookings, there are special notations about whether the yacht's owner and crew are responsive to inquiries from nude and/or gay groups. Of course, you could argue that every yacht should be open to these kinds of charters, but so many of the highest-quality crewed boats are available that it's simply not worth wasting your breath. And if you're bareboating, you obviously can do whatever you want onboard while wearing as much or as little clothing as you like.

A good charter broker can tell you which yachts, crews, and bareboat companies are likely to make you feel the most comfortable in any given scenario, and you will have plenty of options to choose among in virtually every case.

Extended Charters

If you want to charter a yacht for more than a week, special preparations will need to be taken into consideration. Charters of two to three weeks are fairly common occurrences, but extended charters like the 'round-the-world versions mentioned in Chapter One require months and sometimes years of advance planning.

You can't just pick up a phone and have a charter broker book you a year-long charter. She will need time to negotiate and plan with the boat's owner, captain, and crew.

"For us, it was realistically almost a year of planning for a 13-month charter," explains crewed yacht broker Debra Blackburn of Fraser Yachts Worldwide, regarding the 108-foot motoryacht "charter-around-the-world" that I mentioned in Chapter One. "It took me about six months just to find a boat—that's the biggest factor, finding a boat that's willing to make itself available for that length of time. Not only is the yacht owner not going to have any other charters during that time, he's also not going to be able to use his own yacht."

To Blackburn's thinking, any charter longer than about eight weeks requires extra time and planning, and the associated extra effort on the broker's part. Charters that are two or three weeks long, while once considered extended, are becoming easier and easier to arrange.

"These days, it's getting to the point where people are booking Mediterranean yachts for six to eight weeks," Blackburn says. "That's becoming almost common. I'd say anything two months or longer, in terms of a charter, would fit the extended category."

Surf and Turfs

Surf and turf is the nickname used in the industry for vacations that are split time-wise, half on a yacht and half in a land-based hotel or private villa. They're an excellent idea for first-time charter guests who aren't sure how much they will enjoy being onboard a yacht, but who know for sure that they want to give the experience a try.

You can arrange a surf and turf yourself if you're bareboating, simply by asking your bareboat company which local hotels and resorts are the best. In some cases, you will have waterfront options very close to the company's marina base, while at other times you may want to arrange a rental car or taxicab to take you inland for the second half of your vacation. The advance planning is important in terms of reservations, because it can be challenging to coordinate check-in and check-out dates that correlate to the dates you can book onboard your chosen yacht.

The worldwide bareboating company Sunsail actually owns what it calls "sailing resorts," which are waterfront resort hotels that act as home bases for bareboat charters. You can spend some time on land with additional time at sea, or take an instructional charter while the non-sailors in your family stay onshore. There are currently five Sunsail sailing resorts in the Mediterranean (in Greece and Turkey), while the flagship sailing resort is on the Caribbean island Antigua. That resort, called Colonna, even offers several adults-only weeks every year.

If you're booking a crewed yacht, it pays to ask your charter broker which yacht owners also have private villas that they are willing to rent out as part of a vacation package. In some cases, yacht owners keep their boats at docks near their waterfront homes, which go just as unused as the boats themselves when the owners are back at home working. Sometimes you can get a package deal.

Of course, you can also ask your broker to pre-arrange a surf and turf that includes a resort, if that's the kind of vacation you prefer. Many resort destinations, like the popular Ocean Reef Club in Key Largo, Florida, have world-class marinas as well as fancy hotels, five-star restaurants, top-notch spas, and challenging golf courses. You could spend a few days or a week cruising the Florida Keys onboard your charter yacht, then have it drop you off at Ocean Reef on the day you check in for another few days or a week of vacation on land. You could even order the surf and turf at the restaurant one night, just for the insider's joke.

Your charter broker and captain will work together before your charter begins to ensure you can get appropriate dockage at the resort's marina, and to figure out whether any additional delivery fees will be due the yacht's owner for a drop-off point that may be far from the yacht's home base.

Ship-to-Shore Transfers

Just as with cruise ship vacations, you'll need a way to get from the airport to your yacht. You can of course book a regular flight on any commercial airline, coordinating your time of arrival with your bareboat or crewed yacht's departure. From the airport, you can either take a taxicab or, in the case of crewed yachts, await pickup in a private car or luxury van.

There are other options, though, especially in the Bahamas, Virgin Islands, and greater Caribbean, where small, chartered planes are fairly easy to come by. You can book them yourself, or have your charter broker make the reservations for you whether you're booking a bareboat or a crewed yacht.

Chartering a small, private plane may sound like an unnecessary additional cost, but in reality, if you're paying for six or eight commercial airline tickets—especially if you're flying first class—a chartered plane to and from the islands can cost about the same amount, or even less, especially from a major hub like Miami or Fort Lauderdale. And you will have the benefit of having your pickups and drop-offs with your yacht coordinated at whatever time you, your charter broker or your bareboat company chooses, in keeping with whatever itinerary you and your captain agree upon.

Again, it's all a matter of pre-charter coordination, just one more special consideration to take into account.

Preparing to Book

No matter how many, or how few, special considerations you have, they will affect your vacation—just like the size and style of your yacht, the general itinerary you select, and everything else you have learned thus far about private yacht charter. At this point, you have all the information you need to speak the same language as the experts in the charter industry.

If you're like most first-time charter guests, though, all of that newfound information can seem overwhelming. Creating a boating vacation "a la carte" can be quite challenging if you're used to simply picking a predetermined package from a cruise ship menu. In fact, even though no charter brokers will admit as much publicly, many say privately that one of the hardest parts of their job is helping people figure out exactly what they want. The endless options are sometimes paralyzing, especially if you haven't yet formed a crystal-clear picture of exactly what you desire.

This is the time when you may be tempted to pick up the phone and have a bareboat company or charter broker sort through the finer details for you. That's an option, of course, but if you truly want to set your own course, all you need are a few more tips and tools for zeroing in on exactly the right charter for you.

That's what Chapter Eleven will teach you: How to sift through your final choices so that even the most subtle of differences is perfect.

11

Choosing the Right Charter

By now, you probably have at least a hazy picture in your mind of what your perfect yacht charter vacation might include. For instance, you may be leaning toward a sailboat instead of a motoryacht to help keep your costs down. You probably know whom you intend to invite along, and thus what cabin styles would be ideal. You have a couple of special considerations to take into account, such as special diets and a birthday onboard. You may even have picked out a few islands that are must-sees on your wish list.

The challenge at this point becomes trying to choose exactly the perfect yacht from the available listings in a given destination. Whether you're still surfing the Web or you've already requested a few brochures from bareboat companies and charter brokers, you will likely have at least two or three—and maybe more than a half-dozen—yachts to choose among when it comes time to actually book. All of them will meet at least some of your major criteria, and in some cases, all of them will seem ideal.

So, how do you zero in on the best choice when you're so close that you can already feel the salt water on your skin? You start by using your new yacht charter vocabulary.

Accentuate the Positive

Think about what you knew of yacht charter before you started reading *Have the Whole Boat*. Not much, right? Maybe nothing at all?

You're not that person anymore. Yes, you may still feel like a novice wading through a murky sea of choices, but the truth is that if you've read this far, you know 99 percent more about private yacht charter vacations than 99 percent of the first-timers who book them.

That's not just lip service. Consider that you now have a general vocabulary to help you explain how one boat differs from the next, be it as basic as power versus sail or as specific as an express cruiser versus a trawler yacht. You understand the different kinds of charter, and you know whether you need just a skipper or a full crew. You realize that all yachts are built to suit the tastes of their owners, thus making each one full of unique features and cabin styles. You know that not all yachts cruise in all places, and that there are some locations where you will have more choices than others. You understand that prices are often more than they appear to be, depending on what kind of yacht you choose and how you decide to use it. You even know that the people you take along in your charter party will contribute far more to the overall tone and style of your vacation than they ever could on a cruise ship, especially if one or two of them have special needs.

The point is this: You know far more than you think you do about private yacht charter vacations. All you need to do now is simply get used to asking for what *you* want, instead of choosing from a list of prepackaged cruises that some big, world-wide company put together to appeal to the lowest common denominator.

If you're having trouble putting all of your new ideas together in your mind, you can put them together in ink. Start by taking a blank sheet of paper and writing the words "I think I would like…" at the top. Then, make a list of all the things you believe would contribute to your ideal yacht charter vacation—the little things you highlighted and circled in the previous chapters, the details you made notes about in this book's margins, and anything else that comes to mind.

Try to be as specific as possible. "I think I would like to have a fun vacation" isn't going to help you when it comes time to tell the bareboat company or charter broker what you want. "I think I would like to visit the island of Tortola onboard a sailing catamaran that sleeps three couples in queen-size beds and has a full crew" is a much, much better place to start.

Continue listing sentences along those lines until you've filled your sheet with everything you can think of, using all that you've learned thus far. "I think I would like to have a party one night to celebrate my wedding anniversary." "I think I would like to have a chef who knows the South Beach diet." "I think I would like a yacht that has kayaks onboard, and maybe Jet Skis, too, even though they're not as important to me." "I think I would like to spend $5,000 per person for the week, including all the extras like fuel, provisioning, and crew tip."

You can even write "I think I would like to charter one of the biggest, most luxurious, highest-quality brands of yacht in the world, and then take it to a place where I can show it off, no matter what it costs"—but make sure that you mean it. Remember, this exercise is not about creating a $1-million-a-week fantasy. It's about helping you to articulate your desires so that your bareboat company or charter broker can make your dream vacation a reality.

If you have found specific yachts online or in printed brochures that appeal to you, then you should make notes about them, too. "I think I would like the sailing yacht *Angel Glow* because the picture shows a hammock, and I like to read in the fresh air." "I think I would like the megayacht *Blue Harem* because it looks like it has a big, open deck, and I want to throw a birthday party during my charter." "I think I would like the powercat *Aquasition* because the picture of the cabins makes them look bigger than the cabins in other pictures I've seen."

You may not end up chartering any of these particular yachts, but being able to tell your bareboat company or charter broker exactly what you liked about each yacht will help them to find you similar, sometimes nearly identical, yachts that might be available in places where the pictured boats are not. It will also help them to understand the kind of charter vacation you are envisioning—and to suggest yachts that you can't find anywhere online, but that they've been aboard and know are far more likely to appeal to you.

After you've filled your entire sheet of paper, you'll have a pretty clear notion about what you think you want. Next, you need to rank those desires by importance, in case you have to compromise on one or two of your lesser wishes in order to get the ones that mean the most to you.

The High Five

No matter how many items you have on your "I think I would like" wish list, you'll probably have a little bit of trouble ranking them on a scale of one to ten (or on a scale of one to 30, depending on how many desires you listed). In some cases, one wish will be equally as important as the next. In other cases, you just won't know how important something is—like having a wakeboard available on the yacht—simply because you've never experienced one before.

In this case, you might find it helpful to place each of your wish-list items into one of five categories:

- boat style and outfitting
- accommodations layout
- crew attitude and abilities
- chef's specialties
- destination.

The High Five

The goal of this exercise is to place your wishes into five categories, and then decide which categories are most important to you overall. This will help your charter broker or bareboat company find a boat that meets your primary needs first.

Boat Style and Outfitting

I think I would like the big public spaces onboard a catamaran.

I think I would like to have sails on my yacht, but also a powerful auxiliary engine

I think I would like ...

Accommodations Layout

I think I would like to have a twin cabin near the master so my children can be near me.

I think I would like a yacht with a small eating area where the kids can dine alone.

I think I would like ...

Crew Attitude and Abilities

I think I would like a crew member onboard who can teach me how to water ski.

I think I would like a captain who is more fun-loving, rather than formal.

I think I would like ...

Chef's Specialties

I think I would like a chef who does a good job integrating local cuisine.

I think I would like a chef who can make separate meals for my diabetic husband.

I think I would like ...

Destination

I think I would like to be someplace tropical where I need only sandals.

I think I would like to visit islands so small that only yachts can get to them.

I think I would like ...

The truth is, these five categories are the major aspects of any yacht charter vacation. In fact, when I review charter vacations for worldwide magazines, I always emphasize how each yacht rates in each of these five major areas. I call them The High Five.

If you can figure out which of The High Five categories are most important to you, then you will be able to choose the yacht that compares most favorably in your top areas of concern. You will be able to look at a yacht and know whether you are getting everything you *need*, and then compare that yacht to others that suit your *needs* to see what extras they offer in terms of your *desires*.

Let's take a closer look at each of The High Five categories, to help you sort your ideas and better rank them.

Boat Style and Outfitting

The boat's style is what you learned about in Chapter Three. We're talking power versus sail here, the fast power of an express cruiser versus the slower power of a trawler yacht, the monohull style of layout versus a catamaran. If you want to charter onboard a monohull sailboat—and you want no part of powerboating or catamarans at all—then boat style would rank way up top on your list of The High Five.

Outfitting in this case refers to the way a yacht is "fitted out," or finished off after the general hull style has been built. Outfitting includes things like the style of the décor, the kinds of water toys kept onboard, whether there is an elevator, how many cabins have their own televisions, whether there are indoor or outdoor bar areas (or both), how many people the main dining table seats, whether there is a hot tub on the top deck, how many sunbathing areas are onboard, and on and on among the infinite number of choices that individual people have when building a yacht to their own tastes and desires.

In my experience, most of the things that can be called outfitting are less significant than other categories of The High Five. If you're a die-hard Wave Runner fan and you absolutely, positively *must* have a pair of them onboard your yacht, then yes, outfitting will rank higher on your list. And of course, having more updated furnishings and televisions is always nice, no matter what kind of vacation you're taking.

But for most people (and I count myself in this category), the color of the curtains or the fact that there are three sunbathing areas instead of two are optional choices that don't necessarily make or break a charter vacation. For that reason, my advice is to think seriously before ranking outfitting desires toward the top of your High Five list.

Accommodations Layout

As you learned in Chapter Four, a yacht's *accommodations plan* shows its general layout, including the location and size of each guest cabin. There are king-size beds, queen-size beds, double beds, and twins with Pullman berths. Some are better suited for adult couples traveling together, while others are more comfortable for children or single people traveling in a group.

This category in The High Five is pretty straightforward, since most yachts of the same size and style have similar accommodations plans. In most cases, if you determine that you want to be onboard a 70-foot motoryacht, then all you will need to figure out in terms of accommodations is whether one or two couples might be willing to sleep in twin beds, since motoryachts of that size usually have at least one or two twin cabins.

It gets a bit trickier going the reverse route: deciding whether one or two pairs of single people might be willing to share a double or queen-size bed, if that's the kinds of cabins available onboard a yacht that meets every other one of your High Five criteria. Again, that's why you're making a list and ranking these items in order of importance. Only you know what compromises you and your guests are willing to make. If you're traveling with a group of sisters, sharing beds may be no problem at all. If you're traveling with relatives of opposite sexes, the accommodations plan may demand more attention.

Accommodations also become more important in the cases of small children. If your kids are small, say age five or younger, you may want to look for an accommodations plan that has a master cabin in close proximity to a twin cabin, so that the kids can get to you in the night should they have a nightmare or get nervous about anything. In some cases, yachts will only take children at those ages if you also take along a nanny—who will need a cabin of her own near the kids' cabin.

In the case of adults with special needs, proximity can also be an issue. For instance, some cabins have their own bathrooms, while others do not, especially onboard smaller sailboats and bareboats, power or sail. If you tend to make a few emergency runs from your bed every night, you may not be willing (or able) to share a bathroom with others. This would of course rank accommodations toward the top of your High Five list.

Crew Attitude and Ability

One of the things that constantly amazes me about crewed yacht charter companies is that they are always marketing pictures of the boats—when in reality, any good charter broker will tell you that it is the crew, more so than the boat, that typically makes or breaks a fully crewed, partially crewed, or skippered bareboat vacation. In fact, many people who repeatedly book yacht charter vacations often follow a favorite captain from boat to boat as his career progresses. They feel that the yacht itself is secondary to the service the captain and crew provide.

Even less publicly known is the fact that good brokers will not book charters onboard boats where the captain or crew have bad reputations—no matter how beautifully built and outfitted the yacht is. Some captains have been blackballed and even forced out of the industry for treating guests poorly or negotiating prices unfairly, with brokers quietly talking to one another to keep an unofficial tally of known problems.

I believe this is a good thing, even though it causes grumbling about gossip and collusion. Crew attitude and ability have the same effect onboard a yacht charter that they do in, say, a restaurant. If you're at a place with an out-of-sight chef but lackluster service, your food will arrive cold and you won't enjoy your meal. On the other hand, an excellent wait staff that ensures you have whatever you desire can raise a restaurant's profile, even if the chef is merely average to good. Just like restaurant reviewers, charter brokers get paid to know where the service is good—and to steer you away from the places where it's bad.

That a crew will be well trained should be a given onboard a yacht charter, especially one booked through a broker—whose job it is to know the crew personally. In terms of The High Five, crew attitude refers not to good or bad personalities, but to things like outgoing or shy personalities. Some crew love to entertain the guests with everything from extravagant theme nights to personal tours of local islands, while others are far better at blending into the background and offering a more reserved style of service. Either is fine, of course, but if you prefer one to the other, I would rank that toward the top of your High Five. I personally much prefer a gregarious crew whom I can get to know and even befriend in some cases, though for shy guests who just want to be left alone, my favorite kind of crew would be less than ideal.

Crew ability in terms of The High Five does not refer to whether they are trained to run the boat. I have yet to step onboard a broker-recommended charter yacht and encounter any problems with incompetence. Instead, what I mean by crew ability is any special skills that you will need based on your desires.

For instance, if you plan to celebrate a birthday while onboard, you will want to have a crew that excels in throwing parties. (Believe me, some of these crew can decorate with the best land-bound socialites.) If you have a certain medical condition that requires knowledge of more than basic first aid, you might look for a crew whose captain or first mate has additional training, say in the symptoms of diabetes if you are an insulin patient. If you are a certified scuba diver who has yet to master navigation, you will want a crewmember onboard who is a dive master, to lead you underwater or act as your buddy.

The crew onboard the 115-foot motoryacht *Surprise* do their best to bring the South Pacific culture onboard during charters in Fiji. Capt. Carol Dunlop (seated) knows many traditional songs and customs, while other crew members are well respected in local villages and can perform greeting ceremonies that will allow you to go ashore.

A special note about crew applies to charters that take place in destinations where getting to know wildlife and vegetation are key to the vacation experience. In the Galapagos Islands, for instance, I've done two different charters over the span of a few years. I can barely remember the itineraries we followed or the size of the bed in my cabin during either charter, but I can remember very well that one yacht had a far better naturalist as part of its crew—and that the tours and information she provided helped me to enjoy the wildlife, geology, and history of the destination far more.

If you're bareboating, of course, crew attitude and abilities will rank at the bottom of your High Five. But if you're looking to charter anything from a skippered bareboat to a fully crewed megayacht, I'd strongly urge you to rank crew toward the top of your list.

Chef's Specialties

Technically, the chef is part of the crew, but I always give him or her a separate ranking because food is such an integral component of any charter vacation.

If you're bareboating, of course, you'll be making your own meals or choosing restaurants onshore, so a chef's training is not a concern (and should be at the bottom of your High Five). But onboard crewed yachts, just as with cruise ships, you can eat until you literally can't stuff yourself into your pants—or you can decide that you'd rather go the healthy route, which means you'll need a chef to accommodate that desire.

Even if you have unique dietary requests, you can expect terrific tastes and presentation during meals onboard crewed yachts. Here, a chef has prepared a single, specially requested lunch of vegetarian chili with a side of black bean, mango, and ginger salsa.

As was briefly mentioned in Chapter Ten, different yacht chefs have different types of training and abilities. Some have been trained in the finest French sauces at Le Cordon Bleu, while others are focusing on creating Atkins-friendly menus that contain far more than fatty steaks and slabs of butter. You are the only person who knows how picky your fellow charter guests will be and whether any of them need a chef who knows how to follow a particular diet regimen.

Every broker-recommended charter yacht I've eaten onboard has had a chef whose skills varied widely enough to keep me happy and satisfied during the entirety of a weeklong cruise, even when I asked for low-sugar or low-carbohydrate entrees. You need not worry about having foods you dislike at the table—especially if you've done a good and honest job of filling out your preference or provisioning sheet before the charter.

What you need to ask yourself in terms of The High Five is how important it is to you that your chef has specific abilities that go beyond basic requests. I believe that you will find that most broker-recommended charter chefs can accommodate things like low-salt and low-calorie diets. Where things get more complex is in situations where you will only eat Italian food cooked in the traditional ways of Tuscany.

If you're a foodie who demands that level of specificity, you should rank the chef's abilities far higher on your High Five.

Destination

You probably have a general sense of which destination you want to visit during your charter. If you're thinking about the Caribbean, you will probably consider yachts that are available in the north, toward St. Maarten, or in the south, toward Grenada, but you aren't likely to also consider a yacht that's available at the same time in, say, Alaska. You know you want to be in the tropics.

In some cases, you also will know at least one or two islands that you especially want to visit. This is what I mean by *destination* in terms of The High Five. If you absolutely, positively must visit the island of Anguilla during your yacht charter, then your choice of yacht is going to depend more on which yachts are willing to go to Anguilla than on any other factor. Destination will be one of your top High Five factors.

On the other hand, if you know that you want to visit the Caribbean but you don't really care which specific islands you come across during your charter, you should rank destination lower on your list of The High Five and instead focus more on other factors, such as the crew's abilities. Heck, having a good captain who knows the local waters—wherever they may be—can often help you discover fantastic islands you never even knew existed in the first place.

Beyond the Brochure

The point of the "I think I might like" and The High Five ranking exercises is to help you see beyond the brochure when zeroing in on your perfect charter yacht. You understand all too well at this point that the best charter experiences are the sum of many interchangeable parts. It will go a long way if you can help your bareboat company or charter broker understand exactly what is most important to you, so they can match you with the right yacht for your needs.

"The first thing people want to know is what costs are involved," explains Kim Vickery, a crewed yacht charter broker with International Yacht Collection in Fort Lauderdale, Florida. "I talk to them about the charter fee and the expenses involved. I have a form that I provide the client that outlines the expenses—everything, including potential taxes in the cruising area. Then we talk about where you want to go, what time of year. I provide them some examples of boats. We send them our charter catalog. After that, we get into the particulars. Are you outdoor, fun-in-the-sun people, or do you want sophisticated restaurants onshore?

"If they're in the area, say they're in South Florida and they're around the boats, I'm happy to give them a tour," she adds. "Otherwise, it's not always practical to see the boat before you charter it. It's my job to see the boats. If it's necessary, I'll fly out to the boat before the charter and check on it."

I agree that it's the broker's job to know the yachts, but I do believe that if you're a first-time charterer and if it's at all possible, you should get onboard your actual charter yacht before booking your vacation. It's not quite as beneficial, but it is certainly helpful, if you can at least get onboard yachts of similar size and style before booking, if only to get a feel for what the outdoor spaces and indoor rooms will be like.

Simply touring two or three yachts that have a lot in common with the ones you think you might like can open your eyes quickly to concerns you may not have foreseen, such as your elderly mother's inability to navigate spiral stairs—which are, in some cases, the only way to a yacht's top outdoor deck. You also may take the opportunity to actually stand in the smallest cabin's shower, to see if your brawniest friend will have any problems cleaning up at the end of each day's activities.

In many cases, you need not travel to your actual charter destination to see your yacht, or ones that are similar to it. You need only attend a boat show—which is just like a car show or a craft show, with vendors lined up in rows for you to sample their offerings and products. True, the vendors are usually looking to sell boats instead of to charter them, but I wouldn't let that stop you from poking around and seeing as many boats as possible.

You can climb onboard smaller yachts inside convention centers and onboard larger yachts at nearby in-water displays. If your particular charter yacht happens to also be for sale (as many of the larger yachts are), you can usually get a tour of it. In some cases, you can even sample the chef by having lunch onboard with the captain, or at least hors d'oeuvres during a quick get-to-know-you conversation with various members of the crew. A charter broker who regularly books high-end, fully crewed yachts can help you to arrange this type of thing.

Major, Public Boat Shows

Public boat shows are just what they sound like: events that anyone can attend. Again, they are geared toward boat sales, not charters, but plenty of business gets done in both areas.

These shows typically occur in the same places year after year, and in some cases have grown to become quite the spectacle. The mayor of Fort Lauderdale, Florida, once told me over breakfast that his city's annual boat show, when combined with the annual show just down the coast in Miami, draws somewhere in the neighborhood of a half-million people—more than the average Super Bowl, no matter where it's played.

In fact, those two shows in Florida are the best places to start if you want to see boats in terms of both quality and quantity. They're the biggest major shows in the United States, and each one includes far more yachts than you could ever hope to tour in a year, let alone in the four or five days that the shows run. Each show also features sailing and power-driven yachts of literally every style and pedigree, meaning that you can see for yourself the difference between one brand's quality and another's in the exact same size and style of yacht.

Bareboat companies, charter management companies, and independent charter brokers all attend these shows, too, so you can even meet face to face with the people who will be helping you to plan your vacation. In a lot of cases, they will even take you for tours of various yachts they think you might like, introducing you to the crews and pointing out significant outfitting features.

The Fort Lauderdale International Boat Show is held annually at the end of October (usually overlapping with Halloween), while the Miami International Boat Show is held annually in the middle of February (usually overlapping with Valentine's Day). Hotels, airfares, and parking book up fast, so if you plan to attend either show, make your arrangements as far in advance as possible.

Both shows are organized in multiple venues, with smaller powerboats in the convention centers, sailing yachts at one nearby marina, large motoryachts at another nearby marina, and so on. Booking a hotel near your boat style of choice will save you lots of money in cab fares, and lots of blisters on your feet.

For venue details, specific dates, admission rates and additional information about the Fort Lauderdale or Miami shows, go online to a search engine like Google and type in "Fort Lauderdale Boat Show" or "Miami Boat Show." The shows' ownership appeared to be changing hands when this book went to print, and specific Web sites for each event had yet to be created.

Internationally, there are also several boat shows worth considering—if you happen to be traveling near them. Fort Lauderdale and Miami will satisfy virtually every charter yacht shopper's curiosities, so my advice is to stick with them unless you just happen to be overseas during a major international boat show.

The bigger shows near major tourist hubs are in London, England, in January; in Dusseldorf, Germany, in January; in Sydney, Australia, in August; in Monaco in September; and in Genoa, Italy, in October.

Smaller, Public Boat Shows

If you live in America and don't plan to travel to any of the major public boat shows mentioned in the previous section, you still have opportunities to get onboard yachts and meet some crewmembers. Many U.S. cities host smaller annual boat shows that, although not as big and varied as the ones in Fort Lauderdale and Miami, still manage to offer you lots of yacht styles to look at and get onboard.

Some of the better shows to consider attending include Seattle, Washington, in January; Newport, Rhode Island, in September; Annapolis, Maryland, in October; Palm Beach, Florida, in March; New York City in January; and Chicago in January.

Keep in mind that most of these places are not major charter destinations, so actual charter yachts may be harder to come by—even though you may find yachts that are similar in size and style. Also remember that these boat shows themselves are smaller, which means they don't tend to attract the biggest, most luxurious yachts. If you have your heart set on seeing one of those, a smaller boat show is likely to be a waste of your time.

Industry-Only Boat Shows

The charter industry does have its own set of boat shows each year, but unfortunately, charter guests are not allowed to attend. The shows are purposefully set up to allow charter brokers to get onboard as many yachts as possible while interviewing crew and sampling chefs' creations, and the philosophy is (rightly so) that having the general public around would simply grind the whole endeavor to a halt.

I attend the biggest of these shows annually, in Antigua and St. Maarten every December, and in Genoa, Italy, every May. Any charter broker worth his or her paycheck attends them, too, along with at least one or two of the smaller industry-only shows held in Newport, the Virgin Islands, Greece, and Turkey.

There is simply no better place than these shows for brokers to inspect the condition of various charter yachts and meet all of their crew—all the while taking endless notes that they can share with you when it comes time to match your desires with available yachts. If you find yourself working with a charter broker who lets slip that she has never attended an industry-only show, consider hanging up the phone and finding someone who conducts herself more professionally.

It's Time to Book

After all of your ranking and touring and zeroing in, you will finally end up deciding on a charter yacht that is perfect for you. It's a wonderful moment, full of anticipation and expectation of the highest order—and you want to make sure that you book your dream boat through a reputable person who will ensure that you get everything you envision.

It's finally time to pick up the telephone and contact a bareboat company or charter broker. Chapters Twelve and Thirteen will teach you what to look for in reputable agents, as well as what to expect in terms of contracts, provisioning forms, preference sheets, and the general booking process.

12

Booking a Regular, Instructional, or Skippered Bareboat

Should you use a broker for a bareboat or instructional charter?

Ed Hamilton sure thinks you should. He's a well-respected industry expert, a member of both the Charter Yacht Brokers Association and the American Yacht Charter Association. He started in the business back in the early 1970s, when he was a manager for The Moorings, just before it began expanding into one of the world's largest bareboat operations. By 1975, Hamilton had co-founded his own bareboat company, which he built into a fleet of 55 boats by the early 1980s. He eventually became a charter broker—after also working as a charter yacht skipper and a sailing instructor. Today, his agency is one of the few that book as many bareboats as crewed yachts, making him an expert on pretty much every type of charter you could imagine.

In other words, he's the kind of guy you can trust on questions like this.

"It makes sense to use a broker for a bareboat because if you call a bareboat company directly, you're getting their slant on everything," Hamilton explains. "Obviously, even if the company is reputable, they're there to sell their product. We're independent, not tied to any one charter company. We can tell, boat to boat, how they compare. We know the types of boats in the fleets. Because we book hundreds and hundreds of these, we get feedback from every charterer. So we have a very good idea of which companies and which boats in the companies' fleets are working, and which ones are not."

Having a charter broker as a middleman between you and the bareboat company also gives you assistance with contracts, payment issues, and any other problems that might arise. And since it's the bareboat company—not you—that pays the charter broker's commission, you're getting that added layer of protection for free.

"We can often help if something goes wrong," Hamilton says. "We can't promise to get all your money back because the boat was missing a tin [can] opener—some people will try the most ridiculous claims—but with legitimate claims, we can go back to the client and help. We're careful not to make promises, but our job is to try to really inform the client what you can expect. It's a rental car, basically. The thing's being used and abused. But everything should work. It should be clean. If it's not, we can help.

"The other thing is just getting people's expectations in line," he continues. "If you're going with a low-priced, bargain boat, the chances are the boat has gone down through several companies to a budget company. It's a spiral, and the condition of the boat goes down even more, with the budget company not spending as much on maintenance. We watch that sort of thing. If somebody's taking a bargain boat—and we do book a lot of them—we try to get their expectations in line. A lot of times, it turns out that they get just that, a bargain. And it's great. You generally get what you pay for, but there are some lower-priced companies that are good. And we can talk to you about that."

All of which sounds almost too good to be true, which is why you may be thinking: "Of course this guy is going to suggest that I use a broker to book my bareboat. That's how he makes his living."

It's a reasonable concern, and one that I've heard many times before. What I can tell you is that the most cogent discussion I've heard on the docks about this subject left me with the impression that in reality, if you're booking a bareboat or an instructional charter through one of the world's major companies—like The Moorings or Sunsail—whether you use a charter broker or not, your odds are pretty good of getting a fair shake, a well-kept boat, a knowledgeable instructor, and a good or even excellent overall experience. A broker adds a layer of protection, as Hamilton explained, but when the bareboat company itself is on the up and up, you may not need the added distance that a charter broker provides.

It's sort of like the difference between booking a Walt Disney World vacation package directly through the folks at the Magic Kingdom, versus trusting an Orlando-based tour operator who has a special arrangement with a less-expensive motel on nearby International Drive. Will your vacation experience be just as good if you go with the cheaper option? Perhaps. Would it be wise for you to have someone looking out for you besides the tour operator? Probably.

"I don't know why more people don't go through a broker with a bareboat," Hamilton says. "I suppose they just to go the bareboat company's Web site. It doesn't cost you anything if you're using a broker. People should really consider it. We have a lot of bareboaters who even progress to crewed charter, too, over the years."

Proving Your Skills

No reputable bareboat company will give you one of its yachts—power or sail—unless you can prove that you have the ability to operate it. After all, we're talking about vessels worth tens of thousands of dollars, not to mention liability concerns in case something goes wrong while you're at the helm. The bareboat company is going to want proof of your skills as a skipper.

That proof can come in several forms. If you're an experienced skipper—someone who has chartered a bareboat with the same company before, or who owns a yacht and cruises regularly elsewhere—you often can satisfy the bareboat company by simply going on a short *checkout cruise*. These trips usually last between one and three hours, with you showing the company representative that you know your way around the basics of docking, boat handling, anchoring, raising the sails (if there are any), and troubleshooting inside engine rooms (onboard powerboats) or with auxiliary engines (onboard sailboats).

Checkout cruises also give the company representative a chance to familiarize you with your charter yacht's quirks, such as unique helm equipment that might be new to you. Anyone who's driven more than one boat during her lifetime knows that all boats handle differently, and that the people who know a particular boat best can usually offer great tips that will make cruising in general easier.

You can further smooth the checkout process if you can show your bareboat company some form of instructional license that you earned in the past. These include certifications from courses affiliated with U.S. Sailing, the American Sailing Association, and the National Administration of State Boating Law Administrators. There are other course certifications out there, too, and sometimes they will be acceptable to bareboat companies—depending on whether the company recognizes the school that provided them. Worldwide bareboat companies like The Moorings and Sunsail, for instance, have their own affiliated bareboat courses that are designed specifically to prepare beginners for their first charters onboard company yachts.

In most cases, your bareboat company will have you fill out a questionnaire well before you step onboard, usually during the early stages of the booking process. The questionnaire will ask you about your boating experience and instructional certificates in advance, in an effort to smooth the checkout process when you are onboard at the dock.

Keep in mind that a general safe boating course, such as the ones offered locally by divisions of the U.S. Power Squadrons and the U.S. Coast Guard, usually are not enough to get you the thumb's up for chartering a bareboat. In virtually all cases, bareboat companies will insist that your certification include training in a bareboat cruising course, not just in a safe boat-handling class. The general classes may teach you the rules of the road, but they aren't likely to teach you the kinds of navigation skills you will need to skipper a bareboat safely in most waters.

Learning as You Go

If you're new to boating and are interested in skippering your own bareboat, you'll have to learn as you go before you will be ready for a checkout cruise. This can sound intimidating, but I've written about enough instructional charter courses to know that even the most timid of novices can feel confident at a bareboat's helm after a solid week of training from a reputable company.

I was one of those novices a half-dozen years ago, when I signed on for a weeklong instructional charter with Sea Sense in St. Petersburg, Florida. My only prior boating experience had been during my childhood, at my grandfather's lake house in New Jersey. There, I was allowed to paddle the canoe, skipper the one-person Sunfish sailboat, help an adult with the sails on the larger Hobie Cat sailing catamaran, and drive the bowrider powerboat as long as the weather was good. Basically, I'd done the kinds of boating that many people do during family vacations, onboard small boats and in enclosed waterways where I was always within sight, or even swimming distance, of shore.

By contrast, the Sea Sense course was taught in the sprawling Tampa Bay onboard a 42-foot Grand Banks trawler yacht. The boat's engine room was bigger than my entire old Sunfish sailboat, and it had more moving parts than my car (as far as I knew, anyway, given my ability to do nothing mechanical beyond checking the car engine's oil).

I was about as beginner as beginners come, and I can truthfully say that by the end of the week's course, I was troubleshooting fuel-flow problems and RPM drops while plotting dead-reckoning courses and docking against strong currents. I had absolutely no reservations about being in command of that yacht. I knew everything right down to where the flare gun was and how to fire it in case of an emergency. My checkout cruise was flawless.

Real boating expertise comes with years of practice, of course, but my point is that you should not feel intimidated about bareboating even if you have zero prior experience. All you need is the desire to learn and a good teacher.

"We run into a lot of people who don't even know what they don't know," explains Barb Hansen, co-owner of Southwest Florida Yachts in Fort Myers, Florida. "They had a Boston Whaler on a lake in New Hampshire, and they've been boating for 30 years, but it's a different thing. Even if you've boated before, you may be a beginner to chartering. The type and size of boat you're trying to charter is a whole different world. You have not only the boat and the systems and the complexity, but you have tides and currents and weather and navigation."

Still, with the right attitude, most people who sign up for the company's instructional charters succeed. "I'd say 90 percent graduate and can go bareboating," she says. "Our class is a six-day course. It puts people through their paces. We take them from novices and have lots and lots of letters from people who say they never thought they could do it. It's not a day at the beach—there's no time for fishing or diving—but you're out cruising and putting it all into practice. It gets into the maintenance of the vessel. Putting the dinghy in the water. Fiddling with the outboard if it won't start. Checking the engine room and the systems. This is not a mechanical course, but there are things you have to know. You have to clean the sea strainers. Most people can handle this. It's been a small percentage of people who haven't been able to do it.

"About half the people who take the course then go bareboating, and they stay with it," she adds. "They go everywhere, with other companies, too. It opens up a whole world that wasn't there before. You can go to the islands, Alaska, Greece, the Chesapeake Bay, there's just so many places you can go. And as a family, too, if that's what you want for your vacation."

Hansen recommends that families wanting to cruise together get educated together, taking the same course at the same time whenever possible. That way, everyone takes ownership of the idea that boating comes with responsibilities, and everyone feels better able to live up to them underway.

"All of the boating shouldn't just be on one person, to do everything," she says. "A lot of times, it's the guy's idea and the wife doesn't want to come, but a lot of times, if they start out as equals, she ends up doing better. It's not a medically proven fact, but women just have a better sense of steering the boat, chart reading, focusing. It's a lot safer, too, to have more than one person who knows how to run the boat."

Families, or at least couples, who take instructional courses together also tend to avoid the kinds of command and control problems that can crop up during a bareboat charter. If only the husband learns about boating, he will always assign himself the role of captain—and sometimes bellow at his wife and children as if they were slaves meant to swab the deck. I'm not exaggerating here for dramatic effect; many a man's boating dreams have been crushed by his own behavior toward his wife and children onboard. Most experienced boaters can tell you countless stories about sailing into harbors only to find husbands and wives at each other's throats, usually with the husband screaming instructions from the helm while the wife struggles to quickly perform a task that nobody ever taught her how to do in the first place.

On the other hand, if the wife and older children also have a strong foundation in bareboating skills, then every member of the family can take turns acting as the captain, thus gaining confidence and enjoying the boating experience more. Each family member will instinctively learn to treat others in the "crew" the way they would like to be treated when they're not serving as skipper, and family bonds tend to blossom instead of strain.

My advice in this area is quite simple: Sign every member of your crew up for the same instructional charter, whether they're your family or friends. It's the best way to keep the peace onboard, and to make sure everyone feels as comfortable as possible as you sail off in search of exciting new vacation adventures.

It's also the best way to ensure your own safety at sea. If something happens to you and another family member has to take over, you'll know you're in confident hands.

Selecting a Boat from a Fleet

No matter how big or reputable a bareboat company is, it's going to have a variety of boats in its fleet. Some will be older, some will be newer, some will be bigger, some will be smaller—all will have their own idiosyncrasies that can add to or detract from your private yacht charter vacation.

This, remember, is why Ed Hamilton explained earlier in this chapter that he recommends booking your bareboat through a charter broker, whose job includes keeping tabs on which individual charter yachts are being maintained better than others. However, if you've decided to work with a reputable company and forgo the broker's advice, you'll have to select your own boat from the fleet, usually sight unseen.

Price will obviously be a factor in your decision, as will availability in the destination where you want to cruise. The Moorings, for instance, has many different kinds of bareboats in its worldwide fleet, but only certain styles and models are available in some locations.

Regional companies that focus on a single cruising area, like the Virgin Islands, will usually have their entire fleet available for you to consider—depending on how far in advance you book and whether the "better" boats are already taken for your vacation dates. Keep in mind that these regional companies are by definition smaller, though, and their fleets are, too. There may be only one bareboat that has all the newest, fanciest outfitting and equipment, and it's likely to be snapped up fast by other bareboaters who are booking their own cruises.

In general, newer usually means cleaner when it comes to boats, but it does not always mean better in terms of handling and speed. If you don't work with a charter broker, you will have to rely on the bareboat company's opinion of which boat in its fleet will best suit your needs.

My personal preference is to look for the biggest bareboat that fits my budget, with the understanding that it might not be the prettiest in the fleet. I hate feeling squished, and when you're onboard a 30-footer, you're never more than 30 feet away from anybody else on that same boat. I'd rather spend a little more for a bigger boat that holds eight people, even if I might be traveling with only six people, because I know there will be plenty of extra room to move around and find private spaces. (Bigger boats also tend to have bigger cabins, which means more windows and opening ports that provide fresh breezes in the tropics.) I, personally, put space and comfort above brand-new features when choosing a bareboat.

Bear in mind, though, that if you go with the biggest boat your budget allows, you will need to have enough capable people onboard to handle the size boat you select. Two people on an 80-foot yacht would be decadent in terms of roominess, but you definitely might wish you had a few extra people around to handle necessary tasks.

Again, if you're new to chartering, a broker can help you balance these kinds of concerns.

What to Expect in the Contract

Bareboat and instructional charter contracts are just like any other kinds of contracts: They contain lots of fine print that lawyers think up and expect the rest of us regular folk to magically understand.

If you're working with a charter broker, ask her to explain your contract to you line by line, including anything that she thinks is missing or seems out of the ordinary. If she can't do any or all of those things, immediately hang up the telephone and find a more professional broker.

If you're booking your charter directly through the bareboat or instructional company, you'll have to pay special attention to what is and is not included in your contract. Don't assume that something so elementary as full water and fuel tanks are part of your deal. As with any kind of vacation, it's important to iron out these kinds of specifics up front, in writing. Add-ons brought to your attention at the last minute can quickly add to your bill, sometimes doubling your overall anticipated budget.

For instance, there may be different compensation plans due to you if there is a problem on the bareboat company's end. What if the model of yacht you chose is suddenly unavailable? How about if you get the right yacht, but it breaks down immediately through no fault of your own? What if your skipper or instructor has a personal emergency during the middle of your vacation? Will you be due a refund, or money toward a future charter? Or nothing? What happens if a hurricane barrels through during the week when you're scheduled to be cruising? Are there special clauses to consider if you're cruising with a group of more-accident-prone novices in a flotilla?

On a more basic level, is the company stating in writing that it will provide everything you need and want for boating in general? In some cases, a dinghy might cost extra. So may kayaks, snorkeling gear, and other water toys that may be pictured in the brochures. Are cruising guides, navigation charts, and electronic navigation aids like GPS included in the price, or do you have to bring them yourself? How about safety equipment such as lifejackets and a first-aid kit?

If you're chartering in a place like the Virgin Islands, you will need certain marine conservation area cruising permits to visit certain islands. If you're cruising in the Mediterranean, you may have to pay additional taxes called VAT depending on which countries' borders you are within. All of these things cost money, and you need to know whether it's coming out of your pocket in addition to the bareboat's weekly rate. The same goes for airport transfers, nightly dockage and anchoring fees, and any additional assistance you might require while underway, such as towing if you go aground.

Again, a reputable charter broker is a good bet for helping you navigate the contractual minefield of obligations and omissions. To this day, even given all of my chartering experience, I still trust reputable brokers to help me figure out things I may have overlooked no matter what kind of boat I'm planning to be onboard. I've even had brokers who book fully crewed yachts for a living tell me that they use brokers specializing in bareboats to help them book their personal vacations.

If you choose to book the bareboat on your own, even through a company you've used before, be sure you understand every word of the contract before you sign it—and try to anticipate possible problems based on boating you've done in the past.

Insurance

In most cases, your bareboat company will force you to purchase an insurance policy as part of your contract. These insurance policies vary from company to company, but for the most part they cover damage to the yacht itself.

It is your responsibility to ask your broker, or to discern for yourself, exactly what the bareboat insurance policy covers. There may be different deductibles, for instance, based on different kinds of mishaps and where those mishaps occur—especially if you are bareboating in a region where different islands are under the control of different countries. In some cases, the bareboat company will pay the insurance policy's deductible, but in other cases, your personal savings may be on the line.

The Moorings, for instance, specifically states in its policy and its online marketing materials that you, the charterer, will be held liable if damage is caused by your "gross negligence or wanton or willful misuse" of the yacht. What, exactly, does that mean? And exactly how liable might you be? The entire insurance policy deductible? Or the entire cost of replacing the yacht? These are the kinds of details you need to examine in the fine print and negotiate to your advantage if possible.

It's rare for a standard bareboat insurance policy to include medical coverage, though sometimes the bigger companies will offer those policies for separate purchase. Before you turn them down flat, check with your health insurance carrier at home to see whether you are covered for expenses outside of U.S. borders. The last thing you want to do is find yourself with a broken leg on an island with a hut for a hospital—and no idea whether you'll be reimbursed for a helicopter ride to the nearest trauma center.

Some companies also offer travel insurance that is similar to the policies now being sold by some cruise ship lines. These policies help you get your money back, or its equivalent in a future vacation, in case you have to cancel your vacation due to illness, travel disruptions like snowstorms that close airports, and the like. In some cases, a bareboat company's travel insurance will cover airline and lost luggage problems even if you booked your airfare without the bareboat company's help.

If you would like travel insurance but find it is not offered by your bareboat company, talk with a charter broker. She can often help you work something out through a third-party insurance provider.

As with all kinds of insurance, bareboating, medical, and travel policies are complex. If you're chartering for the first time or with a smaller company you've never used before, my advice is to use a charter broker to help you weed through all the variables.

Keeping Costs Down

Most people choose to book bareboats for one of two reasons: They either really enjoy the idea of taking the helm, or they are looking for a less-expensive private yacht charter option. No matter which of those categories describes you, the following tips will help you get the most vacation for your hard-earned dollars.

For starters, if you live near a city like Fort Lauderdale or Miami where major annual boat shows are held, do your online research in advance and then book your charter at the bareboat company's boat show booth. These companies almost always offer *boat show discounts*, such as getting a few extra days of cruising for free when you book a weeklong charter on the spot. In many cases, the presidents or major officials of the company are on hand at these shows, too, so you can shake their hands, collect their business cards, and keep them handy in case you have problems later on during the booking process or the charter itself.

Even if you don't book your bareboat charter at a boat show, you still may be able to get a special deal. When you call your charter broker or bareboat company to make your booking, be sure to ask if there are any discounts currently being promoted. You just may get lucky, especially if you're cruising during the off-season in a given destination. Also check Web sites like *www.CharterWave.com* for special discount opportunities.

Food and drinks are a major expense during any vacation, and bareboating is no different. Still, there are ways to stem your outgoing cash flow. For starters, if you're chartering a bareboat from a well-developed hub in touristy places like the Bahamas or the Virgin Islands, you can almost always find a grocery store and a liquor store nearby the bareboat company's base. This means you can do your upcoming week's shopping yourself—at local prices, especially when buying local brands of beer and wine. Doing your own provisioning this way usually costs less than arranging your provisions through the bareboat company, even if you have to pay cab fare to and from the grocery and liquor stores. Be careful, though, to keep your destination in mind. If you're cruising off the beaten path, you're not likely to find a mega-mart there.

One good way to keep costs down is to use the water as your playground. Renting snorkeling equipment and using it several times a day throughout your weeklong charter will keep the kids happy, active, and far away from souvenir shops on shore.

Also remember that there's nothing stopping you from taking along your own snacks for the week. If you typically shop at bulk stores like Costco, Sam's Club, and BJ's, you can get all the potato chips and pretzels you'll need at a fraction of the cost that you'll pay even at a local grocery store in your cruising destination. You can either stuff an extra suitcase full of these items or ship a box down before your charter. The same goes for specialty items like sugar-free candy and name-brand wines, which likely will be extremely expensive or completely unavailable once you set sail.

If you do choose to provision through the bareboat company, pay close attention to what you're getting. In many cases, you'll have a choice of provisioning packages or a la carte offerings, and in some cases, a la carte will be a better deal because you won't want or need everything in the pre-made lists. For instance, there's no need to pay the bareboat company for a week's worth of dinners if you plan to eat out at waterfront dock-and-dine restaurants, which you can plan for in advance by reading a local cruising guide. There's also no need to stock the boat with tons of premium-priced beer if you plan to snorkel with the kids all day and then visit bars with your adult friends at night.

Packing all your toiletries is another way to keep costs down. There's nothing worse than forgetting to take a basic bar of soap—and then having to pay $5 to replace it when you find yourself at the mercy of tourist shop operators.

Last, you can keep costs down by boating smartly. If you're chartering a bareboat powerboat, for instance, set a limit on the number of miles you plan to cruise each day as a way of keeping your fuel use in check. If you're chartering a powerboat or a sailing yacht, look for free anchorages where you can drop the hook at night instead of forking over fees to nearby marinas. If you plan to eat at waterfront restaurants, read your cruising guide and look for establishments that offer dockage. In some cases, you will even be allowed to tie up at a restaurant's dock overnight, for free, if you're a paying customer at the dinner seating.

All of these little things can add up to big savings, in some cases enough to help you get a bigger bareboat, a skipper, and even a chef, if you want them.

What to Take

Your sense of adventure is the main thing you need for a successful bareboat or instructional charter. Outside of that, it's all about being comfortable and feeling safe onboard.

Most important are local charts and cruising guides, if your bareboat company does not provide them with the price of your charter. You will need the charts for navigation and the cruising guides to tell you about attractions, restaurants, marinas, and anchorages along your course. You can sometimes buy charts and cruising guides from the bareboat company itself, though you're likely to get a better deal if you buy them yourself ahead of time from a marine specialty company like Bluewater Books & Charts (*www.BluewaterWeb.com*).

I also like to take along a general guidebook to the area, like a Lonely Planet or Fodor's title from *www.Amazon.com* or *www.BarnesAndNoble.com*. They usually have basic phrases translated into the local language, along with information about the region's history and local customs that make exploring there all the more interesting.

If your bareboat does not come equipped with a chartplotter or GPS system, you can—but don't necessarily have to—take along a handheld GPS. These can be helpful with navigation, or can at least be a reassuring piece of equipment to confirm the courses you are plotting on your printed charts. Handheld GPS devices are available pretty much everywhere, from marine supply stores like West Marine (*www.WestMarine.com*) to sites you may already use such as *www.Amazon.com* and *www.Ebay.com*. The better models start around $200 to $300 brand new.

Entertainment-wise, you should take any snorkeling or scuba gear you own, along with small water toys that are easy to deflate and carry in a soft-sided duffel bag. Pack books and CDs (if your bareboat has a CD player), along with decks of cards and board games if you want extra entertainment at hand. If you plan to golf and have the stowage space onboard, you can take your own clubs to save on rental fees.

You can take a laptop computer that does double-duty as a DVD player, too, but don't expect to have constant, or even intermittent, WiFi access to the Internet. The same goes for cell phone service, no matter what kind of phone or service plan you have. Remember, you're going to be on the ocean. There are no cell phone towers or broadband cables running to and from your boat.

Also remember to pack your sunblock, any prescription medications, and fluffy beach towels for everyone onboard. (You can buy souvenir towels in more touristy destinations, but don't rely on the bareboat company to provide you with extra-wide, sun-worshipping, blanket-like towels.)

Last, I find that provisioning an extra case of the favorite local beer can go a long way toward smoothing your way when arriving at marinas and when buying fresh fruits and fish from the locals. You'd be surprised at how good a deal you can get on many things in exchange for a cold six pack and a warm smile.

What to Check

There are certain things you want to make sure of between the time you step onboard your yacht and the time you cast off on your vacation. If you've booked an instructional charter, the teacher onboard with you will lead you through a list. However, if you've booked a regular or a skippered bareboat charter—even through a broker—you'll want to take responsibility for checking things over yourself.

For starters, make sure you've been given the right boat. Look for the make and model number on the outside of the hull, such as "Horizon 70" for a 70-footer built by Horizon Yachts. Often, the make and/or model number will be painted on the outside of the hull toward the back of the main cabin, or painted on the transom (the very back of the boat), with both of those locations being clearly visible from the dock. If you cannot see this information on the outside of the hull, walk through the cabins and make sure they are in the same places, with the same number of en suite heads, that you remember from looking at your arrangements plan.

In the rare case that the company cannot provide the boat specified in your contract at the time it is supposed to be ready, refer to the contract clause that entitles you to a replacement boat (hopefully of equal or greater size and value, if you or your charter broker negotiated properly). In some cases, the boat you reserved may have a broken engine or a damaged interior from a previous week's charter, or some similar problem that is outside of the company's control. You have to give the company a chance to make good. Reputable companies always do so in these situations, and less-than-reputable companies often can be persuaded by knowledgeable charter brokers.

After you confirm that the yacht is correct, double-check any new paperwork that the company's representative handed you upon arrival. Be sure that all the printed terms and conditions are identical to what you received in your advance paperwork, particularly your yacht pickup and drop-off times, the complete price for the yacht, provisioning packages you ordered, and any extras you selected, such as travel insurance.

Next, take a look at the yacht's *inventory list*, which should itemize all the things that come with your bareboat. The list should include everything from pots and pans to VHF radio and life jackets. With your inventory list in hand, walk through the yacht and make sure that everything on the list is actually onboard. Point out any discrepancies to the charter company before accepting the yacht, so that you cannot be accused later of stealing or losing the items during your charter.

Another key item to look for onboard a bareboat is its logbook, which should be near the main helm station. The logbook is the place where you, as skipper, will make written notes about your day-to-day itineraries and maintenance, such as checking engine oil.

Bareboat companies take logbooks very seriously, both in terms of ensuring that you stayed within the designated cruising grounds and in terms of proving their case should problems occur. For instance, if the engines die on your watch and the logbook shows that you didn't check the oil a single time during your charter, that logbook can become evidence against you in an insurance lawsuit. Thus, before you set off on your charter, you want to make sure you know where the logbook is and exactly how the company prefers that you make notes in it.

Last, you should reconfirm your return air flight time with the charter company, even if you booked your airline tickets separately. When it comes time to return your bareboat, you will have to do a walk-through with a company representative who will check to see that everything is pretty much as it was when you took the boat in the first place—just like a rental car company does when you drop off your vehicle. You want to make sure the company knows how much time you have between dropping off the boat and getting to your flight, and make any adjustments in your schedule ahead of time to prevent problems later on.

Do not, under any circumstances, leave so little time between your yacht return and airline flight that you have to leave the boat before the bareboat company completes its walk through. You want to be present to address and allay any concerns on the spot, before they can fester into bigger problems that affect the return of your security deposit.

When You Pay

Bareboat companies usually request no payment during your initial telephone call. They typically offer a window of about two weeks between that call and your first deposit-due date, giving you a chance to carefully consider the contracts and other paperwork they send you. When the two weeks or so are up, you will be required to make a deposit of anywhere from 25 percent to 50 percent, depending on the company, to reserve your yacht and cruise dates in the destination of your choice.

The balance of your payment, along with any provisioning costs, are typically due one to three months before your departure date. You may be able to pay in two separate installments, depending on the company's policies and on how much time exists between your booking date and your cruising date.

Your security deposit will likely be due on the first day of your charter, payable at the company's marina base. The amount of the deposit will vary from company to company and from boat to boat, but expect it to be somewhat substantial—sometimes as much as a few thousand dollars. It's wise to put the security deposit on a major credit card, which can be refunded the day you take the bareboat back. Your credit card company can also act on your behalf later on, if you need to dispute any damages for which you are charged.

13

Booking a Partially or Fully Crewed Yacht

Working with a broker may be optional when booking bareboat or instructional charters, but that's not the case with crewed yachts. If you plan to book a partially or fully crewed yacht for your private charter vacation—be it your first or your 50th—then you should do so through a reputable charter broker. Period.

The reason is simple: There are too many variables and legalities involved in crewed yacht charter. You will be dealing with an individual's personal yacht instead of with a company's fleet of boats. You will have as many as a dozen different crewmembers onboard whose experience you will want to verify and whose personalities will affect your vacation. You will be talking about spending bigger money than you would on a bareboat—and in some cases, bigger money than some people spend on their first homes. You will typically be dealing with escrow accounts and wire transfers instead of credit card charges. You will have to work through overseas management companies and with occasionally complex travel details, such as chartered helicopters and transfer boats.

It's just too much insider information for even an experienced charter client to process without the help of a full-time industry expert. Your regular travel agent simply will not do.

"A charter broker knows the business," explains Kirsten Ringsing, a longtime charter broker who books top-dollar crewed yachts from her Monaco office with Fraser Yachts Worldwide. "We inspect the boats, we know what we're selling. A travel agent knows how to sell a package. We do customized arrangements. If you know a yacht's owner, you could book a charter without a broker. But even travel agents, they come to brokers. They don't know how to ask the right questions about provisioning, cruising areas. A travel agent doesn't know anything about yachting. They don't even go to the boat shows. They don't know what to ask, and they make mistakes in transferring information.

"And the broker is free," she adds. "It's the yacht owner who pays the broker's fee. We hold the money, we negotiate the contract, and we are here to protect the client's interests."

As I mentioned in Chapter Twelve, I still rely on charter brokers despite my years of experience and dozens of personal yacht charters all over the globe. It's true that I'm immersed in the industry from a journalist's perspective, but I know that brokers spend much more time than I do interviewing captains, inspecting yachts for maintenance and upgraded features, and working with various management companies. Reputable charter brokers know far better than anyone which people and which boats can be trusted to give you your money's worth, which is why I continue to book all my article reviews and even my personal vacations through the brokers I've come to trust.

Reputable charter brokers also make my life easier in terms of charter planning—a fact worth seriously considering when booking a new type of cruise vacation. Good brokers can tell me in a single phone call which airport I need to fly into, where exactly in the airport the yacht's crew will meet me, how long it will take to get from the airport to the yacht, how long it will take to cruise from island to island, what I can expect to find on each island, what the weather is typically like during my travel dates—in other words, pretty much all the general information I could ever need or want to know.

A good broker also can act as a buffer, or middleman, between the yacht and me should problems arise. That has happened to me only once in my entire career, but I believe in preparing for the worst even while expecting the best. I want somebody who knows her stuff in my corner, just in case.

And all of that, remember, is in addition to the assistance good brokers provide with charter contracts, insurance policies, international legal considerations, boat choices, crew interviews, chef provisioning and meal planning, and the many other things that no charter guest should ever want or need to sort through on her own.

Considering that all of this expertise and assistance comes free of charge to you, the charter guest, I cannot imagine a reason why you would want to book a crewed yacht charter without a broker. The only question I can envision you asking is this: How do you find one of the best industry insiders?

Finding a Reputable Charter Broker

There are three main professional organizations for charter brokers worldwide, and each is tougher to get into than the next. Remember, as you read in Chapter

One, that charter is a close-knit worldwide community of people who have developed and built up an entire industry in the past few decades. The brokers with the most experience and power today don't want just anybody sneaking into their territory and giving their business a bad name. Charter brokers are selective about whom they befriend, what they teach industry newcomers, and when they formally welcome them into the professional fold. Any old travel agent simply cannot gain membership into these three leading organizations. The existing members welcome only those new members who are proving themselves as knowledgeable students of the charter industry.

The groups are best known by their acronyms: MYBA, CYBA, and AYCA. They stand for the Mediterranean Yacht Brokers Association, the Charter Yacht Brokers Association, and the American Yacht Charter Association, respectively. MYBA tends to have members living on the European side of the pond, while CYBA and AYCA typically have members living in the Americas and the Caribbean. Full disclosure here: I became an affiliate member of CYBA in early 2006.

Any charter broker from anywhere in the world can book any charter yacht anywhere in the world, so you should not look for a MYBA charter broker simply because you know you want to book a charter off the coast of Italy. The organizations simply sprang up and grew geographically because brokers in classic cruising grounds decided they needed professional relationships with their regional peers. MYBA formed in Europe, CYBA blossomed in the Caribbean, and AYCA took hold in New England and the greater United States. Many charter brokers are members of more than one professional association, no matter which continent they call home. In some cases, the three organizations work together on issues that affect charter vacation bookings worldwide.

Look for the MYBA, CYBA, and/or AYCA logo on the Web sites of any charter brokers you consider using. Also be sure to outright ask any broker you contact which of these major professional groups she works through. You can verify any membership claim by looking through the list of members on each of the organizations' Web sites: *www.mybamembers.com*, *www.cyba.net*, and *www.ayca.net*.

Also start your search for a broker in Appendix B of this book. There, I've listed the brokers whom I've come to know and trust personally through my own charter and boat show experiences.

Brokers, at the end of the day, are people, and they all have different personalities. You can pick up the phone and call more than one broker at first, so that you can find one whose personality jibes with your own, but once you begin working with a broker, you need not call 16 others to check on the price you get for a particular yacht. In virtually all cases, every broker will get you the same exact price. What your choice of broker comes down to is your comfort level working with the person and the service that she gives you.

If you talk with two brokers you like and need more information before settling on one to work with exclusively, you can ask just five questions that will give you an idea of each broker's experience level and industry knowledge.

Five Questions to Ask

Start with the basics at the top of the following list if you're completely new to charter and have no idea what kind of boat you want or where you want to book it. If you've done a little research online before contacting a charter broker, or if you've chartered before, you can also ask the more specific questions at the end of this list.

How did you get into the charter business?

This is the biggie for me, perhaps the singular question that will help you learn more about a charter broker than any other.

Some brokers started out working on charter yachts, and I have found that they tend to know the business the best. For whatever reason, they know a certain way to ask questions of captains and crew that elicit details and responses far more revealing than the answers those same captains give to brokers who've never worked onboard charter yachts. For instance, these kinds of brokers can often get a captain to talk, as one sympathetic friend would to another, about his boss—the yacht's owner. And from that kind of conversation, the broker will often gain insights into whether the owner is a cheap guy, a tough negotiator, a person who invests heavily in his yacht's upkeep, and so forth. All of those details affect the crew's happiness, the boat's quality, and, in turn, your vacation.

Former crewmembers-turned-charter-brokers also tend to look at the yachts themselves differently, noticing design details and maintenance issues that other brokers might miss. Even more, many brokers who once worked onboard yachts have actually cruised in the majority of major charter grounds—sometimes with the same captains who are still running the yachts. These brokers can give you firsthand knowledge about itineraries, restaurants, shopping, snorkeling, and the like, and they know the easiest ways to get you to and from your yacht because they've done the flights and ship-to-shore transfers personally.

I'm not suggesting that you should work only with charter brokers who started out working on yachts. There are plenty of hard-working, knowledgeable, and talented brokers out there who entered the business from different angles and learned enough to fill volumes upon volumes of books. A lot of charter brokers started out working in management companies, for instance, and can use that insider experience to your advantage when negotiating dates and rates with the bigger companies.

In general, though, the people who've been around anything the longest tend to know the most about it and bring their own experiences to bear. The universe of charter brokers is no different.

What was the last industry-only boat show you attended?

As you learned in Chapter Eleven, there are a few major industry-only charter yacht shows held around the world every year, in addition to various smaller industry-only shows in cruising markets such as the Virgin Islands, Greece, and Turkey. A charter broker's attendance at the industry-only shows signals a certain level of professionalism, a desire to step onboard as many yachts and meet as many crewmembers as possible, and a dedication to making sure the information given to charter clients like you is as up to date as it can be.

You should not expect a charter broker to have attended every single industry-only show out there, mostly for financial reasons. Attending these shows includes costs like airfare, meals, and hotel bookings, all of which often come out of the broker's pocket. Many brokers therefore choose to attend the shows where they stand to gain the most information in a single trip, an investment of time and money that I find perfectly reasonable. A lot of brokers attend the European shows and the Caribbean shows on alternating years, thus keeping current on charter boats and crews in both destinations without breaking their travel-budget bank.

When you ask your broker which industry-only show she attended recently, your hope is that the answer will be St. Maarten, Antigua, or Genoa. Those are the three biggest each year in terms of crewed yachts, power and sail alike, and any charter broker who hasn't attended at least one of them in the past 12 months is probably cutting corners. Not a good sign.

Other industry-only shows a reputable broker may have attended include the ones held in the Virgin Islands, Newport, Greece, and Turkey. Or a reputable broker may have seen a handful of charter yachts at a general-public boat show like those held annually in Miami and Fort Lauderdale.

If your broker mentions one of these other shows, it's a promising sign—but I'd still ask when he last visited one of the three main industry-only shows as well.

Especially in terms of booking crewed yachts, attendance at the three main shows are major benchmarks of professionalism.

Have you cruised in my destination?

If you know which cruising grounds you'd like to visit during your private yacht charter vacation, then you can ask your broker specifically about his personal experience in those waters. A broker who has spent time in a given destination is in a better position to know more about it than a broker who has never before been there.

The best charter brokers do more than simply check out yachts and crews. They go ashore, just as you would in the yacht's dinghy, looking for excursions, restaurants, and activities to recommend as part of your vacation. Here, two crewed yacht brokers head toward the Bitter End Yacht Club in the British Virgin Islands.

In some cases, brokers who started out working onboard yachts will have the most widely varied personal cruising experiences. However, many crewed charter yachts offer brokers opportunities to take half-week *familiarization charters*, known as "fam trips" in the industry lingo. The brokers spend a few days cruising onboard just as you would, only instead of relaxing the entire time, the brokers take notes about the service, décor, food, helm equipment, harbors, typical sea conditions, yacht motion underway, and more. Basically, they're there looking for things to tell you when you request a yacht like the one they're onboard.

These fam trips become especially important if you want to book a charter in an emerging cruising ground. Booking a trip for you in a place like Fiji will certainly be easier for a broker who has been to the islands, perhaps onboard the very yacht you will be able to book yourself (since so few crewed yachts are there at this point).

Well-traveled charter brokers also have an advantage because they have been onboard more yachts than other brokers, and thus have a wider body of knowledge from which to draw when answering your questions. Again, experience counts.

Which of the boats on my list have you been onboard?

If you've done some online research and know which charter yacht you think you might like, ask your broker if he's spent any time onboard. And don't settle for a simple "yes" or "no" response.

Brokers have lots of ways to get onboard charter yachts. The aforementioned fam trips are the best, because they let the brokers see the yacht and crew in action during an extended period of time. However, brokers can also spend time onboard yachts at boat shows, where there are often cocktail parties and private luncheons that allow the chef and crew to show off their training in the areas of food preparation and service. On still other occasions, a charter broker might hustle down to a nearby marina if a charter yacht happens to be coming through his local area and is willing to give him even a ten-minute tour.

Your goal in asking this question is not only to find out whether the broker has been onboard a given yacht, but also to discern whether the time he spent onboard was quick or quality. Any broker worth her salt can tell whether a yacht is generally good or bad after just a few minutes onboard, but the brokers who have spent the most time on any boat getting to know its crew are the brokers who will be able to offer you the best information about that particular charter.

I know from personal experience that yachts I have found to be lovely at boat shows have lost a peg or two in my mental ranking after full-blown fam trips. Why? Because the clean, fresh onboard attitude and ambience sometimes doesn't last for more than the single day a crew has to smile at me during a boat show. Your broker—and thus you—want to know how that yacht and crew are going to hold up during an entire week's charter or longer, especially if bad weather or other factors add stress to the situation.

A broker who has toured a yacht is a good start. A broker who has cruised onboard a yacht should be your gold standard.

What can you tell me about this yacht that isn't in the brochure?

The goal of this question is to challenge your broker's expertise by asking her to give you insider information that you can't find yourself online or in brochures.

Don't expect juicy details about who owns the yacht or how many millions of dollars he paid for it, but do expect a reputable broker to know about the crew's backgrounds, the way one cabin has a shower that's a bit tightly spaced for taller charter guests, or the fact that the captain just added a whole bunch of new water toys to the yacht that haven't been publicized yet.

Again, your goal is to make sure the broker knows the boat—if not on the day you first call her, then certainly by the time you make the actual booking.

Reading Magazine Reviews

Your charter broker, in an attempt to give you as much information as possible about a specific crewed charter yacht or destination, may refer you to a review or article that was published in a marine magazine. (The premier magazines that cover yacht charters are listed in Appendix A.) I have written and edited countless numbers of these articles during my time in the business, so I know a thing or two about how they get put together.

In the most journalistically responsible cases, the magazine will pay the writer's way to and from the yacht, along with any other travel expenses the writer incurs. The cost of the yacht charter itself, though, is borne by the yacht's owner. It's a matter of economics: Most magazines cannot afford to pay $25,000 to $250,000 to produce a single article. Your annual subscription rate would have to make up the difference, and you'd be paying more every month for your magazine than for your mortgage.

This financial relationship between magazines and yacht owners—albeit a practical necessity—does give the yacht owners, via their management companies, a feeling that they should have some authority over what the writer tells the readers. To their thinking, they are footing a good part of the bill and should have influence, if not outright approval, of the article. And those same management companies are also advertisers in the marine magazines, which means they, too, have a financial way of putting pressure on editors and writers to print exactly what they want.

I have yet to hear of an instance when any marine magazine printed an article that was knowingly and completely false—say, complimenting a charter that in fact was disastrous. However, in most magazines you will find stories and reviews that are sunny, that omit minor onboard problems. Many editors stick to the notion that small problems are solvable as long as the magazines tell the company or yacht owner about them, and that there's no need to jeopardize a relationship with yacht owners or major advertisers by putting those small problems into print for you, the reader, if they'll be fixed before you step onboard anyway.

The magazines for whom I choose to write allow me to select the yachts that will be featured, and I skirt these problems of financial intermingling by writing only about yachts that reputable brokers recommend. My thinking is that there are so many good yachts out there that want your charter business, I might as well write about those instead of the lesser yachts that shadier companies might pressure my editors to promote.

Other magazines are not so disciplined, though. For instance, I know first-hand that a magazine with U.S. distribution lets the captains of the charter yachts write the reviews of their own boats, and that the same magazine promotes only the charter brokers who pay a fee, regardless of their experience—without admitting any of those connections to you, the reader. This, obviously, is not the kind of publication you can trust when deciding which yacht might be right for you.

My advice in looking at charter features in marine magazines is to stick to the magazines listed in Appendix A—all of which have been around a while, whose editors I know personally, and which I believe do their best to talk straight with their readers in the face of ever-increasing pressure from advertisers and yacht owners.

And if you come across even the slightest criticism in a magazine article, consider that it might be a watered-down, sanitized version of a bigger problem with the yacht or crew. Ask your broker about not just the stated problem, but also about anything else she's heard regarding it. Nine times out of ten, there will be more to the story.

Reputable brokers know these clues when they see them in print, and they often call writers like me to get the unedited version of events firsthand. That's the kind of broker you want to work with, one who gets to the bottom of things from every angle.

Video Brochures

A recent advancement in charter marketing is the creation of video brochures. They're just what they sound like: downloadable mini-movies that show you the inside of a charter yacht and sometimes introduce you to the captain and primary crewmembers.

Fort Lauderdale-based International Yacht Collection was among the first major management companies to make these videos available to the public, and they've been a big hit, helping charter clients like you get a better feel for a given yacht than any printed brochure could ever offer. I've seen a couple of independent charter brokers walking around yachts with handheld video cameras in the past year or two, as well, which tells me that they are preparing to make moving pictures available to their clients.

Stay tuned for these video brochures to become available in more places, including on this book's companion Web site, *www.CharterWave.com*.

The Preference Sheet

After you place your booking, but before your charter begins, your charter broker will send you a *preference sheet*. Take this piece of paper very seriously. The answers you provide will tell the yacht's crew what kinds of things you like and need, greatly affecting the meals and service during your charter.

"The main preference sheets, they ask you about food, liquor, and medical conditions," explains Suzette McLaughlin, a crewed yacht charter broker in the Palm Beach, Florida, office of Camper & Nicholsons International. "But we just revised ours recently, to make it even more detailed. We have a preference form plus a checklist now, with everything from e-mail needs to brands of suntan lotion that people prefer. Do you need bathrobes and slippers, that sort of thing. With our checklist, it goes to the boat to tell us what they have, and then we send it to the client so that they'll know what the boat offers. That way, everyone knows what's there and what they might want to request in addition."

McLaughlin—along with every other charter broker and yacht crewmember I have ever met—stresses that it's important to be as detailed as possible when filling out a preference sheet. The only way a yacht crew can give you what you want is if you tell them what you want, something you're probably not used to doing if you've only been onboard cruise ships where you have to choose food and amenities from a pre-set menu.

"One of my repeat charter clients actually provides menus," McLaughlin says. "They're extremely detailed. They say the chef doesn't have to follow those menus day to day, but it's to give the chef an idea of how particular they are about their food. Ninety-nine percent of the clients say, 'We like seafood,' 'we don't like chicken,' things like that, which is fine. If you're following a diet, put it on there. Just be honest. Don't be afraid. The more information the crew has, the better service you're going to get. Especially during the busy season or in remote areas, they need to know so that you can get what you want."

Remember, yachts are not hotels with access to supplies from stores on nearby street corners. Even the biggest, most expensive yachts leave their marina bases—which have food markets and wineries—and head off for places where the only other inhabitants are singing birds and colorful fish. All crewed charter yachts carry the basics onboard, but if you know you prefer white chocolate to dark chocolate, you need to say so on your preference sheet. That way, the crew will have time to buy the white chocolate before you and the yacht sail off into the sunset.

Can you change your mind about what you want to eat, or about how you want each day's schedule to go, after you get onboard? Of course. But if you want to add something hard-to-get at the last minute, like fresh caviar in the tropics when the only mode of transportation is a chartered helicopter, then it's going to cost you. Dearly.

What to Expect in the Contract

Crewed charter contracts have become far more standardized in recent years than they used to be. Reputable charter brokers and management companies now typically use forms provided by professional associations including MYBA and CYBA, with those contracts covering everything from the charter's location and dates to insurance liability and warnings about using drugs onboard.

Missy Johnston, a longtime crewed yacht charter broker with Northrop & Johnson in Newport, Rhode Island, has been instrumental in creating some of these documents while working on the contracts committee of AYCA. She knows the ins and outs of charter yacht fine print better than almost any other broker I've met, from liability clauses to legal frameworks that revolve around which country's flag the yacht flies.

"Yacht charter basically falls into two classifications: commercial and private pleasure," Johnston explains. "Commercial is when the owner supplies the crew, and private pleasure is when you charter a yacht and then hire the staff. The difference is liability. They're similar to renting a fully staffed hotel suite versus renting a privately listed villa and then hiring the staff.

"Beyond that, the contract needs to reflect the flag state requirements of the country to which the vessel is flagged," she says. "The charterer should view this as a moving product with various countries' flags moving through various countries' waters—all of which will impact the contract choice. We work constantly in the industry to keep track of every country's changing maritime rules and regulations so that we can give the best contract possible. This is an industry governed by maritime law. There are a variety of differences from what's on land. That's what the charter broker is educated about."

Charter brokers also need to help you sort through which costs are included in the contract and which will be extra. "The contract will reflect the pricing structure, which can be for the yacht and crew only, with all expenses in addition—that allow you to customize your menu and itinerary—or the contract could be inclusive of expenses in certain areas," Johnston says. "It is rare to have all-inclusive contracts, but it happens all the time in certain places, like the British Virgin Islands. It's only a 32-mile area, you're going to get a certain food, they know what it's going to cost."

One of the key contractual phrases I've learned regarding crewed charters over the years is *force majeur*, which means an act of God, weather, or other event that is out of the yacht owner's control. The force majeur clause of the standard CYBA contract states that a yacht's captain has complete discretion to cancel a charter at the last minute, say, if a major hurricane is headed toward the yacht. That's perfectly reasonable to me, but the clause further states that no refund will be given in the case of a weather-related cancellation—scary words indeed when you're talking about a vacation that costs tens of thousands of dollars.

"There are contracts like that out there, with those clauses, and I won't sign them," Johnston says. "This type of travel product is very unique. It requires sophisticated information for the right contract, and that's why you need a charter broker who is knowledgeable and experienced."

Negotiating Tips

I mentioned in Chapter Eight that some yacht owners are more willing than others to negotiate weekly charter rates. This can be sticky territory—and one that some charter brokers and management companies don't like to discuss. It is, after all, in the management companies' financial interest to set the prices for crewed yacht charters as high as the market will bear and then stick to them, earning commissions along the way.

But in reality, there are sometimes deals to be made—and the best charter brokers are always looking for them.

"We have had clients who make offers [for a yacht charter] that we think are unrealistic, and lots of times they've worked out a deal" with the yacht's owner, explains Kathy McErlean, a Connecticut-based charter broker with International Yacht Charter Group. "It's definitely possible, especially in the off-season, or if you can fit a booking in between other charters the yacht already has. Maybe they have an awkward amount of time in between two other charters, like six days, and they need a four-day charter. Then, they may be able to work something out.

"There are some advertised specials, too, that brokers know about," she adds. The important thing is to be flexible. "I was just speaking to a man this morning who is really detail-oriented, an investment banker. He wants everything down on paper. But I had to explain to him that this is just not that kind of cut-and-dried industry. If you're willing to be flexible, you can often find a good deal."

For starters, you can agree to travel during shoulder seasons, when an owner is moving his yacht from one destination to another. A shoulder season in the Caribbean, for example, would be in late spring or early fall, before or after the busy winter months. Since the yacht is headed to or from the Caribbean anyway, you might be able to book a charter starting or ending in Florida without paying delivery fees, no matter which islands you want to visit.

Another good tactic is booking charters that start or end in places where major boat shows are being held. Again, the yacht may be headed to these destinations anyway—including Italy, St. Maarten, and Antigua—which means you might get a deal on some fuel and delivery expenses, along with dockage fees that the owner is paying anyway.

And speaking of deliveries, you can sometimes book charters during those, too. Say another charter client wants to book a specific yacht down in the southern Caribbean, but the yacht is based in the northern Caribbean. That paying customer will fork over the delivery fee to move the yacht to his chosen destination—and you may be able to piggyback on the other client's payment by booking a charter that starts in the northern Caribbean and ends down south, where the other client can begin his trip. Good charter brokers keep an eye out for these kinds of opportunities, and management companies sometimes even put out e-mails asking brokers if they have any clients interested in making these kinds of deals, or in booking discounted charters in far-flung locations to make moving the yacht financially worthwhile in the first place.

In the rarest of cases, if you're willing to change your destination, you can sometimes *make* a few dollars in the whole process. "I once had a charter [to arrange] for a duke in Britain," McErlean recalls. "He wanted to charter a boat on the Amalfi Coast in Italy. The boat decided to stay in the Caribbean instead because the director of *Pirates of the Caribbean* was friends with the owner of this yacht, and they wanted it in the Caribbean so Johnny Depp could use it. The yacht owner paid the duke a substantial amount of money, plus our commission, so it cost him $30,000 to get out of this deal. So the duke was then able to go up in price a little bit with his found money, and our contact in Greece found a great boat for the price. But that boat was for sale, and we didn't want it to get sold before the duke got onboard, so our contact worked with another boat's owner to get that more expensive boat for the same price that the duke could now pay. He ended up in Greece instead of Italy, but he was on a bigger boat and quite happy."

Of course, there is always the option of offering any yacht owner less money for a charter than the printed weekly base rate. Again, a good broker will know which yacht owners are willing to bargain, either all the time or in cases where previously booked charters fell through and a yacht is sitting idle. In these cases, it certainly never hurts to ask for a better deal—and to have a knowledgeable broker doing your bidding.

Insurance

Typically, it is the yacht owner's responsibility to carry insurance that covers the boat itself. The standard CYBA crewed charter contract specifically states that in all cases, the yacht's owner will be responsible for damages that occur because of fire, marine, and collision risks. You need not worry about those things in most cases—unless you are grossly negligent in using the yacht, say, by flicking lighted cigarette butts onto the furniture in the main saloon.

On the other hand, it falls squarely at your feet to worry about personal injuries and property damage that might occur during your charter. If you break your back while scuba diving or fracture your arm while getting into a dinghy, you are almost always responsible for the costs. The same holds true if you lose your fancy new digital camcorder or a necklace dripping with diamonds.

Different kinds of insurance can cover these types of expenses. Your existing health insurance may or may not cover medical expenses outside of U.S. borders, something you need to check before you begin your charter. A good homeowner's insurance policy will sometimes cover property losses outside of the home, but sometimes not. Travel insurance, just as with cruise ship bookings, can cover at least some of your expenses if you have to cancel your charter because of illness, injury, or weather. This insurance is sometimes referred to as a trip-cancellation policy.

There is also something called charter liability insurance, which any reputable charter broker can help you purchase before a crewed yacht vacation. Basically, it covers anything that a yacht owner's insurance may omit as well as protects you in the unlikely event that the yacht's owner decides to sue you (say, in the case of those flicked cigarette butts).

It is extremely rare for a yacht's owner to sue a charter guest, but it does happen. I heard of one case where wealthy rap artists destroyed a yacht's interior during a wild party and then literally threw down a wad of cash and told the captain to go fix the damage. What the superstars didn't count on was the fact that replacing the carpeting, furniture, curtains, and fixtures onboard the yacht would take weeks—and force the yacht to cancel several upcoming charters with other paying guests. Thus, the yacht's owner sued the rap stars not just for actual damages, but also for lost business opportunities, including any repeat business that may have resulted from the already-booked charters.

Big money, indeed—and yet another example of why you should listen to the advice of reputable charter brokers when deciding which, if any, insurance to purchase.

When You Pay

As with all other forms of yacht charter, you pay nothing toward a crewed yacht vacation during your first telephone call to the charter broker. Only after you receive, review, and sign the charter contract does money begin to be exchanged.

Typically, you will be asked for a deposit as high as 50 percent of the total charter price upon signing the contract. In some cases, you can pay this deposit with a credit card, but in other cases, you will need to work with a charter broker to facilitate a wire transfer. (Some yachts and management companies simply aren't set up to handle credit-card transactions, especially for big-money charters.)

No matter how you pay the deposit, it should go into an escrow account instead of directly into the hands of the yacht owner. This offers you a measure of protection and a tool for your broker to use should any problems arise before the actual charter dates.

The balance of the charter rate, along with additional expenses like the provisioning fee (based on your preference sheet), will usually be due one to three months before the actual charter date. This gives the yacht's crew enough time to provision the boat for your vacation, and having the full fee in escrow gives the yacht owner strong incentive to do everything possible to keep the charter dates intact.

During your charter, the captain or a designated crewmember will keep an itemized tally of additional expenses, including such things as satellite telephone use, marina dockage fees, fuel consumption, and rendezvous scuba diving charges. A notation also will be made in cases where you run through your provisions early and the crew needs to buy more, or if they need to dip into the owner's collection of wines and spirits to satisfy your party. In terms of food, there are rarely additional expenses—though I did hear of one charter whose grossly overweight guests demanded five full meals a day, plus midnight snacks, without warning the crew in advance. With wine and spirits, the crew will provision the brands you request, but some charter guests who are connoisseurs can't help but to ask for a bottle of a rare vintage that a yacht's owner might have stowed onboard. If that sounds like you, expect to pay extra.

Any of these additional fees that you rack up will be brought to your attention with an itemized bill at the end of the charter. You should go over them line by line with the yacht's captain, pointing out any discrepancies you notice. If there is disagreement, you should dial your cellular telephone and describe the items in question to your charter broker, who will then take the matter up with the captain, yacht owner, and management company, if necessary. Any remaining funds you have in escrow can wait there until things are ironed out.

If you decide to take a cash tip onboard for the yacht's crew, you should give it only when you are completely satisfied with the final bill. For top-dollar charters where you don't want to carry a cash tip, you can arrange that the gratuity be put into escrow before the charter, with your other funds, and released only on your command at the charter's conclusion.

14

Stepping Onboard and Cruising

My first charter definitely was unlike any vacation I'd ever experienced, and it was especially unique from the cruise ship trips I'd done in the past. It's not as if everyone were suddenly speaking Greek and serving me boiled octopus (although that did happen to me on a later charter near Athens), but I definitely had a sense, during that first charter, that I was in the dark about many small, subtle things that, when combined, would have helped me enhance my experience even more.

Your expectations for your first charter are probably linked, as mine were, to vacations you've done in the past. In some cases, this makes sense. If, for instance, you particularly enjoyed the privacy of renting a villa as opposed to staying in a crowded resort hotel, you will definitely enjoy the same benefit of seclusion onboard a private charter yacht. Yet in other cases, you may be thinking that charter will be a lot like a previous vacation experience that, in reality, it is not. I happened to think that cruising onboard a private yacht would feel a whole lot like being aboard a cruise ship, but I quickly learned that yachts move through the water differently, and that my tactile responses had to adjust.

These are the kinds of little things that nobody tells you about, the things you may wish later that you'd known in advance. It's not that your inexperience will hurt your chances of enjoying your charter—in fact, the excitement of doing something for the first time is half the fun. Still, being "in the know" about some of the smaller things you are likely to encounter may help you feel more at ease as you adjust and settle into the rhythms of cruising onboard your own yacht.

That's what this chapter is all about: Discussing the things that so often go unmentioned except behind closed cabin doors.

Pedicures

I'm a bit of a tomboy. Actually, truth be told, I'm a lot of a tomboy. When I was a little girl, I cut my hair so short that people thought I was my father's son.

When the girls in college were all pledging sororities, I was learning to rappel down mountainsides. When the other brides were shopping for venues draped in flowing flowers, I was looking into renting out a sports lodge and a giant, inflatable bungee basketball game that I could enjoy with all of the kids in attendance.

Given my personality, it should come as no surprise to you that I never had a pedicure until my early 30s. I trimmed and filed, of course, but buffing and polishing were as foreign to me as girdles and petticoats. And so it was that I became frightfully embarrassed the first time I stepped onboard a private yacht charter—and learned that guests are asked to leave their shoes off whenever they are on the boat.

That's right: You will be barefoot or in socks the entire time you are onboard your yacht, even in the formal dining room. You can wear a full-length, diamond-studded gown if you'd like, but matching shoes are verboten. The yacht owners simply don't want the wear and tear on the plush carpeting and freshly washed decks.

Some guests wear socks in the evenings—men often buy new pairs from places like Barneys to make a statement—but most women simply go barefoot day and night, whether lying in the sun or enjoying cocktails in the main saloon. There is a culture that has evolved around this practice, with female guests trying to outdo one another in terms of ornate toenail paint and fancy foot jewelry. Anklets and toe rings change as often as earrings and bracelets, with different sets to match different outfits.

I haven't gone quite that far yet, but I do now stop in for a quick pedicure before any of my charters begin. One basic color is enough for me to feel like a charter pro.

Moving About

The first time I took my sister with me on a yacht charter, she had a little trouble adjusting to the boat's motion. It's not that yachts are generally difficult to move about, but that sometimes, in certain sea conditions, you can feel their motion more than you might feel a larger cruise ship's. You have to adjust a bit, like you might if walking against a stiff wind.

And so, somewhere between Mystic, Connecticut, and Sag Harbor, New York, in seas that were far rougher than usual, I wandered into the motoryacht's main saloon to see my first-time chartering sister trying desperately to make her way toward the front of the boat. Her legs were locked at the knees, with her feet spread apart almost as far as her extended arms. She was moving forward in short bursts, trying to keep her balance while leaning against the boat's rolling motion—and basically falling into furniture left and right. I must say, she looked an awful lot like Steve Martin trying to disco dance on *Saturday Night Live.*

All of which is why I told her to start watching how the crewmembers and I moved around the boat. At virtually every moment during the hour or so when the seas were rough, we had an arm or a leg or our back or even just a few fingers propped against something, to help us stay balanced. It's not that we would've fallen over otherwise, but that we had learned from experience that the body needs a stabilizing element when it first encounters the cruising motion.

A good general rule for first-time charterers is this: One hand for you, one hand for the boat. You can carry anything you want with you, as long as it fits in one hand. The other hand should always be holding a railing or moving along a dresser, just in case you lose your balance while the yacht is underway.

Many people have no trouble adjusting within a few minutes or a day at the most, but if you do, keep your knees slightly bent so your body can move up and down, or left to right, with the boat's gentle motion. After a day or two, you'll be doing this subconsciously. It's the same concept as walking into the wind: Your posture just needs to come into equilibrium with the forces trying to push you into an unnatural motion.

Using the Heads

A *head* is a bathroom compartment onboard a boat. Most yachts have more than one head, with the larger yachts offering one head per cabin along with an additional *day head* or two for everyone's use near the main gathering areas. The toilet is within the head, as are the sink and shower. A toilet onboard a yacht is sometimes called an MSD, which is an acronym for marine sanitation device.

If someone wants to indicate that they're going to use a bathroom onboard a yacht, they typically say, "I'm going to use the head" or "I'm going to hit the head." Thus, if you have a problem with your sink or toilet or shower, it would be appropriate to notify the yacht's crew by saying, "There's a problem in my head." It's simply a bit more classy than blurting out, "I've clogged the ol' flusher and flooded the floor."

When you think of the heads onboard yachts, you should think of the bathrooms inside your house. There are only a handful of them, and if one gets jammed up, it is likely to cause at least a minor problem for everybody inside. The toilets onboard yachts are far more sensitive than the ones inside houses, and most can handle only special toilet paper made specifically for marine environments. Flushing anything else—including tissues, Q-Tips, dental floss, and sanitary devices—will usually cause a major clog.

Now, most yacht crew and bareboat company managers will tell you during your basic introduction to the yacht that you should avoid throwing things into the toilet. What they won't tell you, though, is how embarrassing it can be if you forget this rule. Unlike on cruise ships, where you rarely ever see the people who make up your cabins every day, you will see and even get to know most of the crewmembers onboard your yacht—or, if you're bareboating, the crew will be you. In other words, you will know the name and face of the poor person who has to go undo whatever toilet damage you have done, and you will see him again after he's sorted out the issue.

You may not be the type of person who cares what others think of you, but if common courtesy is part of your vocabulary, you should pay special attention to the rules your bareboat company or yacht crew explain regarding head use. Flush only what's allowed, and avoid embarrassing situations altogether.

Boat Bruises

This is a term used commonly in the yachting industry to describe the small, strange bruises that occasionally appear as if by magic on your arms and legs during a charter.

Boat bruises are not something you will definitely encounter during your vacation. In fact, I get one only on every third charter or so, usually when I'm onboard boats that run into rougher seas than usual. I never seem to know where the bruises came from, and I never can remember what I bumped into in the first place. Like most yachties, I simply wake up the following morning, look down, and wonder what the heck happened.

You can avoid boat bruises by following the aforementioned rule of "one hand for you, one hand for the boat." Always having your body braced or propped against something in rougher seas is a sure way not to bang into things at random.

And, hopefully, you're less of a klutz than I am.

Weird Noises

Usually, newcomers to private yacht charter don't notice any weird noises onboard their boat—until bedtime. Only then do all the boating-specific creaks and wooshes seem to emanate from the walls, like restless spirits coming to life inside an old attic.

The thing is, yachts are designed to look gorgeous on the inside, but—just as with houses—in between what you see on the inside and what you see on the outside lies a world of piping, ductwork, wiring, machinery, and insulation that makes the whole space function.

It's easy to forget this basic fact if all you've ever cruised onboard before is cruise ships, since they tend to be so noisy anyway that the sound of a little water going through a pipe in the wall is no big deal. By contrast, when you're onboard the only yacht in a private cove in the middle of a remote island chain with no civilization in sight, that same sound of rushing water through a pipe can sound greatly amplified, like an X-Wing Fighter scene from *Star Wars*.

If you're a light sleeper, or if you're traveling with young children, make a point of asking the crew what kinds of noises you might hear in your cabin during the night. Sometimes, a person may flush a toilet a few cabins over, and that water may run through a pipe next to your bed. It won't be thunderous, of course—and in most cases, you won't notice anything at all—but it's worth asking about if you are traveling with someone who tends to imagine ghosts in the closets.

Deck Obstructions

When was the last time you thought about where you were going to step next? If you're an avid hiker, this type of thinking might come to mind on a rocky outcropping where every step prevents a tumble, but in terms of everyday life, most of us just put one foot in front of the other and, well, walk. This is just as true onboard cruise ships as it is on city sidewalks, and you may step onboard your yacht without giving it a single thought.

In the case of that yacht, though, you should be a bit more careful. Sailing yachts, in particular, have decks that may be cluttered with things like winches and cleats—metal objects built into the decking itself to help the crew sail the boat. I've walked smack into winches and cleats more times than I care to remember, always with at least one broken toe to show for my trouble. I have yet to completely trip over a winch or cleat, thus taking a tumble onto my head or, worse, over the boat's side, but it has been known to happen, especially in rougher-than-normal seas.

This large sailing yacht sure has a beautiful teak deck, but look closely and you'll see a minefield of stainless-steel hardware that's perfect for stubbing toes. Onboard most yachts, it's smart to pay a bit more attention than usual to where you step.

My advice is simply to watch where you're going, particularly the first time or two that you make your way around the yacht's deck. Think of these obstructions as land mines, and make a mental note of where they are so that you can avoid them during the entirety of your vacation.

Local Pilots

In some destinations, even the highest-qualified yacht captain will be required to hire a local pilot to drive your charter yacht into or out of a given marina. The local pilot requirements do not exist everywhere, vary from place to place, and stem from multiple concerns. Sometimes, an island's government insists on a local pilot to protect a nearby reef that has been marred by other yachts in the past. Sometimes, the local pilot laws are more money-minded, with local governments seeing an easy way to charge a yacht owner or charter client a few hundred dollars as a tax for simply coming ashore.

No matter the reason your captain gives you for having to hire a local pilot, do not feel concerned that the captain himself is unable to command your yacht. You can feel comfortable and safe as the local pilot's (sometimes shabby) boat pulls up next to yours, allowing the pilot to step onboard your yacht and make his way to the helm. In most cases, you will never even speak to him. Sometimes, the whole thing will be over before you even knew it happened.

Seasickness

If you've ever taken a cruise ship vacation, then you probably already know whether you're likely to succumb to the dreaded *mal de mer*. I happen to be one of those unfortunate people who does get seasick from time to time. I've tried every preventive measure in the world, from pills to wristbands to chewing on ginger root. Nothing ever helps, except going green and letting my belly turn itself inside out for a day until I find my sea legs and settle down.

What I've learned during my unfortunate experiences in this area is that the prudent thing to do when you know you're going to blow onboard a yacht is to simply walk to the boat's aft deck and lean over the rail. No matter where the other guests are or where the yacht is headed, the aft deck is the place where long-time boaters and crewmembers go to get their seasickness under control.

The aft deck, you remember from the accommodations plans in Chapter Three, is the space all the way at the back of the boat's main deck. It's often where you step onboard, and it connects to the swim platform, which is usually down a few steps and parallel to the water's surface.

There are several good things about the aft deck in terms of being seasick over its back rail: You're out in the fresh air, the motion of the boat keeps the wind at your back and whisks the evidence into the sea, there is always a railing to hold onto and lean over, you can look up at the horizon and focus on a point to settle your sense of motion, there is usually a freshwater hose nearby (for swimmers) that you can use to rinse your face, you are on the lowest level of the boat (so nobody will be standing unwittingly below you), and the floor is made of teak or a similar material that is easy to hose off.

Your instinct may be to head down below to your cabin when you feel a bout of seasickness coming on, but onboard a yacht, this is the absolute worst thing you can do. For starters, you aren't likely to make it through the main saloon and carpeted stairway in time, and even if you do, you'll be trapped in an enclosed space without any fresh air or a clear view of the horizon. And, onboard most yachts, the cabins are designed to be slept in, not used when the yacht is underway. The sense of motion inside them is far greater than it is in places like the aft deck—meaning that if you trap yourself inside your cabin, the space will only exacerbate your seasickness.

If you're like me and your belly takes a day to adjust at sea, make a mental note of how to get to the aft deck from wherever you are on the yacht. You'll work through the problem in a matter of hours, and you'll look like a pro even in the ickiest of situations.

Also listen to your charter broker, who will know which region's sea conditions are likely to be the worst during certain times of the year. "Depending on where they're going and when, I can say there are good or bad odds of getting seasickness," says Linda Owen of Port O' Call Yacht Charters in Kansas City, Missouri. "Or sometimes, you get a person who wants to go from St. Thomas to St. Maarten, and I just tell them it's really a rough trip and they just don't want to do it. Seasoned crew don't want to do it. I try to guide people about what to expect, that it isn't all as easy as the Virgin Islands."

If you're chartering a top-dollar, power-driven megayacht, be sure to ask about zero-speed stabilizers, which are sometimes called at-rest stabilizers. This recent technological advancement is available only in high-end motoryachts, and it keeps the boat virtually free of uncomfortable motion whether you are in rough seas or at anchor.

They sound too good to be true, I know, but these stabilizers really do function as advertised. I even asked a captain to turn them off once, just because I enjoy the gentle rocking motion of the yacht at night and I thought the boat felt eerily still.

Opening and Closing Doors

Doors onboard yachts have to be more secure than doors inside houses, for the simple reason that yachts move—and nobody wants the doors flying open and closed while the boat is under way.

In most cases, doors to rooms, showers, closets, refrigerators, and cabinets will have some sort of latch that keeps them open or closed. If you don't know about the latches, you can quickly grow frustrated trying to open or close doors that just won't budge, and you may even think the doors are broken. Rest assured they are working just fine. You simply have to find the latch and unlock it.

Sometimes, the latches will be simple hook-and-loop fasteners, like on a screen porch in a summer cabin. Other times, the latches will be of the push-and-twist variety, like on the stall door in a public bathroom. Still other times, the latches will be outright bolts that need to be turned the way you might turn the lock on your home's front door. In most cases, no matter the type of latch, it will be either all the way at the top or down at the bottom of the door.

Larger, more luxurious yachts will have latches of these sorts inside the cabins, but on the doorways leading outside, you are more likely to find electronic push buttons and even motion sensors that open the doors for you as you approach. Your crew on these larger yachts can explain the ins and outs of whichever system is onboard.

Constipation

The first time I cruised onboard a private charter yacht, I felt fine for the first two days. Then, on day three, I started to notice an unusual pressure building in my belly. I spent hours trying to figure out what I'd eaten or done to cause the uncomfortable sensation, and finally I realized that I hadn't had a bowel movement in far longer than my maker ever intended.

That problem worked itself out on day four of the charter, and I figured it was a lone incident that I should chalk up to trying new foods at dinnertime. But then, I had the same problem during my second charter. And my third. I started to wonder if there was something wrong with my system and considered consulting a doctor.

Eventually, out of sheer frustration, I asked a few close industry friends what the heck was going on. They told me that they sometimes have the same problem—and that it's relatively common among people who charter private yachts, as well as among some crewmembers. Nobody seems to know exactly why the constipation occurs, but the best guess I've heard is that the body is so busy learning to react to a new and constantly moving environment that it simply forgets to perform a few other regular functions.

Yacht chefs, it turns out, are quite familiar with the phenomenon. Although it's not usually something they discuss with charter guests, many chefs put a dash of prunes or similar foods on the menu for day three or four of a charter, just to give silently suffering guests a gentle assist.

You can use the same method if you're cooking your own meals during a bareboat charter. Or, if you're on a crewed yacht, do what I do: Tell the chef on day two if you're having problems.

After several dozen charters of doing just that without embarrassment, I've never received anything but a silent nod of understanding—along with a delicious dinner that gets the job done.

Water Conservation

Fresh water onboard private charter yachts comes from two places: watermakers and holding tanks. Usually, onboard the bigger yachts, the combination of multiple tanks and watermakers means there is plenty of water to be had for even the longest of hot showers. But onboard smaller yachts, especially older sailboats, the holding tanks may empty faster than the watermakers can refill them.

What does this mean? It's got nothing to do with survival—you'll have plenty of bottled water to drink—but it does have an awful lot to do with comfort. You could be in the middle of a hot shower, your hair covered in shampoo, and suddenly the flow from the overhead nozzle on your bareboat will simply cease to exist. You'll have three options at that point: Wait for an inordinate amount of time until the watermaker catches up, holler for someone to bring you a few bottles of water, or wrap a towel around your body and climb upstairs for a quick jump into the ocean.

To avoid this problem—again, primarily onboard older, smaller sailboats—your best bet is to practice water conservation. Keep your showers short, don't let the water run when you brush your teeth, and in general try to be cautious about wasting the precious resource.

If you're bareboating, it will be up to you to keep an eye on the levels in the water tanks and to alert the other guests when a problem is looming. In the case of crewed charter, a good captain will let you know if the tanks are getting low. Usually, onboard both types of yachts, you can solve the problem simply by giving the watermakers time to catch up, or by making a quick stop at a marina to refill your freshwater tank.

Naps and Snacks

You will need more naps and snacks than usual when you're cruising onboard a charter yacht. That's simply all there is to it, and you shouldn't be shy about having your fill.

The reason, I think, is that your body is forced to adjust to the constant motion of a new environment, not to mention any time zone changes and long airline flights that you experience en route to meet your boat. Plus, you'll be sightseeing and doing activities like hiking and swimming that you may not be used to, not to mention being catered to so that you can relax and let your body recover from a hard year's work in the office.

One of the great things about having a private yacht, though, is that you can find relaxation wherever you choose, no matter how big the boat is. You don't necessarily have to go back to your cabin to lay your head for an hour in the middle of the day. You can plop down on the main saloon's sofa, on the top deck's sunpad, or wherever else the mood strikes.

"Remember, you've just spent $50,000," says Tim Clark, the senior charter broker specializing in fully crewed yachts with Ocean Independence just south of London, England. "Why are you spending that amount of money? If you've spent $50,000 on a hotel room, you'd have a very nice suite, and you'd damn well do whatever you wanted in that very nice suite. You'll put your feet up and do whatever you want, and you won't think twice about it. With a yacht, you feel like you're going on someone else's boat, and you have to get over that. It is your boat to do exactly what you want to. A good crew should be guiding the guests in a very subtle way, making you feel at home, that you can use the boat in exactly the way you want to use it."

If you're worried that your appetite for snacks might interfere with the size of your waistline, you can ask the bareboat company or chef in advance—on your provisioning or preference sheet—to keep only healthy snacks like nuts, fruits and cheeses around the yacht. Anyone who doesn't plan for this contingency in advance will no doubt step onboard to find crewed yacht candy dishes full of sweet treats that can be hard to resist.

Emergency Procedures

Everyone who's been on a cruise ship knows the emergency procedure drill. You go to your cabin, put on an uncomfortable orange life jacket and find your way to a pre-assigned, clearly marked muster station where you mill about until the captain gives the all-clear over the loudspeakers. It's an exercise in acquainting you with what you should do in case of a real emergency.

Private charter yachts do not have muster stations of that caliber, nor do they have any sorts of drills involving loudspeakers. They do, however, have lifejackets and escape hatches, along with other features that can include life rafts and emergency personal locator beacons (which emit signals to satellites). On the biggest yachts, there are also emergency horns or sirens, along with designated muster areas such as the aft deck dining table.

I've never had a use for any emergency equipment during my dozens of yacht charters, but I always make sure the crewmembers or the bareboat company representatives show me the available safety equipment—and how to use it—no matter what kind of yacht I'm onboard. International law actually requires crew onboard the larger yachts to do safety demonstrations that are similar to the ones you have probably experienced onboard cruise ships, and many crew who have worked onboard yachts for several years have excellent common sense about which cruising areas, marinas, and even specific coves to avoid in some parts of the world.

Additional safety precautions are often in place onboard the bigger crewed yachts as well, such as video cameras that show the captain (on the bridge) who is boarding the yacht's aft deck at any given time. These cameras stay on all night, long after you've gone to bed, with a crewmember "on watch" to monitor the video feed.

Like I said, I've never had a need to put safety measures into use during a charter, but it eases my mind to know the crew or bareboat company have thought them through with my best interests at heart.

Packing Properly

Even though the cabins onboard some yachts are larger than those you may have had on cruise ships, stowage areas are still at a premium—with little extra room for gargantuan, hard-sided suitcases and dozens of extra items that you don't really need.

You want to pack for your yacht charter by using soft-sided luggage, and by taking along only the things that you actually expect to use. Adding five extra outfits to your suitcase because you just can't make up your mind likely means that you will have five extra outfits stuffed into your suitcase on the yacht, since you may run out of drawer and closet space, especially if you choose a smaller sailboat for your vacation.

Onboard a bareboat, you'll have to be even more careful about packing than onboard a crewed yacht, since the latter tend to have a bit more stowage space in each cabin along with extra toiletries, hair dryers, and even rain jackets for guests who forget them. If you're considering a charter in the tropics, try to think along the lines that one good pair of sandals or flip-flops can get you through the entire week, and that you may not need a hair dryer at all if you plan to swim off the boat's aft deck and hold casual barbecues onboard night after night.

While packing lightly is important, also remember that even in tourist-friendly regions like the Caribbean, private charter yachts tend to go to non-touristy areas—which means no stores selling film, camera batteries, and the like. In many cases, your destination will consist entirely of a beach and a wooded trail.

That's lovely for making memories but not last-minute purchases. Remember to pack all your essentials before leaving home.

Unpacking Properly

You may be the type who plunks her suitcase down in a hotel room and digs through it for the week without ever truly unpacking. This lackadaisical style may work for you on land, but it's going to make your life much harder than necessary on a boat.

For starters, your cabin is likely to be smaller than a typical hotel room, and you won't want your suitcase lying around and taking up valuable real estate. Plus, on bareboats, you will not find an ironing board, even in locations like the Mediterranean where having dinner ashore in restaurants is customary. If you leave your clothes folded and crumpled in your suitcase, they will be wrinkled and creased when you wear them.

Still, the best reason to unpack—whether you're on the smallest bareboat or the biggest megayacht—is that if you don't stow your stuff securely, it will fall all over the place when the boat moves. Gingerly placing a glass bottle of perfume on a dresser is an invitation to a stinky disaster. You need to unpack your personal items and make sure they are in drawers, closets, or cabinets where they will not move underway.

If you choose a fully crewed yacht in the top-dollar range, the crew will offer to unpack your belongings for you. This is perhaps the easiest way to ensure that all your belongings will be exactly as they should be when you decide you want to use them.

Arriving Early

If you're booking a crewed yacht where your entire job onboard will be to sit back, relax, and enjoy the ride, then you can plan to arrive the day of your departure with few, if any, worries.

Bareboats and instructional charters, though, are different. I've found that with these kinds of private charter vacations, it pays to arrive a day early—especially if you're traveling through several time zones to your destination. Bareboating and instructional cruises require you to start out well-rested and paying attention, so that you can adjust to being onboard and in command. That's awfully hard to do if you're jetlagged and exhausted.

Some companies will even let you stay onboard your yacht at the dock the night before your charter, thus saving you the cost of one night in a hotel near your departure marina. In other cases, the companies may have an arrangement with a local hotel that provides discounted rates for charterers in this situation.

Be sure to ask about these early-arrival options if you're booking a bareboat or instructional charter. A lot of times, the broker or bareboat company won't mention them, for fear of upsetting you with an additional expense.

Getting Things You Need

If you're bareboating and realize you need something that you don't have, you will have to figure out how to get it for yourself. In the case of something like an extra loaf of bread, this is a pretty easy proposition. In the case of an extra set of charts, you may need to hail your bareboat company's base on the VHF radio so they can point you toward the nearest marine supply store.

Onboard crewed charter yachts, you can always get whatever you need by asking the crew. If there are only one or two crewmembers, such as a husband-and-wife team, simply ask whoever is available. If you're onboard a larger yacht with many crewmembers, you should usually go to the *stewardess* first.

Typically, a crew will include a chief stewardess along with several others, usually women. Their job is to make up the rooms, serve meals and drinks, and be generally attentive to whatever the guests want or need in the yacht's guest areas. If they can't solve your problem, they'll know which crewmember can and will take it up with them on your behalf.

"If you're on a yacht of any size, there will be more than one stewardess," explains Shannon Webster, a former stewardess who now books crewed yachts through Shannon Webster Charters in Flagler Beach, Florida, (and is married to Capt. Dan Webster of the 120-foot motoryacht *Joanne*). "You should always defer to the chief stewardess, who will introduce herself and have a take-charge personality. If you happen to grab the second stew, she can relay a message or get the chief stewardess for you, and usually it's even with little issues like doing a little laundry for you. The captain doesn't want to be bothered with those things. That's what the stewardesses are for. They're the private hosts, the private waitresses, the private chambermaids.

"My advice is to stay away from the captain when he's working," Webster continues. "Most captains welcome charter guests into the wheelhouse and are friendly, but when the captain's trying to dock the boat or anchor or talking to his crew or other boats on the radio, it's not the best time to start asking him questions. Just use common sense. Recognize that he's busy."

Yacht crew are happy to help you with whatever you need, but try not to ask them non-emergency questions while they are docking or maneuvering around oncoming boats. As soon as they have you and the yacht safely on course, they'll be all smiles and back at your disposal.

In some cases, the first mate or deckhand might be able to help you—especially if your request concerns water sports equipment, which they tend to oversee. But as a matter of practicality, always try a stewardess first. You'll likely have your problem solved before you even know it's a problem.

Changing the Itinerary

As you learned in Chapter Five, one of the best things about private yacht charter is that the itinerary is yours to choose. If you enjoy one secluded cove and don't want to move on to the next stop that's scheduled, it's your prerogative to stay as long as you like.

If you're bareboating, you simply leave the anchor where it is and go on about your business. To change the itinerary on a crewed yacht, though, you'll have to have a conversation with the captain.

"If you have a cruising guide or a travel guide of a country and you read something in there that you think would be nice to see, you go to the captain and say, 'Can we go there? Would it be possible to go there?'" explains Gertrud Annevelink, a charter broker with Camper & Nicholsons International in Palma de Mallorca, Spain. "It's always weather permitting, but if he can get the boat there—find an anchorage or a slip in a marina, organize a mini-bus or a tour guide onshore with help from the broker—he will do it. Ninety, 95 percent of the time, the captain can make it work.

"It's within reason, of course," she adds. "If you're in Venice and you want to have lunch in Dubrovnik, that's obviously not possible. But if you're closer to one place and want to change the itinerary to go to another, it's perfectly possible."

To get the captain's attention, you can either ask the stewardess to get him for you, or you can chat with him on the bridge—as long as you've been told that guests are allowed in that area. Onboard smaller charter yachts, especially sailboats, the captain often will be driving the boat from an outside helm station anyway, probably very close to where you're sitting and discussing your options with your fellow guests. You can simply lean over and ask his opinion about your ideal plans.

Riding in a Dinghy

Shore transfers to and from cruise ships are usually handled on "small" boats that hold at least one or two dozen people at a time. When it comes to yachts, those transfer boats really are small, holding no more than six or eight people at a time (the size of the average charter party).

These small boats are usually called dinghies, tenders, or RIBs (which stands for rigid-bottom inflatables, with the letters out of order for some crazy reason). You usually climb in and out of them from your yacht's swim platform, which is at the same level as the dinghy floating on the water. This is true whether you are chartering a bareboat or a crewed yacht, although with sailboats, you sometimes have to step over a rail. In the case of catamarans, you usually climb into the dinghy from a platform at the bottom of the steps at the back end of a pontoon.

Onboard crewed charter yachts, you will have deckhands nearby to help you get on and off the dinghy—whenever you want, because the dinghies leave on your schedule, not a pre-set schedule. In most cases, one deckhand will stand inside the dinghy while another stands next to you on the yacht. The deckhand in the dinghy will reach out his hand and you can grip it or, even better, grab his forearm above his hand. Your hand is less likely to slip from his grasp in this position than it would be if you reached out to the deckhand in handshake style.

Once you're inside the dinghy, you can sit either on a bench seat or on the dinghy's edge, which is a large, inflatable tube. Always keep one hand on a handle or rope attached to the dinghy, since they sometimes bounce a bit, especially if the waters are rougher than normal.

A good dinghy driver (usually a first mate or deckhand, in the case of crewed yachts) knows how to "read" the water ahead and steer into the waves so that the boat goes with their motion instead of against it, thus creating less spray that might get you wet. A good dinghy driver also will approach your yacht's swim platform by steering the dinghy into the wind, so that the dinghy won't be pushed away from the yacht while you're trying to step up and onto the yacht's swim platform.

Showering at Night

Even if you typically prefer to shower first thing in the morning, you'll find when you're onboard a yacht that it is far easier, and more logical, to shower at night. This is especially true onboard bareboats, where short showers once per day are sometimes necessary for water conservation.

Consider a typical day in the tropics. You wake up, maybe do a bit of back-stroke off the yacht's swim platform before breakfast, digest your freshly made croissants, and then head back out into the sunshine later for a bit of water-skiing or kayaking. Soon enough it's time for lunch, which you eat while wrapped in a towel on the yacht's aft deck with your friends in their own bathing suits. Then, perhaps, it's a midday hike onshore and a swim back to the boat in time for a nap on the sundeck, in the breeze, before sunset. Or, if you're not feeling sleepy, perhaps you might enjoy a pre-cocktail-hour cocktail in the hot tub, still wearing your bathing suit from that same morning.

Then it becomes twilight, which is typically when yachties choose to shower, allowing them to clean up and look smart for cocktails and dinner. Come morning, the fun in the sun starts all over again, and you'll still be as clean as you need to be to jump in the warm ocean waters for that starter swim before breakfast.

Being a Good Guest

When you're on a private yacht charter vacation, you of course should relax and be yourself. You truly can do pretty much anything you want, provided you aren't breaking the law or destroying the yacht. It is your boat for the week.

Having said that, there are a few things to keep in mind that will help you be a good guest, and thus make your charter go as smoothly as possible.

For starters, I need to reiterate the problems with taking drugs onboard. Even commonly used drugs like marijuana are a major no-no according to international laws, which state that captains can lose their licenses and yachts can be confiscated if drugs are found onboard. As you read in Chapter Nine, even some of the world's most famous celebrities have been kicked off $200,000-a-week charters because of drugs. No captain is willing to risk his job, or his boss's boat, so that you can get your groove on. Nor is any bareboat company willing to be accused of running drugs simply to protect you and your stash. In most cases, you will be booted from your yacht and left in the hands of the local authorities—which in some countries means not-so-nice jail cells.

The same thing goes for weapons. Don't even think about taking them with you unless you have received prior permission from the captain, say in the case of a charter to a sporting clays facility. In all other cases, the yacht's crew or the bareboat company will immediately confiscate guns, knives, and anything else that might be dangerous, and you may be asked to disembark mid-charter in the middle of nowhere—without any rights to getting your money back or any assistance in getting back home. You will have, in most cases, broken your half of the charter contract. End of story.

On a happier note, one of the best ways to ensure that a fully crewed charter goes smoothly is by relaxing and letting the crew serve you. If you're not used to this kind of one-on-one service, it can feel strange, as if you have a personal slave, but in truth these deckhands and stewardesses have been trained to offer you the highest possible service. If you constantly try to clear your own plate or make your own bed, they will think you are unhappy with the service they are working hard to provide. I've heard more than one stewardess lament and worry over behavior that guests probably thought was being helpful.

Also, if you're on a crewed yacht, get off the boat once in a while for meals. Yes, the chef will cook for you three times a day (or even more) if that's what you want, but he is, in the end, a person, and he does need to sit down and take a break once in a while if he's going to perform at his best. During Mediterranean charters, it is actually customary for guests to have breakfast and lunch onboard but dinner at a restaurant onshore. In the Caribbean and emerging charter grounds, where restaurants can be fewer and farther between, just do your best to take advantage of off-the-boat eating opportunities when they arise. Let your stewardess know that you plan to go ashore when you see a restaurant you might like, so the chef doesn't prepare a meal you aren't going to eat.

Another thing that will tire your crew out and affect the level of service they can provide is a charter party that divides in half, with a few couples staying up late at night and a few other couples getting up early in the morning. Again, it's your yacht for the week, and you can do whatever you want, but the policy onboard most crewed yachts is that at least one crewmember must be awake and on duty whenever guests are not in their cabins. If your friends keep the yacht's stewardess up until 5 in the morning serving drinks, and then you want her to serve you a full breakfast at 6 in the morning, you have to understand that she's going to be tired and not at her best.

Respecting the crew areas is another detail to keep in mind. Remember, the deckhands and stewardesses—sometimes even the yacht's captain—have cabins that are far smaller than yours. Oftentimes, two or three crewmembers share a single, small cabin with bunk beds and a lone shower. These quarters are all the crew have in the way of private space onboard. Think about how you would feel in their position, and try not to wander into their personal areas.

Also do your best to respect the roles the captain wants each crewmember to play. The odds are that you will be smitten with a particular stewardess and deckhand, and you may even want to invite that crewmember along for a round of water-skiing or even drinks ashore. The thing is, for every moment that person is off the yacht, the other crewmembers have to do his or her work. This can cause problems and ultimately affect the overall service you receive. If you want to invite a special crewmember for a special treat, check with the captain first.

Last, in general, respect the yacht. If your bathing suit is dripping, wait a few minutes for it to dry before you go traipsing through the main saloon to your cabin. Don't hurl your soaked bath towels onto your bedspread, and keep those shoes off when you're onboard. There is no better way to look like you belong, no matter what kind of yacht you choose, than by treating the boat the way you would want others to treat your home.

Tipping

Gratuities are one of the most heavily debated areas in yacht charter. Onboard bareboats, the only people you will need to even consider tipping are the dockhands who help you with your bags, get your lines onto the pilings at marinas, fill up your fuel or water tanks, and that sort of thing. (There's also the skipper, of course, if you go with a skippered bareboat.) Crewed charter yachts are different. As with waiters and waitresses, some yacht crew depend on your tips for part of their earnings. The gratuity you offer at the end of your charter is very much on their minds while they are working for you throughout the week.

There is a split between cultures when it comes to tipping onboard crewed yachts. American captains and crew, onboard yachts anywhere in the world, typically expect a gratuity of no less than 15 percent. European captains and crew, by contrast, are often perfectly happy with a gratuity of five to ten percent, even in the Mediterranean, where the charters themselves are typically more expensive.

I have heard of American captains pressuring charter brokers before a charter begins, almost blackmailing them into telling you, the charter guest, than any gratuity of less than 15 percent will result in less-than-stellar service onboard. By the same token, I have heard American charter brokers defend those captains vociferously, saying that European captains should expect the same level of gratuity and that anything less than 15 percent is insulting to a professional crew of any nationality.

It's dicey territory, to be sure. Further complicating matters is the fact that onboard some of the most expensive, most luxurious yachts, the boat owners insist on tips of 40 to 50 percent for their crews—before they will let you book the boat at all. In other cases, with all-inclusive rates, the gratuity may be added to your bill in advance of the charter itself, regardless of the service you receive.

Brokers can confuse you even more, because American charter brokers tend to support higher tipping while European charter brokers suggest lowering the percentage you offer. It's a part of the cultures on either side of the Atlantic Ocean: Americans simply tend to be bigger tippers than people of any other nationalities.

Most charter brokers who book fully crewed yachts tend to agree on only one thing: A gratuity of any size is something that should be given at your discretion, based on the service you receive. It is a thank-you gift, pure and simple.

"Our general rule is that the percentage is between seven and 15 percent, which will encompass European boats and mentality and American boats and mentality," explains Cindy Brown, a knowledgeable and straightforward crewed yacht charter broker in the Manhattan, New York, office of Nigel Burgess. "What we do for our clients, we provide a service where we will lodge funds in escrow for them. They give us a call a few days before the end of the charter and tell us how much they want released, and then we talk to the captain."

Noelle Alice-Fasciato, a well-respected broker with International Yacht Charter in France, puts the recommended percentage at five to ten percent with the following philosophy: "The tipping system came from—initially, 30 to 40 years ago—when crews were not paid extremely well and their main wages came from the tipping by the few clients they had. But this system survived the years even when the crews get good wages, considering the fact that they usually have no real taxes to pay, they live and eat onboard. The funny point is now a reality that can seem a bit bizarre, when the captains decided that the tips *should* be a certain percentage of the charter fee."

No matter how much you decide to leave as a tip—based solely on the service you receive—you can either arrange for it to be held in escrow before your charter even starts (with crewed yachts), or you can deliver it to the captain during the final day of your charter (with any kind of yacht). The most tactful way to handle a cash or check tip at the end of a charter is to take along a thank-you card that you handwrite and have every member of your charter party sign, and then offer the card with the tip inside to the captain when he's not busy driving the yacht or docking it at your final destination.

I usually write a note in my thank-you card that is specific to the charter, saying things like, "I'll always remember the delicious chocolate cheesecake that chef Mike served and the wonderful hike that deckhand Steve took me on when we were on Anguilla." In many cases, the crew keep these cards as proud souvenirs of a job well done.

It is up to the captain to distribute your tip among his crewmembers. If you feel the urge to tip one crewmember more than the others, keep in mind that you see some crewmembers more than others, and thus may grow more fond of them even though other people are working just as hard on your behalf. The stewardesses, for instance, often end up being guests' favorites because they serve all the meals, but it is the engineer who is sweating down below, out of sight, making sure your lights, air conditioning, toilets, and stereo systems are working perfectly.

For this reason, most captains prefer if you simply give them the entire tip, to distribute equitably among their team. Many charter brokers who go on familiarization trips actually request that the entire crew be present for the giving of the gratuity, so they can thank everyone at once and make sure all the crewmembers know they are appreciated.

If you're feeling especially generous, crew do appreciate your leaving behind any recently released CDs or books that you might have finished using during your charter. Especially in the Caribbean, these crewmembers don't typically get access to much more than old Harlequin romance novels and Jimmy Buffett CDs, and they would happily enjoy some fresh entertainment after cleaning up any messes you've left in your wake.

You also can invite the captain and crew ashore for drinks or dinner one night, if they've done an exceptional job and you want to go above and beyond in saying thanks. Most crewed yacht teams will graciously decline your offer and stay behind to work on the boat, but a bareboat skipper or husband-and-wife team may take you up on the offer—and regale you all night with some of the best boating stories you've ever heard.

Settling Your Bill

At the end of your crewed yacht charter, the last matter will be settling your bill. This includes any extra food, wines, onshore expenses, or marina fees that may have come up during your vacation—all perfectly legitimate expenses.

However, this is also the time when you will need to satisfy yourself regarding any problems that may have arisen during your charter. Before you write that final check or give the all-clear for final funds to be transferred by wire, you need to feel confident that you have received the experience you were promised in your original contract.

"At the end of a proper yacht charter, you should get a statement of what exactly was spent so that there are no discrepancies after you've left the boat," explains Nicole Haboush of Allied Yacht Charters in Miami Beach, Florida. "A lot of clients try to get off the boat because they think they've spent too much and they don't want to pay the difference [from their advance provisioning payment], but we have to find the clients and make them pay.

"I tell my clients that halfway through the charter, it's a good idea for the captain to sit down and go over how your expenditures are going," she adds. "See how much fuel you've used, how much expensive champagne you've been drinking, that sort of thing. I've had clients going $20,000 over, but a lot of times if you're going under, at the end of the charter you can use that toward the crew's tip. The captain should have a detailed spreadsheet he can show you, with receipts if you request them."

If anything feels wrong to you, remain on the yacht and contact your charter broker. "If there's something you can't resolve, we would assist you or even call the owner of the yacht," Haboush says. "Sometimes, the owner will even talk to the charterer directly. Before the charter, there should be a good idea of what the expenses will be, but sometimes things happen."

15

Important Insider Tips

As you no doubt understand by now, the industry experts quoted throughout *Have the Whole Boat* know far more about private yacht charter vacations than could ever be written in an entire series of books. Whether they started out as liveaboard sailors, megayacht crewmembers, or even U.S. Navy recruits, these folks know the business of boating. They have much to teach you, whether you want them to help you become a bareboat skipper or plan the relaxing crewed charter of your dreams.

With that in mind, this chapter includes a last few tidbits of advice and information from various segments of the private yacht charter industry.

Bareboating Tips

"I tell people, 'Don't get in over your head,'" says Barb Hansen, co-owner of Southwest Florida Yachts in Fort Myers, Florida. "Make it an enjoyable experience the first time. Maybe you won't turn yourself off, but you may scare your wife or the kids to death. First-time boaters will come and say they want to go [from Fort Myers] to Key West with their wife, their three-year-old, and their six-year-old. That's just a red flag. We talk to them about how it's too far, it's an offshore run, a lot of things can happen, there can be bad weather, people get sick. It's not something that's fun on a schedule when you've got a week of vacation, whether the weather is good or not. My advice is to make it enjoyable.

"That's why I like our area," she adds. "It's easy boating. You're in sight of land, you can anchor out, you can be in a gourmet restaurant at night, if you go aground it's likely to be sand or mud, just things that make for easy boating. It's doing it slowly, and you need time to think about things when you're new to boating, until it becomes routine. Our area gives people a chance to literally get their feet wet. You are going to run aground. Everybody does. You want to do it in a place where you're not going to hurt yourself or the boat."

Barney Crook of TMM Yacht Charters says the same thing. His company offers fleets of sailboats and powerboat bareboats in the Virgin Islands, Belize, and the Grenadines, but for first-timers, he always recommends the British Virgin Islands.

"Most people chartering the first time go to the BVI," he explains. "It's the easiest place of anywhere to bareboat. You're never far away from the base, we can always get to you from the base fairly easily, it's well organized with moorings and ice everywhere. You think about Belize, the facilities aren't the same and it's much harder to provide backup. There's no moorings, you can't pick up ice and water at every stop, you have to be prepared to do everything without backup. You're really out there cruising. For the first time, the BVIs are a lot easier."

In terms of choosing a specific bareboat company to work with, Hansen recommends looking for telltale signs of professionalism.

"There's companies that don't really have an office," she explains. "Do they have a storefront? Are they accessible seven days a week? If they say you can only check in on certain days, like Saturdays, well, who do you call on Sunday when you're cruising and you have a problem? Some places don't have a lot of resources. Especially in a remote area, you want to know you have support."

More than anything, though, she says it's important for bareboaters to be honest with themselves. "If you look at your abilities as a bareboat charterer, you're basically the owner of the boat for the time that you're on it," Hansen says. "You're telling that company that you're qualified to be in charge of that boat. You need to make sure you are able to handle that boat.

"I had a guy who chartered a Grand Banks 32, and I looked at his resume, and I thought he needed a captain. He ended up taking one for the first day even though he didn't want one, and it ended up being very windy that week, and he just freaked out when he set out on his own. He got to his first stop and called and said, 'I shouldn't have done this. This was a mistake.' It turns out his wife was ill, and he thought this would be a good thing for her, but he never told us this, and of course she didn't want to be on the boat. So now he wants to get off and abandon the boat and have us go pick it up, and we had to send a captain up to go get them and the boat, and they went home early.

"So he misled us—and himself—about his abilities and his purpose. He just thought he could do it and that it would be good for his wife. You have to know your limitations, and your skills and abilities. You don't have to be a diesel mechanic, but you have to know what you're doing.

"If you take a course, you will be able to do these things. You'll also know your limitations. You can't just go out and get on a 50-foot boat and take it out.

It's not my requirement. It's you and Mother Nature that require this education. It's for your enjoyment, your safety, and your family's well being. It's just common sense."

When you sign a bareboat contract, you are taking sole responsibility for the yacht throughout the duration of your charter. That includes navigating, engine room maintenance, and more. You are in command.

Crook says working with a broker is a surefire way to get the kind of bareboat that suits your needs and abilities. Still, he doesn't necessarily think that first-time bareboaters need a broker's help—especially bareboaters working with a reputable company.

"I don't think so much that they *should* use a broker, but they can," he says. "Some brokers provide a very good, impartial, overall outlook and view to people who haven't done it before and are having trouble deciding on their own. Brokers are also an excellent resource if you're looking to go someplace out of the ordinary. They can save you a lot of time, just like a travel agent. But today, with the Internet, people can find out a lot of what the brokers know on their own. You just won't know what the broker's other clients think of the boats, or what the brokers themselves think of the boats.

"It's not necessary [to use a broker for a bareboat booking], but it's by all means not bad. If you've never done it before, it's a good way to start. It will help put you in touch with a company that will give you what you're looking for."

Instructional Charter Tips

Doris Colgate, who owns and operates the Offshore Sailing School with her husband, Steve, says first-time instructional charter students need to pay close attention not just to the kind of certification a teaching program offers, but also to the kinds of yachts each charter company uses as classrooms.

"There are an awful lot of schools out there that aren't doing the best," she says, lamenting the lackluster approach to safe-boating education that exists in some places. "Look for a school that has U.S. Sailing Certification. It's the one we adhere to, and Steve was on the training committee that initiated the program. It is not easy to become a U.S. Sailing School. The instructors have to go through a very intensive evaluation. We don't teach people to teach. They have to come to us with a depth of knowledge, which includes single-handing a 26-footer or whatever boat they're working on."

Some sailboat instructional schools use smaller boats in the 19- to 24-foot range, and those classes can cost less, Colgate says. By comparison, Offshore Sailing School's prices are typically the most expensive, and their boats are among the newest and biggest available for instructional sailing.

"I don't think the new sailor understands how important the boat they learn on is," she says. "Our Colgate 26 has a tremendous amount of sophistication, so you can move to other kinds of boats with fewer problems." The idea is that if you start out by learning the most complex systems onboard one sailboat, every other sailboat you ever try to charter down the road will be easier by comparison.

Bill Shermer, co-owner of the trawler yacht-focused Blue Goose Charters on the Chesapeake Bay, also believes that choosing a reputable company with a reputable fleet of boats is key to any first-time instructional experience—especially if you really want to learn anything.

"Most first-timers have a general, vague, romantic idea," he says. "They want to get into the boat and go. But they haven't thought through all the details. The horns of the dilemma are that it's not like renting a car. You already know how to drive a car. It's not like renting a canoe on Lake Winnehaha. You're going out onto the Chesapeake. It's a fairly serious undertaking. Our philosophy is that the more you learn about boating, the more relaxed you'll be, and the more you'll enjoy it. If you're coming for training, then that has to be the top priority, not taking a vacation. You will get to go out on the bay, but you need to be serious about it in the beginning so that you don't make a mistake and la-de-da your way onto a reef or an oyster bed."

Shermer's overarching advice for any first-time instructional charterer is to make sure you know what you want, and simply ask for it. A good instructional company should be able to help you achieve your goals with minimal additional stress beyond the actual boating itself.

"For training, you want to remove as much of the details as possible," he says. "Don't burden yourself with a lot of preliminary worries. Tie in with a company that is going to hold you by the hand. Shop around. You have to have a good idea of what your training objectives are. Then, the company can give you the answers that you need.

"If you ask us, as opposed to asking another company with a set curriculum, you'll get different answers. We tailor our curriculum. We try to remove as much of the anxiety as we can."

David Forbes at Club Nautique in Alameda, California, also tries to take the pressure off first-time sailing and powerboat cruising students—by separating the teaching from the actual cruising, and in some cases by separating spouses from each other. "We do a lot of instruction, and we do a lot of charters, and we do some instructional charters," Forbes explains. "We frankly split it up more. That way, there's no pressure on the instructor or the student to pass [the course] by the end of the charter. One of the things we see occasionally is that it's the husband pushing the wife, and the wife isn't necessarily motivated to do this. We try to separate them, sit down with the wife and set some realistic expectations and goals. If she doesn't necessarily want to get certified, or maybe just learn the basics, we take the pressure off. You can do this your way. That's what this is.

"The marinas are full of people who've done this the wrong way, who bought a boat to see if they like it. You don't have to own the mountain to go skiing. You don't have to own the court to play tennis. In the old days, you had to know somebody who had a boat to go boating. Nowadays, that's not true. You should do this."

No matter what school you choose for an instructional charter, Forbes says, the most important thing is to recognize your goals.

"Some people have no goals," he says. "They just want to see if they like it or not. Some people just want to sail locally. A lot of people want to go rent a boat in the Caribbean, and some people eventually want to own a boat, to go off cruising. All of them are going to benefit from education. A lot of people put a lot of money into boats—gear and electronics and that sort of thing—but not enough money into themselves.

"Generally, people fail before the boat. Become an educated boater. You'll have more fun."

Crewed Charter Tips

Janet Bloomfield, president of Fort Lauderdale, Florida-based International Yacht Charter Group, says the one thing she can't understand about crewed charter guests is their reluctance to talk to a yacht's captain before booking a vacation. Crew can make or break a charter no matter how nice the yacht itself is, and it's important that your personality—more so than your broker's—is a good fit with the personalities of the people working onboard.

"A lot of clients are not interested in talking to the crew," Bloomfield laments. "They just want me to do all the work for them. Now, I might love the crew, but it's personal. I have my own taste. It doesn't mean you'll like them."

Bloomfield typically offers her charter clients two potential yachts, after listening to their preferences and using her instincts about which crew might be the best fit. "My ideal advice is that we'll find the boat, and before we go to contract, that I'll put them in touch with the captain on their top two choices," she says. "It can be on the phone or via e-mail, I'll set it up. The agenda is to discuss the itinerary, who's going to be coming, what is their boating experience—items that I know are of interest to the client, so that they're not only exchanging information, but also getting to know each other.

"What stuns me is that very rarely does the client talk to both captains," she continues. "They usually say the first captain is fine, let's book it. It's just crazy. My philosophy is to get as much information as possible. You need to know who these people are on the boat with you. Especially for a first-time charter guest, the crew is critical."

Bloomfield also says she is continually amazed that charterers don't feel comfortable sticking up for what they want. A crewed charter yacht is supposed to be a highly personalized experience. If you're not getting that experience, something needs to be remedied.

"If something goes awry, the client always worries that if they speak up to the captain, there will be retribution," she explains. "That's why the broker is there. Make me the bad guy. Call me 24/7. Maybe the captain says you can't go anchor in the BVIs. Well, of course you can anchor in the BVIs. Or they won't put the sails up, but it's a sailboat. Some captains forget who they work for. They think they work just for their [yacht's] owner, but when you're there, they work for you. And it's my job to help them remember that.

Photos like this one, of a 120-foot motoryacht circling the tip of an iceberg in Alaska, will make you think about the exciting adventures you can enjoy during your charter vacation. That's all well and good, but don't let marketing brochures get you so excited to book a trip that you forget to ask about important details—such as the crew.

"I had one situation where they had a late lunch, and the guests wanted a late dinner. So the chef, who was the captain's wife, says, 'Okay, we'll have a 7:30 dinner.' And they wanted a 9:30 dinner, but they were afraid to say something. I don't know why. Or at least why they didn't think to call me. I'd let that boat know that they needed to get their act together or I'd never book them again."

Crew are also at the top of the list for Capt. Ray "Rags" Weldon, charter and sales manager for the Fort Lauderdale, Florida, office of Ocean Independence. He, too, wishes more first-time charterers would learn to look beyond the yacht itself and at the service being provided onboard.

"They do tend to go for the pretty, white, new, shiny boats," Weldon says. "I say, 'Okay, your requirements are this, and you have six boats. Your requirements fit all six'—they'll pick the shiny white one every time. But the crew is what makes the charter, not the boat. I never try to talk them out of it, if that's what they want, but I try to tell them that the crew is what makes the boat. A better crew is better service. A better crew is a better vacation."

He also has words of wisdom regarding charter brokers themselves. "Some of the first-time charterers are scared about being ripped off," Weldon explains. "We're basically telling people to send me $10,000 and go stand on a dock, and a boat will show up. There's always a lot of insecurity on the charterer's part. I try to befriend the charter guests. That's the difference between one charter broker and another one. If you like me, and you can see what I'm doing for you, you'll come back.

"Some of these newer brokers, who are more or less just salesmen, they're making a deal. This isn't a deal. This is somebody's family vacation you're doing. The money is irrelevant to what it's all about. It's about intimacy, getting to know the client, and getting to know the boat. My job is to make sure everybody will get along."

LeAnn Morris Pliske, a charter broker with The Sacks Group in Fort Lauderdale, Florida, couldn't agree more. "The price is the price, no matter the boat," she explains. "Like Realtors use a multiple-listing service, we use our listing service. Are rates negotiable? Yes. But we're all going to get the same negotiated rate. If I have a particular relationship with a yacht owner, in a rare, extreme circumstance I might be able to squeeze out a few extra percentage points of savings. But really, your charter [experience] comes down to your relationship with the broker. I know a lot of things about my clients that are not repeatable. But I have to know it to make the charter work. It's how the broker communicates to the crew about the charterer's likes or dislikes that makes or breaks the charter."

Pliske also says she wishes first-time charterers would think beyond the yacht itself when working with a broker. If you're taking the step of booking a yacht instead of a cruise ship, why not also ask your broker to add a private jet charter into the mix to personalize your entire vacation experience that much more?

"People just don't know that they can do it," she says of private air transportation being added to private yacht charters. "People think about a jet, they think that something that can take them across the Atlantic will be cost prohibitive. But when you're talking about eight or ten or 12 people, it's really not any more expensive than first-class tickets. And you have your own plane. And the food you want. And the literature you want onboard.

"On the East Coast, it's very easy to get a jet charter to the Bahamas and Caribbean," she continues. "There are even companies that sell the dead-heads back. That's when the plane comes back empty to its hub. A lot of times we can get hold of them, and they're a third of the regular price. So you can combine all your points of transportation. We even arrange special customs and immigration for our clients. They come out to the airplane instead of making people go into the terminal. I did it in Grenada for a charter of 12 [people] this Christmas, and it was $200 for all of that to happen. It wasn't expensive at all. Their vacation started when they boarded the plane in New York."

Gina Robertson of Yachtstore in Fort Lauderdale, Florida, also says she wishes first-time clients would simply ask for what they dream of having. She started her career booking cruise ship vacations and knows darn well that in the world of yacht charter, you really can get more for your money. All you have to do is make the request, which requires a mental adjustment. It's not about choosing among cruise ship cabins you're offered. It's about demanding what you envision on a personalized cruise all your own.

"One analogy that I use all the time is this catamaran," Roberston says. "There's this great boat, *Double Feature*, a 57-footer. It's no secret that her owner is a very famous female movie producer. It's an immaculate, four-stateroom boat with queen beds for four couples. Two crew, five-star food, all-inclusive for $25,000 a week—and that's with good wine and scuba diving. It comes out to about $300 per person, per day. That's less than a Princess [cruise ship] balcony cabin."

These are the kinds of things that Pliske's clients at The Sacks Group love to learn as well.

"I just recently had a slew of first-time charterers," she says. "One of them was a 60th birthday, and he was gathering multiple generations of his family. He just found us in a magazine and didn't know what he was doing. I love those phone calls. Once they start to understand the economics of it, people start to clue in that this is on par with a five-star resort anywhere—but you're getting multiple resorts, because you get to go to different stops along the way. These people came back and they were just flabbergasted. The guy said, 'God, I wish I hadn't waited until I was 60 to try this.' Those are the phone calls that make my day."

The Last Word

I hope that in the pages of *Have the Whole Boat*, you have learned many things that will help you book your perfect private yacht charter vacation, whatever it may be. But I hope that more than anything else, you have come to see the essence of what yacht charter is in all its forms: a refreshing break from pretty much everything else that connotes a seagoing vacation in today's Age of Capitalism.

Yacht charter is the antithesis of the glossy-brochure, prepackaged, target-marketed, all-or-nothing vacation options that force you to choose one cruise ship over another without really giving you any choices at all. Yes, one cruise ship may be going to Italy while another one goes to Puerto Rico, but at the end of the day, you're still on a ship with a thousand other people on the same schedule, eating the same food, and doing the same excursions for half a day at a time before you have to rush back and start all over again. Sure, you chose the ship. You may even actually want to see one or two of the islands on the itinerary, and you may like some of the shows on stage. But your vacation time—your precious handful of down time from work and stress—really is not your own. You're just one in the crowd, being herded from place to place like sheep.

Now that you have discovered private yacht charter vacations, I hope you feel like I do, like the proverbial rat in the maze who finally found the cheese. We really *can* have it all on the world's waters, often while saving a few bucks in the process.

The boating vocabulary, insider tips, reputable names, and industry information you've come to know throughout this book are the tools you will need to make your own private yacht charter vision a reality. I hope you enjoy regaining control of your on-the-water dreams, and I wish you fair seas as you *Have the Whole Boat* for yourself.

APPENDIX A

Additional Resources

Have the Whole Boat is meant to be a complete introduction to private yacht charter vacations. If you've read this far, you understand how the industry works, the many choices you can make, the assistance you will need from brokers, what your onboard experience will include, and what to do should you encounter problems.

Still, you can learn much more as you delve deeper into specific kinds of charter. Bareboating and basic boat handling, for instance, are the subject of countless books and magazine articles each year. While reviews of actual crewed and bareboat charters are harder to come by, the yachts themselves are profiled regularly in many magazines worldwide. There are books about the yachts, too, including everything from how they're built to how you can buy a yacht and become the captain of your own charter crew.

Here's where to look if you want to find more information.

Web Sites

Currently, the main sources of charter yacht information on the World Wide Web are charter companies themselves—obviously a somewhat biased bunch. I'm working to change that, as is at least one other industry insider.

CharterWave.com. This site is designed as a companion to the book in your hands. It includes links to help you reach reputable crewed yacht charter brokers and bareboat companies, as well as copies of my full-length marine magazine reviews of actual yacht charters around the world—including new information and photos that never saw their way into print.

I continually add information about specific bareboats, instructional yachts, crewed yachts, corporate charters, and charter brokers to the site, making it the Web's only dedicated source of professionally reported information about actual charter experiences and industry experts. My monthly E-newsletter includes information about charter yachts I've visited recently, crew who are offering unique and outstanding service, discounts and deals available on boats of all kinds, and trends I see emerging worldwide.

Features I am adding to *www.CharterWave.com* include tools to help you plan charters, videos of charter experiences that you can download, forums where you can talk to experts and to other charterers about particular boats and crewmembers, and links to exclusive deals and discounts on charter vacations of all kinds.

As with this book, I do not take a cut of the fee from any charter bookings that result from your using my Web site—so you'll know the information you're getting is from an independent source.

SailOnline.com. This site is run by a man who owns three yachts that he offers for bareboat charters through The Moorings. It includes good, general information about chartering bareboats and crewed yachts alike, especially ideas about getting bareboat discounts that only a bareboat owner could conceive.

The creator of the site is the president of an association of several hundred yacht owners (mostly bareboat sailboats in the 35- to 60-foot range). He connects those boat owners to you through a link called "discount charters," where you can place a last-minute offer for a charter booking and see whether any of the association's owners are willing to accept it. That's a good feature if price is your main consideration, but keep in mind that you will have to settle for whatever boat takes you up on your offer, sight and quality unseen—with no broker in your corner should problems arise.

You can try to better your chances for a good charter by asking questions about specific yachts on the Web site's message board, where people who have taken charters exchange information. Site users also typically offer advice about ownership issues for anyone who wants to buy a boat and put it into the charter market, hoping to make a little money.

Magazines

If you're looking for articles about actual yacht charters, your best bet is a boating magazine. Yes, charter stories show up once in a while in general-interest travel magazines, but you could go crazy trying to find them—and they're usually written by people who know precious little about yachts. The boating magazines, in general, do a decent job of covering the charter industry, although their advertising is tied to it, so you'll rarely find criticisms about companies or specific boats unless something goes dreadfully wrong onboard.

On the brighter side, the boating magazines that cover charter do have Web sites with searchable databases where you can find enjoyable features about boats, companies, and destinations that you may be considering. As a bonus, these sites also contain reviews of different styles of new-model yachts, which will further help you to understand various layouts and yacht features.

Please notice that I have not included any charter-specific magazines on this list of reliable resources. While you may find a charter magazine in your local bookstore, I believe the following titles are most honest with their readers.

Power & Motoryacht. This is the nation's leading consumer marine magazine, with nearly 160,000 readers each month. Full disclosure: I work regularly for this magazine, and I'm on its masthead as the charter/cruising editor. My boss, Editor-in-Chief Richard Thiel, is the most ethical editor I have met in the business, even supporting me when I write about problems I find onboard charter yachts—and cost the magazine advertising revenue.

Regular features include bareboat powerboats as small as 30 feet all the way up to the world's largest and most expensive megayachts. Charter is covered in multiple issues throughout the year, and the annual October issue has a "charter/cruising" theme. Note that this magazine does not cover sailboats of any kind.

The Web site *www.PowerAndMotoryacht.com* has a "cruising/charters" link that you can click on to find dozens of articles about actual bareboat and crewed yacht charters that the magazine's editors and I have taken. The site also has a "videos" link that will let you download (for free) narrated tours of actual powerboats and megayachts that may be available for charter.

And, if you want to get the latest gossip about the fanciest, big-money charter megayachts, you can check out the "forums" link to the "megayachts" string. Yacht-spotters from all over the world exchange tidbits here on a daily basis.

Voyaging. This is a sister magazine to *Power & Motoryacht*, put out four times a year. Full disclosure: I am the editor of *Voyaging*, deciding which stories get covered, who writes them, and how the information is presented. The features are focused on destinations from the viewpoint of cruising to them onboard 30- to 70-foot powerboats. Note that this magazine does not cover sailboats of any kind.

Voyaging is a cruising magazine as opposed to a general boating magazine. You will not find reviews of new boat models, for instance, but you will find ideas about fun and interesting places to go boating. Most features include a "charter options" sidebar that tells you where you can book bareboats and smaller crewed powerboats in the featured area, and some of the articles themselves are produced onboard bareboats, instructional charters, and crewed charters.

This magazine's Web site is *www.VoyagingOnline.com.*

Sail. This magazine has the same parent company as *Power & Motoryacht* and *Voyaging,* but an entirely different editorial staff—who are experts in and devoted entirely to sailing. Full disclosure: I've written one or two small items for *Sail* on a freelance basis.

You'll find bareboating and cruising articles in this magazine's pages, and its Web site, *www.SailMag.com,* has a "charter cruising" link that takes you to feature articles about charters the magazine's writers have taken. There is also a "learn to sail" link that will connect you with instructional charter companies worldwide.

Yachting. This monthly magazine is the main competitor to *Power & Motoryacht.* Full disclosure: I was the executive editor of *Yachting* from 2000 until 2003. Charter is covered in regular issues throughout the year, and the March and October issues each carry a "charter/cruising" theme. Note that you will find powerboats and sailboats in this magazine. Increasingly, the focus is on higher-end yachts as opposed to bareboats. There has been a recent shift away from reviewing actual charters, with general information about destinations and yachts now filling the magazine's charter sections.

The Web site *www.YachtingMagazine.com* has a "charter/destinations" link where you can find stories about charters the magazine's editors have reviewed (with a few of those stories written by me). You'll also find a searchable database there that connects you to *www.CharterIndexOnline.com,* a compilation of worldwide charter yachts that boat owners pay to be listed in, as a marketing tool.

Cruising World. This is a well-read magazine among sailboat owners who enjoy cruising worldwide, though the editors do also run occasional features about bareboats and chartered yachts. Note that this magazine does not cover powerboats of any kind.

Its Web site, *www.CruisingWorld.com,* has a "charters" link that will take you to news stories about various charter company happenings and discount offers, as well as to a listing of bareboat and crewed charter contacts around the globe.

PowerCruising. This is a sister magazine to *Cruising World* and a direct competitor of *Voyaging.* It is written primarily for powerboat owners, and it includes new boat and gear reviews along with stories about destinations and charters. Note that this magazine does not cover sailboats of any kind.

As of this writing, the magazine's Web site, *www.PowerCruisingMag.com,* did not have a specific link to information about bareboats or crewed charters. However, the site does have a "destinations" forum where you can communicate with powerboat owners about places where they like to cruise.

Showboats International. This is a high-end, luxury yachting magazine that prominently features the world's most expensive sailing yachts and power-driven megayachts. You will not find bareboating or instructional charter information here, nor lower-priced fully crewed charters.

Historically, the charter articles in *Showboats* have been reviews of charter yachts, as opposed to reviews of actual trips taken onboard them. (The stories talked about furniture and construction details, not of crew service and chef's offerings.) However, *Showboats* recently got a new editor who enjoys taking the actual charters, so you may see more high-end charter reviews here in the future. You also can find industry news and notes about charter brokers in this magazine.

Its Web site is *www.Showboats.com.*

Boat International. This is the main competitor to *Showboats,* and as such focuses on high-end, fully crewed charters. You will find articles about sailing yachts and power-driven megayachts alike, but you won't find bareboating and instructional charter information here. Again, it's top-dollar only.

Boat International USA (the American version of the magazine) recently added a "Mediterranean charter" issue to its annual editorial mix, indicating that it intends to publish more features about charter in the future. It also regularly runs industry information about charter brokers and companies.

Their joint Web site is *www.BoatInternational.com.*

Books

If you plan to take a bareboat or instructional charter, there are countless how-to books out there for you to read. Most are written with brand-new sailboat and powerboat owners in mind, but the skills are all the same, so the books will be good reference materials for you. Most are available at sites like *www.Amazon.com* and *www.BarnesAndNoble.com*, as well as at the remaining brick-and-mortar bookstores that still have boating sections.

Other good sources for how-to boating books are *www.BluewaterWeb.com*, the home page of Bluewater Books and Charts, and *www.WestMarine.com*, a superstore chain for boat owners whose printed and online catalogs have entire sections devoted to books and videos. You also will find cruising guides at both these stores, listed geographically and packed with boater-friendly information about various regions and waterways (that charter guests of all kinds can enjoy).

There also are a few books to be had about yacht interiors and design, if you want to see the insides of different styles of boats (only some of which are available for charter). These books are sometimes glossy compilations of boating magazine articles, with lots of nifty details about how much the boat owners paid for the chandeliers and that sort of thing.

Unfortunately, there is a dearth of books about crewed yacht charters, and about the history and basics of the overall charter industry. That's why I wrote *Have the Whole Boat* and created *www.CharterWave.com* as a continuing source of new information for newcomers who simply want to book an enjoyable vacation without having to read through page after page of engine room instructions.

Following are short summaries of books that I've found helpful in recent years.

Chartering A Boat: Sail and Power, written by Chris Caswell and published by Sheridan House. Caswell is the charter editor for *Yachting* magazine, and he is a friend of mine in the marine journalism business. His book is the only other general introduction to bareboat and crewed yacht charter that I have found on the market, and it offers his expertise in three parts: The Basics, The Skills, and Charter Areas. Anyone looking for a crewed yacht vacation will want to skip the middle section of the book, which applies to bareboaters, but the general information about cruising areas and seasonal weather applies to all kinds of charter guests. Caswell also has a nifty way with words, so the book is easy to read.

Chapman Piloting & Seamanship, 64th edition, edited by Elbert S. Maloney and published by Hearst Books. This is the bible of boating, pure and simple. It contains more than 900 pages of information about everything from hoisting appropriate flags to determining which boats have the right of way in cruising situations. Every true boater keeps a copy onboard.

Colgate's Basic Sailing, written by Stephen Colgate and published by Offshore Sailing School Ltd. This is the textbook used for the Offshore Sailing School's Learn to Sail course. It's written by one of the school's owners and is based on his more than 35 years of teaching experience. Lots of excellent, hands-on, how-to information in here.

Sailing: A Women's Guide, written by Doris Colgate and published by McGraw Hill. This book is by the "better half" of the husband-and-wife team who run the Offshore Sailing School. Her book helps beginning and expert female sailors alike to level the playing field alongside their male counterparts.

Practical Seamanship: Essential Skills for Modern Sailors, written by Steve and Linda Dashew and published by Beowulf Inc. This book goes into detail about everything from technical difficulties to anchoring off coral reefs without damaging the environment. It also has lots of checklists that enhance the learning process for most beginners.

Start Powerboating Right!, written and published by U.S. Sailing. This book is written with beginners in mind, as part of the company's training-manual series and in conjunction with its instructional charter courses. Subjects include engine systems, navigation, boat handling, onboard emergencies, and more.

Powerboating: A Woman's Guide, written by Sandy Lindsey and published by McGraw-Hill. As with Doris Colgate's book for beginning women sailors, this powerboating book keeps women's natural strengths and learning tendencies in mind when discussing everything from onboard systems to basic handling.

Classic Yacht Interiors, written by Jill Bobrow and Dana Jinkins and published by W.W. Norton & Company. Bobrow is the former editor of *Boats International USA* and the current editor of *Showboats*, while Jinkins is a longtime yacht photographer. Together, they show you the insides of motoryachts and sailing yachts from 30 feet to more than 300 feet long.

The Superyachts, published annually by *Boat International* magazine. The most recent (2006) edition of this book includes nearly two dozen insider tours of the world's finest luxury yachts, along with a look at two high-end charter destinations. It also contains a register of the world's largest yachts, plus information about boatbuilders. A sister book, *The Megayachts USA*, focuses on luxury yachts built for the American market.

Charter Companies

Some of the bigger, crewed yacht companies put out thick, glossy booklets known as *charter annuals*. They include information about how to book charters, along with suggested itineraries from charter captains and details about various charter yachts in each company's fleet.

While these publications are marketing materials as opposed to unbiased sources, they do contain a lot of good information if you're looking to book a fully crewed yacht charter. Look for company contact information in Appendix B for Camper & Nicholsons International, Fraser Yachts Worldwide, Nigel Burgess, and Yachting Partners International—the companies that historically have produced the fattest, most information-rich charter annuals.

APPENDIX B

Where to Call for Bookings

Your regular travel agent may have served you well in the past, but you will need the specialized knowledge of a leading bareboat company or a reputable charter broker to help you plan a private yacht vacation.

All of the companies and brokers mentioned and quoted in *Have the Whole Boat* are industry leaders—people my colleagues and I trust year after year to help us set up trips for major magazine features, and people I believe you can trust in organizing any kind of private yacht charter vacation, anywhere in the world. If I personally have not worked or would not work with a company, I have not included them in this book.

Having said that, there are countless companies and brokers out there, and some of them may be quite good even if they're not referenced in the preceding pages or the following alphabetical listings. You have learned enough in *Have the Whole Boat* that you can ask smart questions and, hopefully, tell for yourself just how knowledgeable and experienced a given company or charter broker might be.

Bareboats and Skippered Charters

The companies listed alphabetically in this section all have their own fleets of sailboats and powerboats. This means you can book directly through them if you decide you do not want to use a charter broker.

Blue Goose Charters

Bill Shermer, a retired U.S. Navy commander, now goes by the nickname "Mother Goose." He co-owns this small trawler yacht operation on the Chesapeake Bay, offering training, bareboat charters, and skippered charters onboard five different boats. Blue Goose has been in business for more than 20 years and is based in the easy-to-reach hub of Baltimore Harbor. Learn more at *www.Blue GooseCharters.com.*

Charters Northwest

This is a company recommended to me by another that I work with frequently. It's based in the Pacific Northwest's San Juan Islands—one of my favorite cruising areas—and offers monohull sailboats and powerboats (no catamarans). Adding a skipper to any of the two-dozen yachts in the company's fleet will cost you about $225 extra per day. Check out the company's Web site, *www.ChartersNorthwest. com,* for details on basic rates as well as special offers that change regularly.

Club Nautique

This Northern California company has been in business since 1980. It offers nearly 50 sailboats from 25 to 54 feet long, plus a handful of trawler yachts from 32 to 43 feet long. The company offers different levels of membership that can give you, among other things, 35-percent discounts on California charters, 25-percent discounts on instructional courses, flotilla charter opportunities, and reciprocal discounts with other cruising companies outside of California, including some in the Caribbean and Virgin Islands. Or you can stay local and cruise up the Napa River to the edge of wine country. Log on to *www.ClubNautique.net* to learn more.

NauticBlue

NauticBlue is the powerboat arm of The Moorings company, offering 32- to 46-foot monohull powerboats and powercats for bareboat and skippered charters in three regions: the Bahamas, the Virgin Islands, and Greece. An interesting note about NauticBlue monohulls is that they often can supply small motoryachts and express cruisers, which get you from island to island much faster (albeit with higher fuel costs) than the trawler yachts you can charter through other companies. Learn more by logging on to *www.NauticBlue.com.*

Southwest Florida Yachts

Vic and Barb Hansen—longtime cruisers who love to fish, scuba dive, and sail—have owned and operated this company since 1984. They offer bareboats from their Marinatown base in North Fort Myers, Florida, and from a second base at the Burnt Store Marina on Charlotte Harbor. The company has sailboats and trawler yachts that you can cruise east along the Okeechobee River, or north and south to places like Tampa, Sarasota, Captiva Island, Sanibel Island, and the Florida Keys. If you learn to bareboat through their sister company, Florida Sailing & Cruising School, you'll get a discount on your first charter. To learn more, log on to *www.swfyachts.com*.

Sunsail

This British-based company is now under the same ownership as The Moorings, bringing the world's best-known bareboat and skippered charter companies together in ways that continue to evolve. Sunsail has two divisions, one that runs its resorts and another that oversees its sailing schools and charter operations. The company is focused on sailboats, with more than 1,000 monohulls and catamarans ranging from 30 to 70 feet long, although powercats in the 34-foot range are also starting to show up in the fleet. Destinations are worldwide, and you can combine your charter with a stay at one of Sunsail's land-based resorts. Airfare can be part of your package deal as well. To learn more, go to *www.sunsail.com*.

The Moorings

Since 1970, The Moorings has been helping people realize their bareboating dreams. Its 700 or so monohull and catamaran sailboats range from 32 to 62 feet long, and the company includes a full-service travel agency that can help you plan your trip from door to door. Destinations are worldwide, with annual events like regattas and races that you can join if you would prefer to sail with other, more experienced cruisers nearby. The skippered charter option is called a Moorings Signature Vacation, and it also includes a chef. You can get discounts on bareboats if you learn to skipper them yourself through the sister company Offshore Sailing School. For more information, go to *www.moorings.com*.

TMM Yacht Charters

I have not personally experienced a charter with this company, but it comes highly recommended by other companies that I do know well, and it offers something a bit harder to find: bareboat charters not just in the Virgin Islands, but also in Belize and the Grenadines. It offers monohulls and catamarans, sail and power alike, that range from about 30 to about 60 feet long. Captains are available for skippered cruises, and prices for individual boats are listed in easy-to-understand grids on the company's Web site, *www.sailtmm.com*.

Trawlers in Paradise

As the name of this company implies, it has a fleet of trawler yachts—ranging from 36 to 46 feet. The company also is starting to branch out into powercats, including a four-stateroom 43-footer. The owners/operators are Tommy and Denise McCoy, who have lived in the Virgin Islands and worked in the charter business for two decades. They charter only powerboats, and they sell them, too, including well-known brands like Grand Banks and Nordic Tugs. Rest assured they can help you with pretty much any problem you might encounter. Their Web site is *www.TrawlersInParadise.com.*

VIP Yacht Charters

This Virgin Islands company is based on St. Thomas, and it offers pretty much every kind of boat out there: monohull sailboats, sailing catamarans, monohull powerboats, and powercats. Some of the powerboats are trawler yachts, while others are small motoryachts that offer a bit more speed. If you decide you like cruising with this company, you can consider its Yacht Ownership program, a fractional deal in which you get four to six weeks onboard annually while VIP Yacht Charters handles maintenance year-round. Check out *www.vipyachts.com* for details.

Virgin Traders

Based on Tortola in the British Virgin Islands, Virgin Traders has more than 20 monohull powerboats and powercats available for bareboat and skippered charters. The yachts range in size from 44 to 56 feet long and cruise at a variety of speeds, some in the 10-knot range and others twice as fast. If you decide that you enjoy chartering with Virgin Traders, you can also look into its fractional ownership plan—which gives you a ten-percent ownership interest in an 82-foot, $3.5-million motoryacht that you can use year after year. Learn more at *www.Virgin Traders.com.*

Instructional Charters

Some of the companies listed alphabetically below are affiliated with bareboat companies, while others are standalone teaching operations. Be sure to ask which companies are currently offering which types of certification, which you learned about in Chapter Fifteen.

Blue Goose Charters

As previously mentioned, this bareboat company is based on the Chesapeake Bay. The training is tailored to the trawler yachts the company offers for charter, making learning here a good choice if you want to book that kind of boat in this particular place. Your skills will transfer to other trawler yachts elsewhere in the world, but you may need to take one- or two-day refresher courses with other companies in order to book their bareboats later on. Learn more at *www.Blue GooseCharters.com*.

Chapman School of Seamanship

Charles F. Chapman may be a new name to you, but he is considered the master by many boaters. In fact, the two-plus-inches-thick *Chapman Piloting & Seamanship* is considered a bible among skippers of all skill levels. The school that bears his name is based in Stuart, Florida, and has trained more than 15,000 boaters since 1971. Some are interested in learning to bareboat, while others want to make careers out of becoming captains. You can receive training on powerboats or sailing yachts, earning certificates from the American Sailing Association and Chapman Powerboat Certification. Both are respected by other bareboat companies worldwide. Learn more at *www.chapman.org*.

Club Nautique

As previously mentioned, this bareboat company is based in Northern California. You can start out small with the company's Discover Sailing program, a one-day introduction to cruising that comes with a $100 discount toward a longer skipper's course. You can take the longer instruction onboard monohull sailboats or trawler yachts, with certification from U.S. Sailing that will satisfy other bareboat companies worldwide. The firm's Web site is *www.ClubNautique.net*.

Florida Sailing & Cruising School

This is the sister company to the bareboat operator Southwest Florida Yachts, based in North Fort Myers, Florida. It offers monohull sailing and trawler yacht powerboat courses, and graduates receive a discount toward their first bareboat charter. Your certification will be through the American Sailing Association as well as the National Association of State Boating Law Administrators. You should be able to apply your skills toward other bareboat charters with other companies worldwide. Go to *www.flSailAndCruiseSchool.com* for details.

Offshore Sailing School

Offshore Sailing School is a standalone operation that works in partnership with The Moorings and NauticBlue, providing discounts on bareboat sailboats and powerboats for graduating students. The owners, Steve and Doris Colgate, have been teaching people to sail since the mid-1960s. Today, they offer certification through U.S. Sailing that you can apply to other bareboat charters with other companies worldwide, as well as a "Fast Track to Power Cruising" course that began operating in the Bahamas and Virgin Islands in the summer of 2006. Women's-only courses are available for sailors, as are courses recognized by the American Council on Education—which means college credits for some students. Locations are in the Northeastern United States, Florida, the Bahamas, the Virgin Islands, and on the northern Caribbean island St. Maarten. Check out *www.OffshoreSailing.com.*

Sea Sense

This company is all about women training women onboard sailboats and trawler yachts alike. Sea Sense has been in business since 1989 and now offers courses in Florida, New England, the Chesapeake Bay, the Great Lakes, San Francisco Bay, the Pacific Northwest, and along the Intracoastal Waterway. You earn a Sea Sense Certificate of Completion, which is recognized by a good number of bareboat companies worldwide but that may require you to take a one- or two-day refresher course, depending on the company you choose for your bareboat. If you pre-arrange your course, you can take along your husband or son—but men are not invited on liveaboard women's-only courses. The company's Web site is *www.SeaSenseBoating.com.*

Sunsail

As previously mentioned, Sunsail is one of the world's powerhouses in terms of bareboat charter. It has sailing schools in the British Virgin Islands, Thailand, Australia, England, Scotland, and Spain's Canary Islands—all designed to help you learn what you need to know before chartering one of its bareboats in any location worldwide. Some of the introductory courses even include flotillas, so you can take your own helm while cruising alongside other students. Learn more at *www.sunsail.com.*

Partially and Fully Crewed Yachts

As you learned in Chapter Twelve, there are several major professional associations for charter brokers worldwide. Look to work with members of CYBA (Charter Yacht Brokers Association), MYBA (Mediterranean Yacht Brokers Association), and AYCA (American Yacht Charter Association).

Keep in mind that any charter broker can book any charter yacht anywhere in the world, regardless of which company the yacht uses for its management services. It's sort of like the situation with real-estate agents, where there is a central database of available properties that anybody can sell.

There have been some accusations that charter brokers working for yacht management companies push charter clients toward only the boats in that company's fleet, since the brokers sometimes get an additional commission for booking an in-house yacht. Does it really happen? Probably. Do you need to be aware of it? Of course. Does it happen with every single charter broker working for the management companies? Definitely not. The brokers I have quoted throughout this book are people who have stellar reputations for booking yachts managed by all different companies all over the world, no matter what logo is on their business card. You can trust the brokers I have named to give you a fair and honest effort.

Also remember that some charter brokers who specialize in crewed yachts have a strong background in bareboats and can help you with those bookings, too. Many brokers will help you book any kind of yacht you want, since they earn their livings from commissions paid by yacht owners of all stripes. If you should happen to call a charter broker who specializes in one kind of yacht when you need another—say, if you get a top-dollar crewed yacht broker when you're really looking to book a bareboat—the broker will usually refer you to a colleague she trusts in that area.

A1 Yacht Trade Consortium

Rosemary Pavlatou is my broker of choice at this fast-growing company, which manages a handful of charter yachts and focuses on bookings in Greece, Turkey, and Croatia. Pavlatou is a British ex-pat and a naturalized Greek national, and her bilingual expertise helps to close the gap between Western travelers' expectations and the developing Eastern Mediterranean marketplace. Learn more at *www.a1yachting.com*.

Alaska Yacht Charters

Owned by Geoff and Debbie Wilson, this is a two-motoryacht operation focused exclusively on charters in—you guessed it—Alaska. The Wilsons run *Alaskan Song*, a 95-foot motoryacht, while their business partners, Stacey and D.K. Williams, run the 90-foot motoryacht *Alaskan Story*. They are not charter brokers, but rather crewed yacht owners/operators. The two couples have more than 50 years' combined experience cruising in Alaska, and 82 percent of their business is from repeat clients. That speaks volumes. Check out *www.AlaskanSong.com*.

Allied Richard Bertram Marine Group

This company is primarily focused on new yacht sales, but its in-house broker, Leslie Adams, is a highly professional charter expert who can help you with bookings onboard yachts managed by other companies. She's based in one of the company's two Fort Lauderdale, Florida, offices and is featured on the company's Web site, *www.arbmg.com*.

Allied Yacht Charters

The lovely and talented Nicole Haboush runs this Miami Beach, Florida-based company, which manages a handful of smaller crewed motoryachts. Haboush offers bookings onboard her own fleet, as well as with any other charter yachts managed by other companies worldwide. Learn more at *www.AlliedYachtCharters.com*.

Angela Connery Yacht Charters

This is the company of independent charter broker Angela Connery, who is based in Salem, Massachusetts, and has been booking charters for 16 years. I see her regularly at industry-only charter boat shows around the world, and she's the type who leaves the cocktail parties early so that she can get a good night's sleep and focus on her work—of inspecting yachts and interviewing crew with an eye toward helping to better serve you. Her Web site is *www.acYachtCharters.com*.

Ann Landry Yachting

Ann Landry is one of those legendary charter brokers who has been around a long time, understands the ins and outs of booking all kinds of yachts, and knows the score on everybody in the business going back more years than they care to remember. She is an utmost professional who spent many years working for the worldwide charter companies before launching her own charter broker agency in early 2006. Contact her in Fort Lauderdale, Florida, through *www.AnnLandry.com.*

Ann-Wallis White Charter Yacht Consultants

This is the business of independent charter broker Ann-Wallis White, who is based in Annapolis, Maryland. Her core expertise is in booking small- to medium-sized sailing yachts, but she can help you with whatever kind of charter vacation you desire. If you're an animal lover, she's a good broker to work with because she, too, has a soft spot for pooches and can help you find boats that will let you take yours onboard. She doesn't have a Web site, but you can reach her by calling (410) 263-6366.

Aris Drivas Yachting

Drivas is based in Piraeus, Greece, just outside of Athens, and markets himself as the man to know when it comes to chartering luxury yachts in that emerging charter ground. He's very personable and also is fluent in English, often serving as a source of information for U.S.-based brokers who cannot inspect Greek yachts in person. Go to *www.GreekYachts.gr.*

Bartram & Brakenhoff

This company's main focus is on selling brokerage boats, but it is also the home base of Pila Pexton, who manages the company's small fleet of charter sailing and motoryachts while booking charters onboard the hundreds of other yachts world-wide. Pexton works out of the company's offices in Newport, Rhode Island, and is a smart, charming person with whom to do business. Go to *www.BartBrak.com* for more information.

BCR Yachts

BCR is based in Antibes, France, in the heart of the Mediterranean yacht charter industry. The company manages a handful of charter yachts and does brokerage sales, in addition to booking charters. I like to work with charter expert Sussie Kidd, who has worked as a yacht captain herself and who speaks both English and French. Learn more at *www.bcryachts.com.*

Beadon Yachts

This company is the home of Jacqui Lockhart, who manages a handful of luxury motoryachts along with the well-known *Mirabella* sailing yachts—the 131-foot

Mirabella, the 137-foot *Mirabella III,* and the 247-foot *Mirabella V* (the largest single-masted sailboat in the world). She also can help you with bookings onboard any other yacht managed by any other company. Go to *www.Beadon Yachts.com.*

Camper & Nicholsons International

CNI is one of the worldwide powerhouses in yachting, offering everything from new yacht-construction and sales assistance to charter management, marketing, and crew placement. Its Web site, *www.cnconnect.com,* has an excellent searchable database of luxury crewed charter yachts, as well as information about itineraries and a basic guide to chartering. My favorite CNI charter brokers in America are Suzette McLaughlin, Barbara Dawson, and Diana Mares, all in Palm Beach, Florida, and Agnes Howard, who is based in Fort Lauderdale, Florida. Overseas, I like working with Anne Sterringa and Gertrud Annevelink, both based in Palma de Mallorca, Spain.

Carol Kent Yacht Charters

This Boston-based agency books everything from one-day local cruises to multi-week charters around the world. Kent is a longtime broker who serves on the board of directors of the Charter Yacht Brokers Association, and her years of experience show in her professionalism and knowledge. Learn more about her at *www.CarolKent.com.*

CEO Expeditions

This is a two-motoryacht operation, not a charter broker agency. I've cruised onboard both yachts, the 120-foot *Kayana* and the 100-foot *Katania,* in Alaska and the Pacific Northwest. They both offer a reasonable amount of luxury at an attractive—and, often, all-inclusive—per-person price. Learn more at *www.CeoExpeditions.com.*

Churchill Yacht Partners

Churchill is a relatively new charter management company built up in the past few years by experts who left other, bigger companies after decades in the business. Sandy Carney was the founding charter broker at Churchill, and she's still there today, based in Newport, Rhode Island. She's one of my favorite people in the business, a straight talker who knows her stuff. Go to *www.Churchill Yachts.com.*

Crewed Charters

Verna Ruan founded this St. Thomas-based charter booking agency in 1982, after she decided she could make a better living booking yachts than working onboard them as crew. She's currently a major player in the Charter Yacht Brokers Association, and she attends not only the major industry-only shows in the Caribbean and Western Mediterranean, but also the smaller shows in places like Greece, Turkey, and the Virgin Islands, all with an eye toward being an expert on destinations worldwide. Her Web site is *www.CrewedCharters.com.*

Custom Charter Yachts Ltd.

Based in White Plains, New York, this charter booking agency includes brokers Sandy Acker and Candy Isdale, two well-respected members of the charter community. Acker's husband, Ed, is also a well-known broker, while Isdale's husband, Dooie, is a high-ranking member of the prestigious New York Yacht Club. They have no Web site, but you can call them at (914) 682-6379.

Ed Hamilton & Co.

Ed's claim to fame is his exceptional height—you can't miss his nearly seven-foot frame walking down the docks, and he knows better than any other charter broker which boats will be the most comfortable for tall men. He's based in Wiscasset, Maine, and has eight staff members ready to help you book everything from bareboats to crewed yachts. His Web site has an interesting feature: yacht prices broken down into per-person weekly rates. He recently helped a friend of mine book her first-ever charter vacation, and she had nothing but rave reviews. Go to *www.Ed-Hamilton.com.*

Edmiston & Co.

This is another large, worldwide company, offering everything from new-yacht construction advice to charter yacht management and top-dollar vacation bookings from offices worldwide. Charter broker Chris Craven is based in Monaco, and I always find him a pleasure to speak with at industry-only boat shows. If you live in California, note that Edmiston is the only major charter company with offices in Beverly Hills. Learn more at *www.EdmistonCompany.com.*

Elaine Stewart Yacht Charters

This is the company owned by independent charter broker Elaine Stewart, a delightful and knowledgeable woman who is based in Roswell, Georgia. She takes great pride in offering personalized service, chatting as long or as little as you'd like about whatever kinds of yacht vacations interest you. Check out *www.Caribbean Sailing.net.*

Flagship

If you're looking for a smaller crewed yacht in the Virgin Islands, Flagship is probably the company that represents it. Most of its fleet is monohull sailboats, but the number of powerboats it offers is increasing—and you can often get all-inclusive rates. I trust the longtime general manager, Pamela Wilson, who has been with the company for more than a decade. Go to *www.FlagshipVI.com.*

Fraser Yachts Worldwide

Fraser is a powerhouse company with worldwide offices and services that include everything from new-yacht construction advice to brokerage sales and crew placement. Its Web site, *www.FraserYachts.com,* has a terrific database that you can search either by charter yacht or by charter destination. The man in charge of the charter division, David LeGrand, has big ideas about expanding crewed charter vacations into new and exciting markets—and I consider him a visionary to watch. My favorite U.S.-based brokers are Diane Fraser in Newport Beach, California; Liz Howard in San Diego, California; and Jan Henry, Debra Blackburn and Robin O'Brien in Fort Lauderdale, Florida. Overseas, I like to work with Kirsten Ringsing in Monaco, Costa Lourandakis in Greece, and Allan Jouning in New Zealand.

Global Yacht Charters

This is a charter booking agency whose principal, Gordon Stonehouse, has been in the business for years. He's based in Palm Beach, Florida, and regularly attends major industry-only shows so he can help you book charters onboard yachts worldwide. Learn more at *www.GlobalYachtCharters.com.*

Hinckley Crewed Charters

Tina Hinckley is the independent charter broker at this company, which works in cooperation with the boatbuilder Hinckley Yachts—formerly owned and run by Tina's husband, Bob Hinckley. She's based in Southwest Harbor, Maine, and regularly attends worldwide industry-only shows. She knows even the smallest emerging markets well, and she can help you book everything from the smallest Hinckley sailing yachts to the world's largest top-dollar megayachts. Her Web site is *www.HinckleyYacht.com.*

International Yacht Charter

This charter booking agency in Cannes, France, has several brokers on staff, but I like Noelle Alice-Fasciato the best. Fluent in English and French, she is one of the straightest talkers I've ever met in the business. She won't hesitate to tell you what she thinks of a given yacht or captain, even if it may cost her your business. The company has no Web site, but you can reach Noelle by e-mailing NaYacht Charter@wanadoo.fr.

International Yacht Charter Group

Liveaboard husband-and-wife sailors Derek Holding and Janet Bloomfield founded this company just a few years ago and have quickly become knowledge-able about a wide variety of yachts worldwide. Janet is a pleasure to work with, as is a newly added charter broker, Kathy McErlean, who is based in Connecticut. The company's Web site, *www.InternationalYachtCharterGroup.com,* is one of the best in the business.

International Yacht Collection

This Fort Lauderdale, Florida-based company is a worldwide powerhouse that focuses on the management and sale of power-driven megayachts, but whose charter brokers can help you book any kind of yacht in any destination you choose. Operations Manager Larry Ebbs has worked hard to make the company's Web site, *www.YachtCollection.com,* eminently searchable, and he was one of the first in the industry to create video brochures that let you take virtual tours of various charter yachts. My favorite brokers at IYC are Mark Elliott, Steve Elario, Katie Macpherson, and Kim Vickery, all highly professional and very knowledge-able. Elliott spends a good part of the year living on St. Maarten, so he has exceptional knowledge of that cruising area.

Interpac Yachts

Interpac is the company owned by independent charter broker Beverly Parsons, who has been chartering since 1969. She's based in San Diego, California, has lived in the Pacific Northwest and Mexico, and is a founding member of both the Charter Yacht Brokers Association and the American Yacht Charter Association. More than 85 percent of her business comes from repeat clients and referrals, and she's one of the few brokers who has attended the industry-only charter boat show in Turkey every year for the past quarter-century. Learn more at *www.Interpac Yachts.com*.

Jody Lexow Yacht Charters

Jody Lexow is an independent charter broker who's easy with a smile, and who is a seemingly endless source of industry information. She's based in Newport, Rhode Island, and can help you book whatever kind of charter you want—though she is particularly knowledgeable about canal barges in Europe. She's also a hoot to sail with, if you ever get the opportunity. Go to *www.JodyLexowYachtCharters.com*.

Jubilee Yacht Charters

Louise Dailey started this independent charter broker agency in Darien, Connecticut, in 1982, before moving her home and work to Osprey, Florida. Her partner, Chick Trayford, opened an office in Delaware in 2005, after many years in Newtown, Connecticut. I know Dailey better, and I find her to be a straight talker who is active in setting ever-higher professional standards for the industry as a whole. The company's Web site is *www.JubileeYachtCharters.com*.

Luxury Yacht Group

This is a continuously growing company that offers yacht management as well as crewed charter bookings. Its president is Rupert Connor, a native of England who has lived in Florida since 1999. He takes a very hands-on approach, and you just might find yourself talking to him instead of to an assistant should you book a vacation onboard a top-dollar yacht. The company's Web site, *www.LuxYachts.com*, features a lot of good information.

Meridian Yacht Charters

Nick and Jenny Trotter are the husband-and-wife team who run this Irvington, Virginia-based charter booking agency. They can help you with bareboat as well as crewed yacht bookings, and they have unique experience in planning tandem and corporate charter events. Nick used to work for Caribbean resorts, so he has a keen eye for surf-and-turfs, too. The Trotters are good, honest people who always leave me smiling. Learn more about them at *www.MeridianYachts.com.*

Merrill-Stevens Yachts

This major yacht sales and repairs company with offices in Florida and California recently acquired Koch, Newton & Partners—one of my all-time favorite charter companies for organizing excellent story-making cruises. The entire KNP charter team is now working with longtime industry expert Lynette Hendry under the Merrill-Stevens flag, including the savvy and hilarious charter broker Sue Flammia. Check out *www.KochNewton.net,* which was still the main source of charter information when this book went to print. Alternatively, go to *www.MerrillStevens.com.*

Nautor USA

Based in Newport, Rhode Island, this company is the home of Carolyn Cox Titus, who previously co-owned the independent agency Cox Marine. Carolyn is quick with a smile and thoroughly professional, whether talking about a 45-foot powerboat or a 145-foot sailing yacht. She's based at Newport Shipyard. Go to *www.NautorSwanCharters.com.*

Newport Yacht Management

Tom Rowe and Patty Martin run this Rhode Island-based company, which serves as the home of the annual summertime industry-only charter boat show. Rowe (not related to charter broker Ted Rowe) handles NYM's charter division, drawing on his extensive knowledge of yachts and the personal cruising miles he's logged along the entire Eastern Seaboard as well as in Bermuda, the Caribbean, the Greek Isles, and the Great Lakes. Learn more at *www.NymYachts.com.*

Nicholson Yacht Charters

This Cambridge, Massachusetts-based company is the eponymous booking agency of Julie Nicholson, a longtime and well-respected broker who is just one in a long line of Nicholsons to serve worldwide vacationers looking to experience private yacht charter vacations. The company also has offices on Antigua, where it has hosted an annual, industry-only boat show for decades. You can learn about the Nicholson family history, as well as the company's charter offerings, at *www.YachtVacations.com.*

Nicholson Yachts of Newport

Karen Kelly runs this booking agency in Rhode Island, independently of the similarly named Nicholson Yacht Charters. She's a charming and smart woman who has been in the business for years, booking everything from powerboats to sailing yachts. She also manages my first-ever charter yacht, the sailing catamaran *Angel Glow*. The company's Web site is *www.NicholsonYachts.com*.

Nigel Burgess

Based in London, this company is a worldwide powerhouse with additional offices in Miami, Florida; Manhattan, New York; Athens, Greece; Palma de Mallorca, Spain; Seattle, Washington; and Monaco. It offers everything from new-yacht construction advice to charter bookings, and touts itself as being the world's large-yacht specialist. Big-money charters are all you'll find here, though lower-priced alternatives may soon become available through the company's new smaller-yacht partner in Miami, called Oceanstyle. Ask for the forthright charter broker Cindy Brown in the New York office, for the knowledgeable Neil Hornsby in London and for the best-dressed multilingual broker I know, Gaye Joyeux-Bourgeois, in the Monaco office. Learn more at *www.NigelBurgess.com*.

Northrop & Johnson

I can't say enough good things about Missy Johnston, the Newport, Rhode Island-based charter broker associated with this worldwide yacht management and charter booking company. Johnston has organized charters for me onboard everything from sailboats to megayachts over the years, always without a hitch. I trust her judgment and recommendations without question. Another broker I like to work with, Sandy Taylor, recently joined the company as well. You can contact them both through *www.NandJ.com*.

Ocean Getaways

Based in Portsmouth, New Hampshire, this company books regular charters as well as corporate-incentive charters for groups as large as 200 people. Company President Trish Cronan attends many boat shows, always with a smile. Learn more at *www.OceanGetaways.com*.

Ocean Independence

This worldwide yacht management and charter firm has made a lot of moves in the past few years to lure talented individuals from independent and big-name companies alike. Those new hires include Capt. Ray "Rags" Weldon, a hilarious and smart broker who used to own his own company in Florida, and Tim Clark, a charming Brit who is working for Ocean Independence in the United Kingdom. Learn more at *www.OceanIndependence.com*.

Port O'Call Yacht Charters, Ltd.

This is the agency of independent charter broker Linda Owen. She's a sweet and hard-working woman based in Kansas City, Missouri—and is one of the few reputable brokers you'll find anywhere in the landlocked Midwestern states. She's been booking charters since 1987, and her attitude at industry-only boat shows is always one of utmost professionalism. Her Web site is *www.Port-O-Call.com*.

Richleigh Yachts

The name of this charter booking agency is a combination of Rich and Leigh Ford, a Fort Lauderdale, Florida-based, husband-and-wife team originally from South Africa who have been in business since 1989. Before becoming brokers, they served as yacht crew, which means they know a thing or two not just about boats, but about standards of service. Go to *www.RichleighYachts.com* for more information.

Robert J. Cury and Associates

This Fort Lauderdale, Florida-based company specializes in brokerage yacht sales, but it also manages a handful of charter yachts under the watchful eye of Nicole Caulfield. She's a gem of a person who worked onboard megayachts with her husband, Capt. K.C. Caulfield, before going ashore to become a broker. She knows the ins and outs of yachts and service from every imaginable angle. You can contact her via *www.RjcYachts.com*.

Robert Laska Luxury Yachts

This is the independent charter booking agency owned by Bob Laska, who has more than 25 years' experience in the business. He attends the major industry-only charter shows regularly and books charters in addition to helping clients buy and sell yachts of all kinds. Check out his stylish Web site at *www.rlaska.com*.

Select Yachts

Ann E. McHorney founded this St. Maarten-based charter agency about 20 years ago, after working as crew onboard sailboats and motoryachts from 40 to 170 feet long. She also has a degree in restaurant management and studied at Le Cordon Bleu, so she can really talk turkey about the best yacht chefs. Contact her through *www.selectyachts.net.*

Seven Seas Yacht Charters

With one of the best Web sites in the business—*www.SevenSeasCharters.com*—this Nokomis, Florida-based company is the home of broker Tim Nelson. He's a fun and dedicated broker who specializes in charter yachts more than 100 feet long, and I've enjoyed my cruises with him onboard megayachts in various locations.

Shannon Webster Charters

Shannon is one of my favorite independent brokers in the industry: honest, friendly, and extremely knowledgeable. She draws on her previous experience of working onboard yachts, as well as everything she learns from her husband, Capt. Dan Webster, in his work as a charter megayacht captain. Every charter she has arranged for me has been outstanding. She is based in Flagler Beach, Florida, and her Web site is *www.ShannonWebster.com.*

Sunseeker Charters

The owners of this British-based company are David Ward and Stefan Wertans, longtime owners of their own Sunseeker yachts who know the ins and outs of running these fast-moving powerboats well. They pride themselves on booking not just terrific crewed charters, but destination "experiences" that include whatever you want onshore, be it in-kitchen tours of the finest restaurants or front-row seats at a sold-out play. Learn more at *www.SunseekerCharters.net.*

T. Rowe Yacht Charters

You met Ted Rowe in Chapter One of *Have the Whole Boat*, where I explained his longtime work in the charter yacht industry. Suffice to say that if he's good enough to be one of my main sources for this book, he's more than capable of helping you book whatever kind of charter you'd like. His credentials as the current president of the Charter Yacht Brokers Association are also impressive. Contact him through *www.TRoweYachtCharters.com.*

The Marine Group

Marian Walker is the face of charter at this company, which has offices in Florida and Alabama and specializes equally in new yacht sales and construction. Walker can help you book not just crewed yachts, but also bareboats and instructional charters, if you'd like to try different things. Learn more at *www.MarineGroup.com.*

The Sacks Group

DJ Parker, one of the first female charter yacht captains in the world, is my favorite broker at this Fort Lauderdale, Florida-based company. She knows more about boats, crews, and destinations than I could ever write in an entire series of books. Parker's fellow brokers at The Sacks Group, Leann Morris Pliske and Barbara Stork, are also great ladies whom I'd trust with my best friends' or my own bookings. Company President Jennifer Saia started out working onboard yachts herself, so she knows the ins and outs of chartering from both sides. All of these brokers are available through *www.SacksYachts.com.*

Tom Collins Yachts Worldwide

This is the company of independent charter broker Tom Collins, a super-nice guy who has worked on and around boats for several decades. His knowledge is deep both in terms of bareboats, which he used to run, and in terms of luxury crewed yachts, which he now books regularly. His extensive personal experience cruising around the Bahamas and the Caribbean also bring considerable weight to itinerary suggestions, and I always enjoy his recommendations for the best new laid-back cruising tunes as well. Learn more about his Miami, Florida-based company at *www.TomCollinsCharters.com.*

Windward Mark Yacht Charters

This is the business of independent charter broker Joyce MacMullen, who is based in Tequesta, Florida. You learned about her in Chapter One; she's the visionary who created the industry's first database of charter yachts. She is a font of information not just about current available bookings, but also about the history of the industry itself. MacMullen has no Web site, but you can reach her by calling (800) 633-7900.

Yachting Partners International

This European company offers everything from yacht construction services to charter yacht bookings, and the combined knowledge of the partners is impressive. My favorite in-house people to work with on crewed yacht bookings are Alex Braden and Catherine Ambrogi, both based in France, and Mike Everton-Jones, who works from England. Check out *www.ypi.co.uk.*

Yachtstore

Gina Robertson, based in Fort Lauderdale, Florida, is the broker I know at this Internet-based charter marketing and booking agency. We have yet to work together on organizing a charter, but her attitude at industry-only boat shows is highly professional. You can contact her through *www.YachtStore.com.*

About the Author

Award-winning writer, editor, and photographer Kim Kavin is one of the world's foremost yacht charter experts. She has been onboard hundreds of yachts in dozens of locations worldwide, formerly as executive editor of *Yachting* and currently as charter/cruising editor of *Power & Motoryacht* and editor of *Voyaging*. She also writes regularly for luxury lifestyle magazines including *Elite Traveler, Celebrated Living, Palm Beach Illustrated,* and *Traveler Overseas,* as well as for additional consumer marine magazines including *Offshore* and *International Yachtsman*.

Kim is vice president of Boating Writers International; a member of the American Society of Magazine Editors, the American Society of Journalists and Authors, and the Society of Professional Journalists; and an affiliate member of the Charter Yacht Brokers Association. She holds a bachelor's degree from the University of Missouri-Columbia School of Journalism and is a graduate of the Dow Jones Editing program.

She lives in Long Valley, New Jersey, with her husband and their two nosy hounds, Floyd and Stella.

Index

978-0-595-40365-3
0-595-40365-4

Printed in the United States
91760LV00006B/232/A